MW01615119

Norbert Blei

NEIGHBORHOOD

NEIGHBORHOOD

Norbert Blei

Ellis Press
1987

Published by Ellis Press, David Pichaske, editor, P. O. Box 1443, Peoria, Illinois 61655.
Typesetting by Peregrine Cold Type, St. Paul, Minnesota.
Design and lay-out by David Pichaske.
Painting on dust jacket by Chick Peterson, Ephriam, Wisconsin. Used with the permission of the artist.

ISBN 0-944024-00-9

FIRST EDITION
1   2   3   4   5   6   7   8   9   0

For Herman Kogan and John Fink, who first gave it light;
my mother, *in memoriam*, who taught me the language;
my father, who defined the boundaries;
and the people of the neighborhood, who gave it heart

Neighborhood

Yet once you've come to be a part of this particular patch, you'll never love another. Like loving a woman with a broken nose, you may well find loverlier lovelies. But never a lovely so real.
　　　　　　　　　　　—Nelson Algren

Prologue: The Neighborhood of Nostalgia

There were silver fish swimming in dark wooden barrels outside the meat markets on Cermak Road in Cicero then. Rabbits, beautiful and dead in their brown fur, hung by their hind legs from under the awnings. Sawdust floors. White enamel meat cases that people leaned into. The sawing, chopping, cleaving of bones. Sharp-pointed knives on wavy, worn butcher-block tables, carving through and around red meat, trimming white fat. Brown eggs, beige eggs, grainy eggs; slabs of bacon, strings of sausage, smoked hams; tubs of lard. The bloody handprints of laughing butchers in once-white aprons. Czech spoken here: praszky, jaternice, debrecinky, buchta, Nazdar! *The smell of fresh sausage, dill pickles, garlic, caraway, warm frankfurters.*

A neighborhood of senses.

Near the Villas show, in front of the Leader Store, an organ grinder played while a monkey in a red jacket skittered around the wide sidewalk, tipping his hat, begging for pennies, shaking the hands of awe-struck children who had never touched a wild animal before. The memory of that tiny paw touching their palm would last forever.

Wooden streetcars, blue and white, clanked, sparked, wound their way back and forth the center of Cermak Road (22nd Street) through Cicero and Berwyn, each piloted by a uniformed motorman on the front platform, one hand clutching the wooden-knobbed steel lever which set the car in motion on silver rails, while a conductor made change on the rear platform, distributed transfers, yanked a cord above that rang a bell, and called out the streets: Central, 58th Avenue, Austin Boulevard . . . .

After Harlem Avenue it hummed through woods and wild-flowered prairie, bridged a running river, swayed through tall grasses, windows wide

*open to the drifting landscape and sweet smells of nature, then vanished with
a spark into deepest Africa: lions, tigers, elephants, gorillas and giraffes — the
Brookfield Zoo, far beyond the neighborhood territory.*

*Seats on the streetcar were the color of woven straw, and when they were
filled with passengers, people stood balancing themselves by clutching a steel-
handled corner of the seat or holding a leather-looped strap from above, their
bodies swaying into each other, rocking, suddenly lurching forward and
backward in the aisle, flowing with each momentary motion of the car as the
motorman engaged or disengaged the current. In winter coal burning stoves
kept the passengers warm.*

Streetcars blessed the neighborhood night like a religious procession. .
By day they resembled harmonicas.

*The neighborhood was a current, a circular field of motion. Much coming
and going. Everything stood still, yet everything revolved (by the hour, the
day, the season, the year) and came back to you. You departed and returned.
And you were the same but different.*

*The Douglas Park El (fire-white sparks and eerie blue flashes; put a penny
on the rail, a nail, a washer, and marvel at the transformations under
screeching iron wheels; touch the third rail and be "automatically"
electrocuted, dead) stopped at 58th Avenue (my stop, my street) and for 3¢
you walked through the wooden station (paid the cashier, bought candy from
the news vendor, stood inside by the stove in winter) then boarded the El when
it came, and stood on the open platform between cars with the conductor (in
spring and summer, if he let you) as the El rolled along at ground level past all
the landlocked stations ... Central, Laramie ... waiting for that exhilerating
climb beyond Cicero Avenue, after Kildare, into the sure flight above Pulaski,
over and into Chicago (past grey wooden porches and second floor*

clo,theslines, black iron fire escapes, backyards of morning glories, white curtains flying through open kitchen windows, men in their undershirts drinking beer on stoops, children playing in alleys, the smoke and gritty smell of factories, rows of women at sewing machines, huge open barrels of pickles, other neighborhoods . . .) and around the steel-girded, skyscrapered heart of the city, looping Chicago and then back home to 58th Avenue. (Sometimes to remain in the car, hopefully unnoticed, to the very end of the line, Oak Park Avenue, anxious to ride the El to the Loop again . . . and again . . . and again . . . especially on Saturdays and school holidays.)

The El was the streetcar in ascension, the dream of flight made real, our first view of a falling-away small world through the eyes of a bird, the cockpit of a Flying Tiger, the vision of an angel. A celestial connection.

Then back to earth again.

The streets and sidewalks were holy, magical, and above all, real. Real in a way, in time, only memory and imagination hold true.

There were two inches of cream in the neck of the glass of milk bottles left behind the back door each morning. You could hear the bottles, sprinkled with ice shards, rattling in the crates in the truck, in the hands of the milkman holding the metal basket as he made his way from the street down the gangway.

White sheets, smelling of bleach, flapped in the sunny wind of backyard Monday morning clotheslines weighted down with overalls, shirts, aprons, house dresses, rag rugs, towels, socks, chenille bedspreads, all propped up with long wooden clothes poles. Basements of cement washtubs, wooden washboards, and cranky hand-wringers where handkerchiefs and socks wound themselves into knots upon the rollers, always getting stuck. Basements smelling of Fels-Naptha, Rinso, Lava soap, and starch. And the magic of the waterlogged wooden wash stick, fishing a lost sock or handkerchief from under the soapy-grey waters of the tub.

Fresh fruit and vegetables — to be picked through, to be tasted, to be weighed — stood in bushel baskets and orange crates outside small food stories along Cermak Road, the aura of earth, the farmer, the countryside about them. Gunny sacks of onions, potatoes, and coffee beans — the blending of aromas. The doorways of the bakeries emitted the warm odors of fresh bread, houska, and coffeecakes. Every corner tavern reeked of stale beer, wafting through open doors and windows, the morning after the night before.

Peddlers came down the alleys shouting their wares . . . "Sweet corn!" Junkmen with cracking whips, perched high on green wooden wagons pulled by tired clopping horses, filled the air with cries of "Ragggss and ironnnn!"

The neighborhood world was immediate, always within human range. People coming and going. The "ding . . . ding . . . ding" of the bell on the red-wheel-spoked cart of the old Italian knife and scissor sharpener, pushing his way down the sidewalk from house to house. Shooting stars (catch them in your hand!) bursting from the sharpening wheel as he pressed the blade's edge to the grindstone.

The truck that dumped a cacophony of black diamond coal sparkling on the street early on an August morning, leaving a black coalman alone with a gleaming shovel and a wheelbarrow. It took hours of sweat for him to reduce the pile to a smudge on the street, wheeling it down the gangway to the window of the coalbin, sweeping the street and sidewalk clean, finally disappearing down the block in an afternoon sun, the shovel shining over his tired shoulder.

If you were very lucky, the iceman still stopped at your house (the ice cart in the front window printed in bold letters ICE and the amount) or the house next door, parked his open truck on the street, flung the black tarp off blocks of blue ice so blinding clear in the morning sun you longed to crawl inside and live forever in such crystal radiance. Instead you waited to make your move, and watched the iceman in his leather apron grasp a block of ice with steel-tonged vengence, lift it, slide it, work the weight of it to within striking distance of his jabbing artful pick, as he chipped it down to size and shape, perhaps divided it in half, then turned into it backwards, hefted it to his leather-padded shoulder, and bore the frozen weight of the world on his back, side-stepping all the way down the gangway to the kitchen icebox.

Which was the signal to climb aboard the wet wooden bed of the truck, quickly gather the shards of ice that slipped in your hands, numbed your fingers, froze your tongue, teeth, and roof of your mouth, but soothed your summertime throat like no glass of lemonade every would.

Everything experienced — seen, touched, tasted, consumed, entered — returned a body transformed. A neighborhood time of wonder.

The boundaries of the town of Cicero were fixed: Roosevelt Road (12th Street) on the northside; Lombard Avenue on the westside; Pershing Road (39th Street) on the southside; and Cicero Avenue (48th) on the eastside. Within the rectangular township was an amorophous bunch of smaller communities (smaller rectangular neighborhoods) called Warren Park, Clyde, Boulevard Manor, Grant Works, Parkholme, Hawthorne, Drexel, etc. each with its own boundaries of streets. Most Ciceronians knew which community they lived in and could point or give reasonable directions to Grant Works, Warren Park, Hawthorne. It didn't matter that much because it was all Cicero, a town bounded by Chicago on the north and east; Stickney on the south; and Berwyn to the west — common enough territory of the same ethnic traditions, sharing the same main street (Cermak Road) and transportation (the Douglas Park El) that the boarder crossing (Lombard Avenue) was rarely though of as such. In civic improvements, one always copied the other, sooner or later.

When the old babickas in paisley babushkas, carrying brown paper and black cloth shopping bags, went to the stores on Cermak, they came from the basements, bungalows, two-flats, and small houses north and south of Cermak Road, and moved up and down, back and forth both sides of the street from Cicero Avenue to Harlem, within their proximity.

But the lifeline was Central to Oak Park Avenue, the meat markets, milk stores, bakeries, fruit and vegetable stands, building and loans, banks small department stores, shoemakers, many with names they could relate to: Pavlicek's Drug Store; Ruzicka, Kobzina, Sekera and others for furniture; Sebesta, Shotola, Verners, and many more for meat; Pancner for Bohemian books, Bohemian greeting cards, stationery, Czech crystal, kind of a center for Czech culture in Cicero (a similar Pancner's in Berwyn); and funeral homes like Clasen, Cermak, Chrastka, Marik, and Svec, where Bohemian families expressed certain loyalties and traditions, preferring one funeral home over another . . . Marik, for example, because that's where grandpa was waked and all the family.

Though the boundaries of the town were fixed, streets, addresses, directions were of less significance to a kid than the fact that Western Electric (the tower, the huge green and red sign that glowed from the roof at night) marked the spot where Chicago began; the Sanitary District (which you could smell when the wind blew from that direction) and the race tracks (Sportsman's Park and Hawthorne) and the Burlington Railway (home of the Silver Zephyr) and the Red Arrow (famous jazz joint) was south; the factories, the Dutch settlement, the Town and Ritz shows, Columbus Park were north and also Chicago; and Cicero turned into Berwyn just after the Olympic show and Sokol around Lombard Avenue across the street from the Hole in the Wall tavern at the "Chinks," where your father took his white shirts to be laundered and starched by a Chinaman who lived behind a curtain in the back of a shop always warms and smelling of steam and pressed cotton.

These became your markers in the neighborhood, and later your memories. How you feared going into the Chink's alone to pick up the starched white shirts, because of tales your father told of his own youth working as a bank messenger in Chicago's Cinatown. Long dark stairways, red dragons and swords. How you feared going into the Chink's alone with your father's ticket (what if you didn't have enough money?) and the Cinaman said something to you, and you could never understand him through all of his smiles and bows.

The Olympic show was on the main drag, and so was the Berwyn, which you often frequented. But your real neighborhood show was the Villas on Central and Cermak where you first discovered romance and adventure both on and off the screen . . . usually in the last row, with your arm both on and off the back of the seat beside you, flirting dangerously around the shoulder of a neighborhood girl who might, just possibly might, rest her head against your cheek. And you knew this was love for sure. Forever.

Dressel's was where your mother ordered your chocolate whipped cream or strawberry whipped cream birthday cakes because Dressel's was known for their whipped cream cakes. You hung out at Kalavoda's Ice Cream Parlor even though your Uncle Bill's favorite was Frejlach's strawberry ice cream and malted milks.

Your mother bought your school clothes, Easter clothes, summer clothes at Jack's Men's Shop and your shoes at Glasser's where you could look through an X-ray machine and miraculously see all the bones in your feet in a blue glow. For years your mother bought all her clothes at Sarah's and later De Mar's while your father shopped for his clothing in the big department stores downtown, where he worked and rode the El every day from 58th Avenue to the Loop and back for more than 40 years. On rainy afternoons you would meet him at the station with an umbrella and walk home together down the wet sidewalk huddled under the big black umbrella. Under his arm he carried the final edition (Red Streak) of the Chicago Daily News.

If you lived around 18th and 58th Avenue, you were more or less in the center of things. The neighborhood appeared even smaller. You didn't even need Cermak Road because there were corner milk stores, grocery stores, candy stores, taverns and drug stores all within a short walk or a bike ride. Ben Darda's butcher shop was on the corner of 57th Court and 21st.

Every day you crossed 16th Street on your way to St. Frances of Rome School, and every day the smell of fresh bread from the ovens of Kadlec's bakery hovered over the prairie lot on the corner of 58th and 16th. On winter mornings you could taste the bread in the air.

On the corner across the street was the Fountain Inn with its beer garden, where you sat outdoors at wooden tables and benches with your parents and neighbors on Friday nights in spring smelling roses and beer, eating potato pancakes, watching water spill from the fountain, counting stars hung in the tree tops high above the beer garden, the neighborhood, the whole world, till you drifted off to sleep, your head resting in your mother's lap.

Some of the neighborhood, some of the memories take on the quality of dream at this stage in a writer's life. Like Frederico Fellini's "Amarcord" they reveal a reality beyond real, visions haunting and vivacious in the rememberer's heart. Like Gabriel Garcia Marquez's One Hundred Years of Solitude, to live again on Macondo, one must profess a faith in miracles. To acknowledge the myth. One loves a place, even a neighborhood, for all that it promised.

Once there was a funny little man, unshaven, in round wire-rimmed glasses, who went up and down the alleys with his toolbox, singing in Bohemian, fixing faucets, toilets, anything that required a wrench. You never knew from which back yard he would apear singing, talking to himself. He joked with the neighborhood kids in Bohemian while they made fun of him in English *because his actions always suggested too much beer — which was often his payment. He was known only as Mickey Mouse. "Hey, Mickey Mouse, can I have a penny?" we would beg. "Mickey Mouse, dance for us," we would taunt him. And Mickey Mouse would take a playful swipe, maybe spin around, stumble, and swear at us. Shout in Bohemian. Finally turn back on us and disappear down the alley or in some backyard, still talking to himself.*

In the middle of the next block there lived an old woman called the Radio Lady. She was a huge woman, fat, with thick white arms and blue-knotted veins in her legs. She wore faded flowered housedresses and worn felt slippers. There were moles on her face, and her eyes were green. Her grey hair was bunched in tortoise-shell combs on the back of her head, strands of it always falling over her forehead. She sat on a stone slab railing on top of the steps of her unkempt house, staring at everyone in the neighborhood who passed by, saying something to them whether they listened to her or not. Older people ignored her, but she captivated innocent kids.

"I have a radio in my room," she would begin, "and I can hear everything you say in your house. I hear all your lies. All the bad things you say, all the bad things you're going to do. I'm going to call the police." If you were a kid, you went home in fear of what the Radio Lady could do, certain the police would come to your house, arrest you, and put you in jail, all because the Radio Lady could hear everything you said and listen to your secret thoughts. She could even see inside your house.

Many blocks away lived the Monster Man, who appeared at the playground every spring, was part man and part boy, actually a man living in a boy's body of undetermined age. His arms stuck out from him like wings, and he dragged one foot when he walked, his head always turned toward one shoulder or another. He mumbled nonsense when he talked, and we could not look him in the face for fear he might come close. He like the swings most of all, where he could hang over the seat and move backwards and forward using his hands and feet. When we saw him approaching we would yell, "The Monster Man is coming! The Monster Man!" and lock him outside of the playground. He would put his fingers through the steel fence like claws, hang on and grin as we taunted him from inside, which is how we played with him. All winter long we never saw him. Once in a while we would speculate where the Monster Man was. I envisioned him chained in some dark basement, waiting for spring.

In another part of the neighborhood on Austin Boulevard (where the "rich" people lived because the houses appeared more palatial, the landscaping more formal) was a modern white brick home surrounded by an iron fence. Just inside the fence and running around the entire grounds (the house sat in the middle) was a small-gauged railroad track of the kind found in children's amusements parks. Neighborhood legend held that a famous clown lived there. For years as a child I would slowly walk that fence, trailing my hand along each iron bar, peering in, hoping to catch a glimpse of the clown and the train. I like to think that once I saw the engine. But I never saw the clown, never saw anyone ever enter or leave the house, never saw anyone. Yet at night all the windows were lit, and I imagined that somewhere behind those curtains sat a clown eating dinner, reading the newspaper, or lying in bed. And somewhere, perhaps under the house, a small train gleamed in the darkness ready to make a run down the rails.

Neighborhood people kept a trained eye on passing life from behind the curtains and Venetian blinds of the front windows of their house facing the street and both sidewalks. Many times, day and night, someone would be watching someone pass by, something going on in or across the street. It wasn't being nosy or a busybody so much as a real need to turn one's back periodically on the household with all its demands, frustrations, sameness, and look out the window to see what was going on in the world. Sometimes to even imagine what might be going on.

I remember the woman who often walked past our house on the sidewalk across the street. No doubt someone else in the household spotted her first through the Venetian blinds and said something with a smile, or in a whisper, or in another language (which grownups were always using to protect the privacy of their words) that piqued my interest and left me wondering. There was a call to the window (maybe a first name) whenever she was seen passing by. No other information was provided, only the furtive peek throught the blinds at a woman walking the other side of the street.

She was of medium height, brown hair, ample hips. She wore high heeled shoes, nylong stockings, straight, tight dark skirts, bright blouses or pastel sweaters that clung to her pointed breasts. Her lips were bright red, her cheeks almost orange, and there was a darkness around her eyes (natural or cosmetic) that suggested both wantonness and melancholia. She carried a purse which swung with her long, swift, brusque, unwomanly strides. From a distance she was not beautiful so much as attractive, determined. She seemed to have no time for anything as she stepped through our range of vision, her shoes often signaling a metal tapping sound, especially in the early evening or late at night. There was no other history to her: not a name, address, or destination. She existed only in our eyes where we kept her within range, left to right, right to left, moving in and out of our window of vision, through the neighborhood, deep into our imaginations.

I was an adolescent when I first became aware of her, feeling somewhat confused. Why the commotion? What's the deal? By the time I reached high school, she took on a new meaning, though I never met her face to face. I see her now as part of my neighborhood rite of passage ... that pane of glass separating innocence from desire. She would remain a mystery that would grow more poignant in the years to come.

The neighborhood conjured images, wonders, stories that never ceased: tales of the gypsy camp on 39th and Harlem. Gypsies who camped there with their wagons and horses and sat around campfires making music, telling stories, always on the lookout for unsuspecting neighborhood children to steal. Stay away from the gypsies, or you might never see home again!

The gypsy campsite would later become Fairyland Park, our own neighborhood Riverview, year before theme parks and Disney covered the U.S.A.

And there were the hobo jungles along the railroad tracks.

And the fire station just down the block on 15th and 58th Avenue where real firemen in suspenders and black boots really played checkers and cards in the firehouse, constantly washed and polished the red engine, slept upstairs, and slid down a brass pole on the sound of a fire alarm. Caught them in the right mood they would marshall the neighborhood kids to the second floor and let them slide down the shiny brass pole as well.

Backyard wonders of rock gardens with falling water and colored lights; the man on the next block who filled his whole yard with handmade, brightly painted windmills of every design. The whole garden spun colors in a breeze.

The ongoing romance (to a kid) of the gangster. We had the legacy and legend of Al Capone. We looked with pride to the 20's and 30's, talked the Hawthorne Hotel and the Alton (old Capone headquarters) and the 4811 Club. Bookies and stripjoints and gangland slayings. Everyone knew someone who was connected to Capone or had a story of the Syndicate to tell.

"Just on the corner across the street from me," I would tell friends, "lived one of the boys, Joey 'The Dove' Aiuppa, Cicero's latter-day Mafia boss. And guess what? I was his paperboy."

And there was midnight mass at St. Francis of Rome on Christmas Eve, when being a Catholic kid in the neighborhood seemed the most magical thing of all, impossible to explain to other kids of other faiths. Nuns in their garb with beads in their hands; priests in their cassocks waving their hands in the air to extend blessings. Some of us were altar boys (dressed like miniature priests) mumbling Latin like archbishops: 'Gloria Patri, et Filio, et Spiritui Sancto Sicut erat in principio, et nunc, et semper; et in saecula saeculorum" amazing everyone. Some of us were choirboys.

The candlelit church on Christmas Eve; the ringing of the bells three times, Sanctus, Santus; priests in their glowing chasubles; statues of Mary and the saints staring into your very soul; flickering red votive candles; light reflected from the tabernacle, the chalice, the crucifix all glittering and gold; incense wafting above the kneeling penitents; finally the communion with God, the small white host like a snowflake on the tongue. Beyond the heavy church doors, a Christmas night of fresh snow and stars, walking the quiet neighborhood home after midnight mass and invited by good Slovenian neighbors and parishioners, the Zbasnik's and Tomse's, to feast on ham and sausage, a table overflowing with homemade bakery and wine. And then to sleep and dream, feeling you would never be nearer to God than now.

All of this was very long ago. All of this seems only yesterday. It was one time on the very edge of another. A time of boyhood on the edge of young manhood. A time of prewar on the edge of war on the edge of postwar. A time of firelight on the edge of electricity — the gateman at the 58th Avenue El station still coming out of his shanty at night to hang red kerosene lanterns on the lowered gates. A time of iceboxes giving way to refrigerators. A time of radio giving way to television. A time of people sitting on front porches talking to the neighbors who passed by, yielding to a time of abandoning the porches, locking the doors, drawing the blinds, and sequestering themselves in a TV room. A time of hand-painted signs giving way to neon; of brick streets giving way to asphalt; of concrete lamp posts topped with huge balls of milk glass casting an intimate light on front lawns and streets giving way to sodium lamps hovering somewhere above, laying an alien glow upon the whole neighborhood. A time when the men of the neighborhood burned huge piles of leaves along the curb in autumn and children ran throught the dense and pungent clouds of white smoke yelling, "Superman!" A time when children made toy boats of wood, cigar boxes, clothes pins and rubberbands to float down all the rivers which appeared along all the curbs in the neighborhood after heavy rains which flooded basements and blocked sewers. A time of a neighborhood of many voices, many ethnic traditions, many small businesses, everything mixed, intermingled, shared, which shaped one's humanness, one's spirit for living in ways forever lost as neighborhoods gave way to suburbs, family businesses to franchises, shopping streets to shopping malls where we appear lost in a culture of consumption, self-gratification. A computerized consciousness isolating all our human instincts to technological "programs" (designed by state and corporate powers) denying our real need for real life.

When I first thought I might become a writer (my junior year at Morton High School and all through Morton Junior College) the neighborhood held little interest for me. It was the place one had to escape to become a writer. There were other worlds out there to be experienced, other lives to be lived (love, marriage, work, higher education, Chicago, Mexico, Europe) and eventually recorded in short stories, novels, and nonfiction.

Yet it was to the neighborhood I returned for material early on (a first short story published in a literary magazine around 1962; a first feature story, "From Central to Harlem, A Little Bit of Bohemia" published in the Chicago Daily News, *March 6, 1965). And it was to the neighborhood I would return time and again, even after leaving it for good in 1969.*

When I began to explore it as a young writer freelancing for his life in the pages of Chicago newspapers and magazines in the 60's and 70's, I looked through a different pair of eyes, I had a vision different than what I've used to recapture in this prologue through memory, image, the heightened sense of reality a short story writer or novelist might employ.

Story, through, was always my center, even as I began to explore the possibilities of nonfiction, of "real" stories in my own neighborhood. I would seek out the past, go to these people, places, celebrations I remembered in the neighborhood, and I would observe what was there, what was left, and I would ask questions, I would listen, let people talk, be themselves. I would fill a whole notebook with my scribbles, then go home, sit at my desk the next morning, and try to shape what I experienced with accuracy, details, voice, humor, compassion, love, with some sense of art, some sense of life beyond the daily newspaper or monthly magazine.

Some of these people and places in the neighborhood are no more. Time has indeed passed. Some of the businesses along Cermak Road have disappeared or changed hands. A number of the people (Shorty the Locksmith, Tony the Shoemaker, others) have died. The neighborhood is not the same. Yet when I go back and walk the streets with my father, who still lives there, I feel at home again.

In the minds of some, nostalgia is a weakness, old fashioned, a desire to cling to a time that is no more, or never really was. A longing of the heart. Perhaps. 'Nostalgia,' Webster explains, comes from the Greek word "nostos," meaning "a return home." Meaning, in a medical sense, "a severe melancholia caused by protracted absence from home." Suggesting, finally, "... yearning for return to or of some past period or irrecoverable condition."

TOWN OF CICERO ILLINOIS

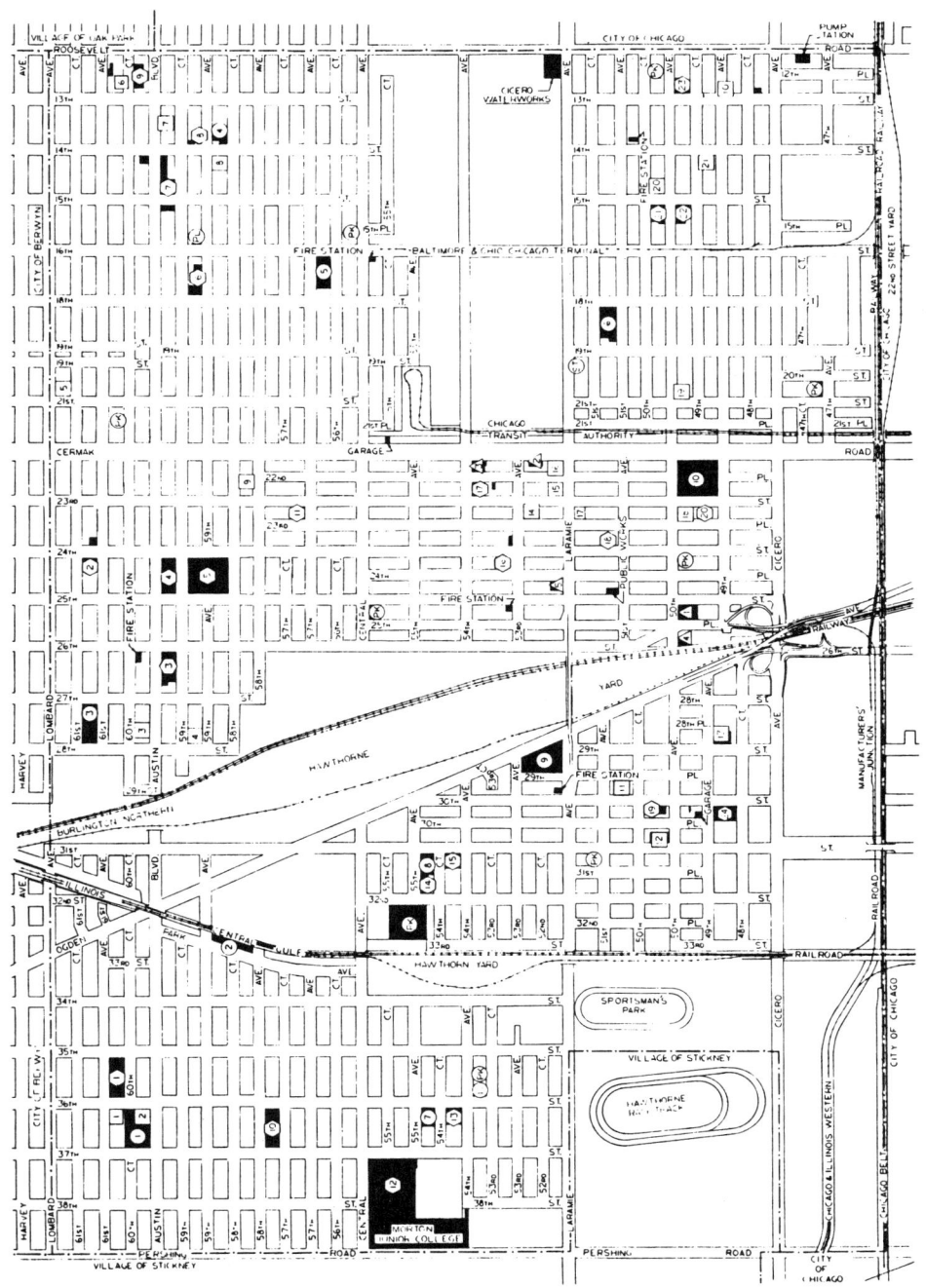

Bohemia on Cermak Road

Bohemia may still be a part of Chicago, a section of the Midwest, or a mythical kingdom behind the Iron Curtain, but my Bohemia is a river of restaurants, savings and loans companies, bakeries, butcher shops and bargain stores, and it is called Cermak Road. It flows from Central Avenue west to Harlem, engulfing everything and everybody. Other nationalities continue to thrive here, but the temper is Bohemian.

All gangways, sidewalks, alleys and side streets lead, eventually, to Cermak Road. On Saturday morning, market day all over America, the Bohemians rise early and drive, walk or cycle to the stores. To get there first and be home before everyone else is the eternal Saturday adventure.

Being first at Mid-America Savings and Loan (where they serve free coffee and homemade *kolacky*) means you won't have to stand in line while the old lady behind you tries to read the balance in your pass book. Of course there is always the satisfaction of meeting a neighbor and talking over all the things Bohemians usually talk about: money, death or some other Bohemians. All these offices in the area serve as a kind of meeting place, probably a carry-over from the town square in the old country. You won't see any of the Bohemians in their colorful old costumes. But the paisley babushkas are still used, and so are the homemade shopping bags, the loud language, the laughter. And an old Bohemian stands in the corner carefully counting his money.

Other Saturday morning adventures consist of a stop at the newsstand for the Denni Hlasatel newspaper and then off to one of the bakeries or butcher shops. Sometimes husband and wife split up at this point, one to find bargains in meat and vegetables, the other to get fresh bread from the bakery.

Modern supermarkets have had little effect on the Bohemian way of life. They, too, have been absorbed by the people. Much of the help speak Czech. Weekly sales cater to the Bohemian's pocketbook. And there are still a few fruit and vegetable stores left for the old-timer to come in and feel the apples, peel away at the lettuce and sort out the good potatoes. Dill and mushrooms are always on hand to satisfy individual tastes. The small meat markets, with real butchers in bloody aprons, stand solidly amidst the chrome and white supermarkets. After all, you can't speak Czech to a freezer full of meat that has already been cut, cleaned, packaged and priced. And the butcher, Joe Svoboda, has good meat. "Yeah, I use to know his sister from the old neighborhood. He makes all his own sausage, you know. His *jaternice* are the best on Cermak."

Bohemian baking cannot be equaled except by another Bohemian with a slightly different recipe, a slightly different touch to the old, old heavy delicacies. All Bohemians bake, but never enough. "Who knows, maybe company will come tonight? You better stop by Fingerhut's or Vesecky's and get a big *kolac* and some rye bread. Maybe get a *babovka* in case Uncle Charley comes."

There are many bright, glittering snack shops on Cermak Road, but few Bohemians do more than take a brief glance. They also stay away from the fancy restaurants that draw visitors looking for Bohemian foods and atmosphere. The only kind of restaurant that matters is the small, family-operated affair which for the Bohemian is like eating at a friend's house. The wife cooks, the husband waits on tables, and the conversation is Czech.

"Frank's Restaurant — Bohemian Cooking" has been in business since I could read. For years there were just two little neon signs — "Restaurant" — that hung in two windows everlastingly steamed up. Outside, a more modern sign now hangs above the door. Inside, there is the same long counter, ten stools usually occupied by four or five Bohemians, at least six tables, an old wooden high chair, and Frank himself, round, red, bald and wearing a white apron, and the lady in the back who cooks, smiles and never sits. Aromatic clouds of sauerkraut hang in the air, with occasional whiffs of roast pork and dumplings, tripe soup, homemade bakery and coffee.

"Pelikan's" is no longer run by the gentle old man with the white mustache, whose spotted dog of indistinguishable breed forever padded behind him. Someone has taken the dusty stuffed animals out of the front window. The whole place has been remodeled. Inside, it is lighter than before. The menu is no longer written by hand. I miss the dog under my feet. But the name remains. It's still called, "Pelikan's." The food is still Bohemian and homemade. And so are the people.

The Bohemian home is all that I have said of Cermak Road and then some. It is good cooking, heavy bakery, cleanliness, saving a dollar, the family, gossip, pinochle, Pilsener with lots of talk, lots of hollering.

It is sometimes a two-flat house (an investment, of course), usually a bungalow (the old standard of wealth), and, less frequently now, the basement of a one-story house. The "Bohemian-in-the-basement" is not a myth, not really a very funny joke. It was a way of life for a people whose only faith was security. Maybe they learned this in the old country. Maybe the depression taught them, yet inside the heart and head of every Bohemian is the passion to save things — buttons, rags, rusty nails, paper bags. "You never know when you might need them." To keep everything fresh, new, untainted, untried is the way to live. There is a certain distrust in making a beginning. Live in the basement, save on electricity, save on heat. In the old days, just a stove, a light or two, an ice box, a round oak table protected with a flowery oilcloth, enough wooden chairs for the family and friends and the smell of food. Upstairs, a museum of good furniture, slipcovers on the sofa, newspapers on the kitchen floor, oriental rugs and maybe some crystal from Prague. All of it shined, dusted, rubbed every week. All waiting for a time, for something or somebody.

The house is painted inside and out every year, so it always looks like new. The back yard, forever neat and trimmed. Flowers? Of course — roses and peonies. And as soon as they start making a mess with their petals, out they go in the alley. The alley? The concrete parks of Bohemia. The children's playground for baseball and hide-and-seek and the great sport of alley-picking. "Look what I found behind Rucka's house! A lamp! So what if it's cracked. All I need is a bulb and some cord. Let's go all the way down the alley to Cermak to see what else there is!"

They say my Bohemia is notorious for other things — especially a section called Cicero. But I wouldn't know. I walk down Cermak, eat Bohemian food, drink Pilsener, and read the Life newspaper . . . just like a Bohemian.

The Bakery

There are almost as many bakeries along Cermak Road in Cicero and Berwyn as savings and loans. And both get their fair share of Bohemian investors — the bakeries probably coming out a little ahead on Saturdays only because they are open longer, and the returns are sweeter.

Nobody knows what it is between Bohemians and their bakery. They just never seem to get enough of it. Take the average Bohemian family with a mother and a grandmother in it, and you have a small bakery in itself. Grandma conjuring up all the old recipes in her head, mother watching and following closely in her footsteps. "How much salt in the houska, Babi (grandma)?" Silence. Grandma tastes a fingerful of batter and scatters a magic handful of salt.

Friday night is usually baking night in the neighborhood. And no matter how many housky, kolacky, or coffeecakes are on the table Saturday morning, someone in the family will usually be told, "Stop at Vesecky's (or Fingerhut's or Vales' or Stetina's or Minarik's) for some Bohemian rye ... maybe a poppyseed babovka, too." Let it be known, all cheap Bohemian jokes aside, when it comes to bakery, the Bohemians are spendthrifts.

At 8 o'clock on a Friday night, Jim Vesecky Sr. sets the ovens going behind his bakery at 6634 Cermak. "I'm just starting on the rye now," he says. "About 30 quarts in a mixing kettle. I'm kinda filling in tonight. Two of my bakers are out; Harry Rauch is sick and Jerry Kadlec is on vacation."

Old man Vesecky is as happy a baker as you could find anywhere. He's a heavy-set man, 62 years old, whose whole life is baking.

"I've been on the street 41 years. Started in 1929 during the Depression, at 6234. My father was a baker, too. My son Jim went to college and everything,

graduated. Went downtown to look for a job a couple of days in a row. It
didn't look too good, I guess. Going back and forth every day . . . working in a
office. 'Pa,' he said, 'I'm going to be a baker.' If that's what you want, okay, I
said. We're partners now, the two of us."

When you deal with bakers, you deal with recipes so big they boggle the
mind. Jim, I ask, what's the recipe for Bohemian rye? And Jim smiles and
starts a soliloquy on rye that raises like the very dough itself:

"Well, there's the long rye and the square rye and the bucket rye; and then
there's the round rye which we call Orbit rye. Orbit rye is a white rye. The
medium rye is darker. The mix for rye bread is ¾ rye mix plus Bohemian
flour, a bleached white flour. You can't put all rye in there because then you'd
have bread like a panny cake. For the Orbit rye you use two bags of medium
rye (100 pounds to a bag) and 1 bag of spring flour and blend it together, 4 to
4½ pounds to a quart; ½ ounce of caraway to a quart; 1¼ ounces of salt to a
quart and ½ ounce of yeast to a quart.

"First, though, you gotta start with the sponge, what we call the sponge, for
real sour dough flavoring. It's made three or four hours before the dough is
really mixed, a combination of yeast and rye dough to give a strong flavor.
That's what gives rye the real sour taste. That's with all the ryes. Then the
mixing . . . I do it mostly by touch, you just about know the feel of it. You let it
raise then about an hour."

Jim, I say . . . one loaf. I was thinking about one loaf of rye . . . .

"That'll give you about 24 2-pound Orbits in a batch, 70 1-pounders, 10 3-
pounders. Long ryes, about 12 3-pounders, 150 1-pounders, and 60 square 1-
pounders. One loaf? . . . I don't know. You'd have to break it down some
way."

After the rye batter, Jim starts on the apple slices. He opens three 6-pound
cans of apples. He begins rolling out the dough with a steel rolling pin,
sprinkling the flour, clapping his hands like magic. "You gotta grease and
dust the pans with crumbs. That way it gets a better bottom."

Houska is one of the Bohemian favorites. It's hard to describe. It's eaten
like bread but tastes like coffeecake. How do you explain houska to non-
houska people, Jim?

"Oh, it's like a rich coffeecake twist with raisins and nuts. Lots of people put
fruit in it. You eat it plain, you eat it with butter, you smear jelly on it."

I try again while he's working the apple slices. . . . What's the recipe for
houska, Jim?

"Twenty quarts . . . water or milk. Twenty ounces of salt, a pound and a
quart. Fifteen pounds of sugar, 15 pounds of butter or shortening, 100 pounds
of flour, 6 pounds of yeast, 5 quarts of eggs, 40 pounds of raisins, 10 pounds of
nuts, cashews and sliced almonds."

I'm almost afraid to ask. How many housky, Jim?

"Around 160. We get to the housky later in the morning. You'll see. Bread first. Rye. Then white bread and buns. Then coffeecakes, then houska."

There is the smell, always the smell of dough and flour. And to the apple slices now is added the sweet scent of cinnamon as the old man continues his work with the two pans of slices, moving back to the can of flour, sprinkling it carefully over the top of dough, running the steel rolling pin over the edge of the pan to cut off the excess dough; then letting out the air with a pricker ("An antique," Jim laughs) — something like a scrub brush with nails instead of bristles — and then brushing the top layer of dough with a mixture of eggs and water. "Bake 'em for an hour," he says. "Later, we ice 'em."

It is only 9:20 p.m. and the bread dough and the apple slices are ready. He starts on some pies . . . 10 large, 10 medium and 12 small pies every day. Also, for Saturday, 24 custard and 24 pumpkin pies. Some of these have been prepared the day before. So at 9:30 he puts pies and apple slices into the small oven to bake for an hour.

The first baker, Al Bren, comes in carrying his apron at 9:31 p.m. Jim keeps talking about the bakery business . . .

"During the week, the bakers come in at 2:30 a.m. The hardest part is getting up. The wives? Hell, they have nothing to say about the hours jsut as long as they get the money.

"You got to always keep up, come up with something new for the people. I read a lot of these bakery magazines . . . try to come up with some new coffeecakes. I go to these conventions for bakers. If I come back with maybe one new idea, its worth it. The customers lots of times remind us of the things we used to make, different breads maybe, so we try again.

"We make a lot of good bakery. Saturday morning, you know, I don't know where the hell all the people come from. Lot of times, I wonder, how the hell can those people wait out there like that holding a number? I can't stand around in a store that goddam long. I get nervous. They must feel they ain't going to get the stuff or something."

Al, in white apron, white T-shirt, white pants and socks, Class A regulation baker's uniform with standard white paper overseas-style baker's cap, begins moving racks around, looking for trays. Then it's Al and Jim, together now, working across from each other at the center table where all the action takes place . . . "the bench," the bakers call it. Al kneading the pile of rye dough in the bin beneath the sliding tabletop bread board. Then lifting the dough out, both arms full of folding-like sacks, and placing it all to the right of him.

"Make about 24 of those," Jim says. And that's about all he says to a baker who knows the business of bread. Al begins slicing and scaling the ryes at 2-pounds, 4-ounces apiece.

Freddie Elftmann, baker No. 2, comes through the back door at 9:45 p.m.

Al begins rolling the chunks of dough he has scaled into small, round loaves, two at a time, two at a time, one in each hand, really laying into them. All you smell is flour. He moves strenuously with legs, back, arms, shoulders, hands, neck, head ... even the eyes roll up. Dough is no pushover. It takes a lot of muscle to work into shape.

At 9:50 p.m., baker No 3, George Strnad, comes in with his apron.

Jim, Al and Freddie all working the Orbit rye now. Jim placing them, four to a pan.

Freddie is a tall, thin man with straight, long hair neatly combed and an assortment of tatoos on his arms. There is an aura of the master sergeant about him. And all you hear now, Freddie and Al working across from each other, is the clicking of the scales and the plopping of rye dough as it is cut and shaped into 1-pounders of bread. Flour flies everywhere.

Jim Bruzek, baker No. 4, a semi-retired baker from Cicero, steps in at 9:55, filling in for Kadlec, the vacationing baker. "Now we're bringing in the heavy-weights," jokes Freddie as Bruzek ignores the remark and heads down to the basement to put on his working clothes.

One rack is filled with 15 pans of bread loaves. Jim Bruzek comes on the scene and uncovers a huge kettle of dough that has raised four or five inches above the rim, just as George Hruska Sr., the fifth baker, enters the shop at 10 p.m.

The old man moves the rye to the proof-box (a steam box) to raise it some more before going into the oven.

Now four bakers are at the bench rolling dough. Jim Bruzek, the heavy-weight, rolling like jelly himself, a man expressing complete joy in his work, shaking all over, both his hands moving furiously, even his head and eyeballs lost in a steady staccato of bread, bread, bread ...

George Strnad wears a little white skull cap on the back of his head ... the only baker in the batch with an original headpiece. He looks like a serene monk in the kitchen of a quiet monastery contentedly doing the Lord's work. He handles the dough like an offering ... while Freddie goes after dough like a precision machinist ... while Bruzek rolls into it because he really loves the feel of dough, and all the world is soft and sticky ... bread, bread, bread ... boom, boom, boom ... bounce, bounce, bounce ...

George Hruska Sr. begins rolling the long ryes at a second table while the other three bakers halt momentarily to lift and dump another kettle of dough on the bench. Freddie lays into it immediately, with a slicer that fits neatly in a man's fist ... chop, chop, chop ... All the bakers begin rolling the dough into round loaves which will be easier to roll later into long ones. At 10:15 the tables are filled with loaves of bread.

Al is the hardest baker to keep track of, a wiry little man who is always everywhere, forever running from bench to oven to steam box to empty rack to sink and back to the ovens. He belongs in an old-time movie.

Freddie, the take-charge baker, gives a few close-order drills: "Start pounding these out next, George, you get five squares." Then silence again except for the sound of dough being cut, being scaled . . . the wonder of it all as Jim and George and Al slap it down, stretch it out, fold it, knead it, roll it into sausage shapes. Silence . . . What do bakers talk about? Nothing, at the moment. They're too busy pounding the hell out of the dough.

It is 10:30 p.m. White bread and buns coming up next. And then the coffee-cakes.

Al is up to more of his capers. He is hopping around from steambox to oven to tray. He is sharpening knives, cutting dough into pieces, checking the round ryes in the steamboxes. He is taking hot pies out of the oven, moving around like a nervous Stan Laurel. Ah, the aroma of hot pumpkin pie. Al is in two places at one time, preparing the round ryes for the oven . . . brushing ("washing") them ("strong") with straight eggs, puncturing them, then placing the pans into the oven for almost an hour. Al giving each load his undivided attention, touching, watching, closing the oven door for the final bake.

Back to the center bench where George Hruska Sr. is rolling out dough

(butter dough) for coffeecakes, adding lumps of shortening, folding the whole piece over once, twice, sprinkling flour, rolling it wide with the pin, folding it again, really stretching the body over it, sprinkling another wisp of flour. "Freddie, how do you want them? Split 'em like always?"

"Yeah, split 'em."

George Strnad is working on buttercrust buns. There's a warm, white, sweet, salty, floury, doughy madness to the bakery now as bakers appear and disappear before your eyes. There are bakers everywhere — behind you, in front of you, beneath the tables, pushing racks, unloading ovens, closing steamboxes, feeding the sheeting machine and talking now, occasionally talking almost to themselves ... "

"Tell him about the home brew you're making, George ..."

"Jim Bruzek can eat a whole coffeecake himself ... "

"Just tell him how many bottles of beer you drink ... "

"Five quarts a day ... that's not much ... for a baker, five quarts a day ... "

Poppyseed buns, plain buns, buttercrust buns, salty horns, hot-dog buns ... George Strnad, in white skullcap, having a holy good time rolling out the bun dough into long, snakey pieces and then tying them into knots. "Kaiser rolls," he whispers and smiles ... "Kaiser rolls. Next, small houska or twists." ... George dancing an in-place twist himself as he ties his fingers in the dough.

Al is now roughing up the long ryes for the oven, washing them with egg, breaking them with the quick slice of a knife across the dough ... "Let the gases out ... let them breathe ... " puncturing them with a handle of nails.

Eleven-fifteen p.m. and the bakers are still working the bread and buns. Freddie is rolling hot dogs in dough for pigs-in-the-blanket ... "About 20 dozen," he says. Jim Bruzek is making poppyseed buns, putting the stripes on them, patting them down. Poppyseed, poppyseed, poppyseed ... only the Bohemians understand poppyseed. "Bohemian bakery ... poppyseed," smiles Bruzek. "I worked for a bakery once in Wheaton. They don't even know what the hell poppyseed is in Wheaton." Old man Vesecky nods his head and dumps a 30-pound box of Extra Fancy Golden Raisins into a mixing bowl big enough for a man's bath.

Eleven-thirty p.m. Al is taking out the round ryes ... and how round and rye and crusty-crackled brown they are. Freddie is scaling the dough at 12 ounces for coffeecakes while George Hruska Sr. is busy rolling the dough for white bread.

At 11:45 a dour George Hruska Jr. (a cousin of George Sr.), the sixth baker, the cake man, comes into the bakery. ("He doesn't like to be called Junior," whispers Jim Vesecky Sr. "He's just plain George.")

By midnight more than 100 loaves of rye bread have been baked, with God knows how many more in the ovens, the steamboxes, with buns coming up next and then white bread. Al is in tune with the temperature of the ovens, 355 degrees. Al, at midnight, is a whirling white blur, ever rising.

And now, the coffeecakes.

George Strnad and Freddie make the first soft move — 12 long, cheese coffeecakes. Then George Hruska Sr. and Jim Bruzek begin warming up, rolling into 20 almond coffeecakes . . . Jim spreading it all out . . . is there no end to the stretch of dough?

Jim Vesecky Sr. stands by the ovens, adding streussel to more coffeecakes. And all the while, Just Plain George Hruska, the cake man, is busy gathering his pans and forms.

Coffeecakes, coffeecakes, coffeecakes: 800 to 900 coffeecakes on Saturday . . . more than 50 varieties. You begin to run out of names for them . . . What are these called? "Road bricks." And these? "Cow Flops." The bakers have an essential working man's sense of humor . . . they call them as they shape them.

Twelve-twenty a.m. Picture a table lined up with 24 long, fruit coffeecakes — cherry, peach, apple, pineapple, blueberry; a cart loaded with cans of apple, cherry, prune, cheese, poppyseed, blueberry; Bruzek and George Sr. juggling some jellyrolls; Vesecky Sr. making custard pies; Just Plain George Hruska carrying 36 pints of fresh strawberries for his cakes; while Al is shoveling out the long ryes, 3, 6, 9, 12 at a time . . . 12:35 a.m.

Al is behind. The heat is on. Al is always behind around this time as the bakers begin to gang up on him and fill rack upon rack of doughy, fruity, nutty, sweet delicacies awaiting the final touch of the oven, being emptied first now of the final batch of rye.

Talk to the bakers . . . slow down the coffeecake crusade. "WGN," Jim Bruzek says. "WGN, Franklyn MacCormack, the baker's best friend. When I had my own place, I used to listen to him all night long. I love baking. I've been doing it all my life. I get a kick out of it You see what you make . . . the whole thing, what you do with your hands. I got out of it when it got to be a rat race. There's got to be an end to making money sometime."

At 12:45 a.m. Jim Vesecky Sr. begins stacking the freshly baked bread into the service case which opens Vasecky directly into the store — the only visible connnection between the bake shop in the back and the store in the front. When the service case is filled, Jim goes into the darkened store and begins placing some of the bread on shelves for the customers. Surrounding him, the soft smell of warm rye . . .

Meanwhile, Just Plain George is busy with his cakes, frosting them, decorating them with trim, putting them into the refrigerator . . . while old man Vesecky returns from the front to fill 24 pies with pumpkin . . . while George Hruska Sr. makes 12 cherry/pecan coffeecakes with George Strnad lending a hand, cutting each roll in half, giving the two pieces his touching twist.

"Strnad!" Freddie calls out . . . and Strnad rushes over to help him lift a burden of dough the size of a man . . . Strnad bending over it, his arms buried up to his elbows in dough. He retrieves his hands and pats the dough gently, like a man expressing his affection for a woman's behind.

Al? Where's Al? What's he up to now? Does the baker never break?

"I don't sleep on Saturday," he says. (Today is Saturday! What happened to Friday night?) "On Saturday I ride my bicycle. Sometimes I put it in my car and go down to the lake and ride all around the lakefront, even up to Lincoln Park. On Sunday I play ball with my son. He's 23 years old. I play ball with my 23-year-old son to help him get his arms back in shape. He was in an explosion in Viet Nam. Life is cheap over there."

At 1:15 a.m. all the bakers are scaling off dough for coffeecakes, still more coffeecakes.

Orders. On the front table, hanging from the front wall, lists of orders:

—2 dozen chocolate jelly rolls for Pavenza
—1 poppyseed loaf iced for Novy
—2 surprise coffeecakes for Prohaska
—1 apple cinnamon raisin coffeecake for Marek

Cakes:

—4 tier pound cake, 16, 14, 12, 8 (layers/diameter) Golden Anniversary, 1 ornament for Samec.
—2 tier pound cake, 12, 8, pillar in between, Silver Anniversary, 1 ornament, for Arnaskus

Jim Bruzek is now at the center bench with 250 "pockets" of dough to be filled systematically with poppyseed, cheese, prune, apricot, then pinched closed and set in a round pan, three of each kind. What kind of coffeecake you call that? "Surprise coffeecake. Can't tell what's inside till you bite it. If you like apricot and you get poppyseed instead, you get a surprise."

Says old man Vesecky in passing: "I got a lunch in the oven. I got the meatloaf in there. I should have put it in sooner, but I was too busy." He sets down two cold quarts of Meister Brau. One quart he brings to the bench for George Hruska Sr., who acknowledges the bottle with a nod of his head.

Al is now putting coffeecakes into the oven. Jim Bruzek is now (2 a.m.) making poppyseed babovka ... rolling it, dropping the dough around a cake form with a hole in the middle, basting it, puncturing it with the pointed end of a file.

Two-fifteen ...the smell of strawberries. Just Plain George has four pans filled with strawberries. George Strnad joins him and begins slicing the strawberries with the sharp edge of an open can, mixing them in a bowl fit for the gods, then plunking down handfuls of strawberries for the lower layer of a whipped cream cake.

Says old man Vesecky: "Lotta work in a bakery, huh? I always say, stuff got yeast in it, you gotta move."

George Hruska Sr. pours himself a beer while finishing up on cinnamon bread with Bruzek. "I used to roll these goddam things out all by hand," says George to Freddie, who is working the sheeting machine for them. Freddie finds the machine more interesting than the comment and so ignores it.

Two-thirty a.m. and Jim Vesecky Sr. walks to the front table with a tray of hot meatloaf. Ah, the smell of hot meatloaf with onion. Jim grabs a loaf of fresh rye from the rack and begins making sandwiches, slicing the meatloaf into thick pieces.

Just Plain George is at the lemon chiffon and chocolate custard pies now. At 2:35, George Strnad is plopping strawberries on top of cheesecake while old man Vesecky is passing out the sandwiches. Two-forty-five, Just Plain George Hruska is piling rack upon rack of strawberry cakes into the refrigerator. Two-forty-six, Jim Vesecky Sr. brings out two more quarts of Meister Brau. Everybody eats . . . nobody has time to eat anything. The bakery itself seems to be rising in its own heat.

On with the coffeecakes! Freddie is making a tableful of round ones that are either all cheese, all poppyseed, half apricot and half cheese or one-quarter cheese, one-quarter prune, one-quarter apricot and one-quarter poppyseed.

"He's a swastika, watch it!" George Strnad continually jokes about Freddie.

"You know what's wrong?" says Freddie. "Years ago I was your apprentice."

Through it all, directions, orders of any sort are scarcely heard. Nobody is really telling anybody what to do next. All the bakers *know* what's next. All the baking is being done. One man constantly, unconsciously, helps the other.

Al, how do you keep track of what goes in and comes out of those damn ovens?

"I don't know. I've been doing it for 45 years. I was a cake decorator for 20 years, but you go nuts at that. Women don't know what they want. Time for a change. So I go to the ovens."

Three a.m. finds Jim Bruzek working on "pizza" coffeecakes — cheese, apricot and prune dolloped out from the finger, squeezed out of the other hand like child's play. Where oh where does all the dough come from?

Fifteen minutes later Freddie begins scaling houska. Bruzek rolls it and begins filling up a pan. Strnad and Hruska Sr. join in, 1 pound 13 ounces, 1 pound 5 ounces, 15 housky to a tray.

At 3:20 a.m. the second member of the Vesecky family walks in. Jimmy Jr., the baker's son, the only baker in the place (the only one on Cermak Road?) with a collage degree. Jimmy starts immediately on the houska, slicing the loaves in threes, preparing to braid them, three strands of dough on the bottom, two on top.

Three-thirty a.m., everybody makes houska.

Jimmy Vesecky Jr. is a tall, quiet, extremely mild-mannered individual who looks much like his father. He has a degree in accounting from De Paul University, but he likes to bake. What's more, he understands and respects the family tradition of good bakery.

"We have about six small grocers who'll be coming in soon," he says. "It won't be long before my mother will be down here getting those orders ready." Mother and Father Vesecky live, of course, above the store. Where else would a neighborhood baker hang his apron? The work that a man does, the things that are most meaningfully made with the hands are traditionally done close to home.

At 4 a.m. you would expect the bakers to be slowing down, but they are going at it with even greater gusto! All eight bakers bending, rolling, slicing, scaling, cutting, moving trays and racks loaded with bakery. Four a.m. and not a single man has even yawned! Not one baker has leaned against a table for a moment's rest!

"Should I go ahead with that second dough, Jim?" asks Just Plain George of Jimmy Jr.

"In about 15 minutes," he replies.

At 4 o'clock in the morning, Al breaks out of the bakery, running out the back door with two trays of cinnamon bread to cool off on the next door porch railing. "Oh, how I like to get out and get some of that cool air!"

After 4 a.m., after the houska, the cycle is almost complete as the bakers begin with the white dough again for bread and buns. Al has his coffeecakes to keep him going, but he is catching up. At 4:05 Mrs. Vesecky, the mother of all the shop, quietly walks in and says, "Good morning, boys," to all the bakers.

In the meantime (about time?) a little temper has flared . . .just when it seemed all bakers worked at the same temperature. Just Plain George Hruska is not too happy with the cinnamon bread. "Look at it! It's like a pancake!" Jim Bruzek says it's not the rolling. Jim Vesecky Sr. says it should be handled more carefully out of the oven. Just Plain George shakes his head and mumbles to the cinnamon bread, coaxing it back to shape.

Mrs. Vesecky is slicing bread in the front store, packing orders for the six grocers. "This batch of white bread is going to be the last thing we bake today," says the old man.

Four-thirty a.m. Cleanup time. Al is sweeping around the ovens; Jimmy Jr. is scraping old dough off the floor; Jim Bruzek is washing his hands at the sink; George Strnad is wiping a stack of baking sheets; Freddie is brushing flour off the tables; George Hruska Sr. is sweeping the floor. Just Plain George is at work with his cakes, cutting and filling them with pineapple, covering them with whipped cream. Four-thirty a.m., Helen, the first of the salesladies, enters the shop with a "Good morning" to all.

"How'd you sleep last night, Helen?" asks Jim Sr. with a smile.

"I won't answer because I know you'll take it the wrong way," she says, and all the bakers laugh, probably taking it the wrong way.

For a windup, the artistry of Just Plain George, the whipped-cream-cake man smearing it on in the final minutes of a baker's morning. Doing the fancy stuff now, squeezing cones into ornate squiggles around the cake; shooting the whipped cream on the layers of a strawberry cake, putting on the top layer, then plastering the whole thing with whipped cream. Just Plain George now stacking whipped cream pies in the refrigerator; now slicing bananas, building himself a banana cream pie to end all banana cream pies — the careful peeling of each banana, the quick, sure slices, the delicate drop of them on top of the filling.

Just Plain George wild in a world of whipped cream — whipped cream pumpkin pie, whipped cream strawberry coffeecake, whipped cream almond and prune coffeecake, whipped cream, whipped cream, whipped cream . . .For encores, the cake man stuffing delicately baked shells for cream rolls.

Mrs. Vesecky and Helen place the hot coffeecakes on pans and begin filling the counters of the front store ...First, it's Mrs. Vesecky with a rack of hot rolls ...Then it's Helen putting out the pies....Mrs. Vesecky again ...

"Yeah, the buns go into the oven now, same as last night," says Jim Sr. And you realize a whole night has passed; it is Saturday; Vesecky's Bakery will be open in an hour: people will begin coming in for their bakery, almost 700 of them before the day is over.

Only Jimmy remains to do the wedding cakes. And somewhere between 5 and 7 in the morning, the action shifts from the back of the bakery to the front store.

At 6 a.m. the Berwyn street-cleaning machine brushes its way past Vesecky's front curb. There are only a few lights on in the store, but there is a feeling that the bakery is open. Helen can be seen filling the front window with every conceivable kind of coffeecake till even the glass glistens with icing.

At 6:02 the first customer walks down the street and steps into Vesecky's for a loaf of rye bread. The lights go on....The second man comes in and buys a surprise coffeecake and a loaf of white bread. "For breakfast," he says. "That should do it." These are the sidewalk customers now, people close by in the neighborhood. "I want a dozen kolacky," says a woman. "Six with cheese and six prune."

Soon the cars begin to pull up. Soon there will be 30, 40, 50 people in the shop at one time. The coffeecakes and bread will move out of the store faster than they were put into the ovens.

You always leave a bakery shop like Vesecky's with more than you came in for. Like the old man out front this very minute, shopping with a small list from his wife ...one small round rye, six poppyseed buns ...and ends up buying an apricot and prune coffeecake besides because it looks so good. So the wife will give him hell when he gets home, so what? He's got his coffeecake.

"You look like a man who enjoys good bakery," says Jimmy, after my long day's journey into a night at Vesecky's. "Here, take some home for breakfast."

At the back door of a house in Berwyn I meet my mother in law, who wonders where her sleepy-eyed son in law has been all night.

"What did you buy so much bakery for, when I baked fresh houska last night?"

I shrug my shoulders.

"Where did you get it?"

I nod my head and hand her the goods. She opens the plain white bags one at a time, studies the rye bread, feels the houska, peeks at the size of the kolacky, and says one word:

"Vesecky's"

Neighborhood Games

We joined hands, 10 or 15 of us, forming a human barrier at each end of the asphalt lot next to the school. Maybe 150 feet separated us and knots of smaller kids who would inevitably get caught in the danger zone of our game.

"Who should we call this time?" we whispered. Unanimously we called the one kid we always called, the one kid we all hated — a tough, smart-aleck kid named Jerry.

"Red Rover, Red Rover, let Jerry come over!" We braced ourselves, checked our footing, squeezed hands till they hurt and you could feel the sweat. From the other side, a fat, blond haired kid released himself from the line, smug in his own notoriety based on bullying everyone, and began a lumbering jog toward our line in search of the weakest link to crash through and maybe break a few arms.

He headed for Louie. And at the moment of impact, we doubled up behind Little Louie and watched Jerry totter and then kiss the asphalt with a bounce and a thunk, and with minimum casualties to our side. He didn't cry. (He never cried.) But we had brought Fat Jerry down again, and the feeling was something special in our childish hearts. We had won! We screamed and jeered and danced around him, till he was able to rise and get his revenge on us. We would cry. But that was the game. And then the bell rang.

I don't remember my first childhood game or just how it came about. But it must have been Hide' n' Seek or just plain fighting. Maybe I poked the kid next door in the mouth just for the hell of it. Or maybe he poked me. And then we became friends.

Games, though, always games. Playing in front of the house, playing in the backyard, in the alley, in the street, in the corner prairie, in the park. Games defined us at an early age and, most importantly, had nothing to do with grownups. Games were the only things that made sense in a world of forever going to bed too early and getting up too early, eating meals with the family, going to school, to church, to visit the relatives on Sunday afternoons.

I don't see many neighborhood games being played anymore, and I can only wonder why. Blame it on the times, and the adults. In regulating games, we've taken the fun out of growing up, and destroyed imagination along the way. Either we corral the kids in planned playgrounds of the latest colorful equipment, or we decree entire old neighborhoods "unsafe" and re-establish our lifestyles and values in the predictable frontiers of suburbia, where oneupmanship is the only game in town. Then we wonder what's wrong with our kids. Hell, they've never had to use their imagination to survive or taste joy, for one thing.

Games destroyed time. Games gave us the first edge of ego (or is it macho in these chauvinistic times?), determining precisely how, in what way, at which game we were better than the kid next door or down the block. What's more, we often played for blood, though we didn't look upon it that way. Winning or losing (even how you played the game) were secondary to the very thrill of playing the game.

We grew up while playing games, though we never wondered what we were growing into. Psychologists would explain this to us later in adulthood, when most of our playing would be analyzed as game plans, and our physical energies reduced to spectatoritis and machines that made sport of us.

We played three games at my parochial school, where gym or sports of any sort were unheard of. We play Red Rover in that asphalt lot adjacent to the school, and we played Horse, and Buck-Buck in a well worn prairie across the street.

All three of the games were against school rules. We could be punished for playing them (a ruler across the knuckles and hind end, or an hour after school writing "I must not's" till the hand eventually fell off).

To this day I don't know what we were supposed to do during recess except maybe mill around outside with our hands clasped, praying for a vocation to the priesthood, or maybe asking St. Peter (more likely Satan) to please pay a sudden call on Fat Jerry and take him to his just reward.

You must not play Red Rover, you must not play Horse, you must not play Buck-Buck, you must not throw snowballs, you must not fly paper airplanes out the window ... you must not, must not, must not ... or!

But in a child's world, the threat of punishment merely increases the pleasure. To play Horse (knocking one or more kids off the kids' backs, tugging and ripping shirts and jackets and pants ...) with the added excitement of possibly being caught by Old Battle Ax herself, was something close to the sublime. "I dare you to ... " was another wonderful spur-of-the-moment game.

Buck-Buck was played with two teams and a telephone pole or a tree. If your team was forming the line of bent backs to carry the load of the jumpers on the other team, you placed your biggest man as the lead man to hold onto the telephone pole while the rest of the guys strung out behind him with bent backs, five, six, seven lengths, awaiting the onslaught. When the teams switched, you saved the big kid for the very last jumper. You had your whole team piled high on the backs of the others, and then you called Bruno to bring down the house.

Oh the pain, the excitement, no matter which team you were on. Everybody was a hero in Buck-Buck! "Come on Bruno!" And big Bruno would begin his lunge like a bear, leap his damndest, and crumble every kid in the class who was brave enough to relish the purpose of the game: suffering. And, of course, joy.

Oh, there were rules to the game. Like the call, "Buck-Buck, how many fingers up?" And the other team was to guess before sending on the players. But rules didn't matter in most of our games. Just the agony in winning or losing, and the danger of getting caught.

Just plain sidewalks were incredibly conducive to childhood games. If you started with "Step on a crack" and then graduated to Hand Ball, by the time you were in the upper grades of grammar school you were usually addicted to the last sidewalk game you would ever play. And that involved gambling. Lagging Pennies it was called. You stood two squares back, your right foot parallel to the line ("No hunching!"), carefully held a penny between your thumb and first finger, then gently, ever so gently, let it go with a body motion and calculated drift toward the second line. To land on top or as near to it as possible. Anyone landing behind you, you beat — and kept the penny.

Pennies, in time, changed to nickels, dimes, quarters, and halves. You began, then, to understand the feel of gambling ...

But there were always the steps. Concrete, stone, or wood (stone was the best). You got yourself a rubber ball, put one or two kids behind you, and you played Stoop Ball.

Poor kid's baseball, when you didn't have the bat, the ball, the glove, the diamond, or enough kids to make two teams. You marked off certain distances from the steps. A single was maybe if the ball bounced (before the fielder could catch it ... Out!) beyond the sidewalk. A double was in the grass. A triple was beyond the tree. A home run was in the street — if the fielder could get to it before a car got to him.

The batter held the rubber ball in his hand, stood sideways to the steps, kept his eye on where the outfielder(s) was playing him, held the ball tightly in his right hand, and either hit the ball lightly against the steps for a cheap shot Texas leaguer, or slammed it passionately into the step with all his strength.

The beautiful smash, the ultimate thrill, was to slam the ball precisely on the edge of a stone step. There would be this mellow sound to the ball, something like "wonk" when it hit the edge perfectly, and you could feel and see the ball sailing up and even beyond the street. "Yeahhhhhhh! Home run!"

In the alleys we played Kick the Can . . . not too exciting. Or we tried to play softball on the narrowest baseball diamond in the world. Only the ball would inevitably land in a yard with a mean dog in it — usually a chow who was trained to eat kids; or with a mean neighbor who would not return the ball unless we moved the whole game farther down the alley or he would call the police because we were disturbing his tomato plants. So we moved the game. A few days later we would innocently return to the same old spot, but this time we'd include the Crabby Old Man as part of the game. If the Crabby Old Man gets the ball you're not only out, but you "automatically" lose the game. "Automatically" was one of our favorite game words. Some kind of disaster was always happening to us . . . "automatically" changing the whole course of action.

Mostly, though, we used the alley for the most exciting game of all: junking. Who could find the best stuff that nobody else wanted? I once brought home, in the course of just two summer days, a China lamp, a Philco radio, short-wave and all, without tubes; a box of old Kayo soda bottles (worth 2 cents apiece), a stack of 78 r.p.m. records, including a classic song: "Where Do Ya Work-a John? I Push-a Push-a Push."

They tried to put us in playgrounds, predictable places with swings, slides, seesaws, all painted an institutional green. The whole setting was cyclone fenced, barb wired and padlocked, open only at the discretion, and soberness, of Old Joe Vacek. Sometimes he'd open it at 1 o'clock in the morning, sit inside on the bench, and wonder why the kids never came.

The last time I saw my old playground it was still locked. But there was a kid who had climbed inside to fly a kite. Now there was a kid who understood playgrounds.

Neighborhood games, of course, were seasonal, with spring and summer being the best of times. You could play outside till the streetlights went on. And the streetlights went on later and later in summer.

In the fall, everybody was outside raking huge piles of leaves onto the street, along the gutters. These we flung ourselves into with abandon, burrowing and burying ourselves into the very depths. Later in the evening there would be the ritual of burning the leaves. Nothing will ever equal the sad, sweet smell of burning leaves. Aside from the wonder of fire, which held us to our innermost selves like some kind of vision, there was the majesty of smoke. Huge billows of it, which we wore like cloaks to make us invisible.

"I'm the Shadow!" "I'm Superman!" "I'm Captain Marvel!" I'm anything but human and adult.

We made orange crate scooters out of a 2x4, an orange crate and one roller skate. We attached sticks for handles, nailed tin cans for headlights, and hummed down the sidewalks, through the alleys on them till the vibrations tickled us and made our teeth rattle.

No playground could ever provide this. No playground could ever equal an empty prairie on the corner, or a foundation that had been dug in a nearby lot where a new house was to be constructed.

And no game would ever quite equal the final stages of Hide'n'Seek, which had slowly evolved into a boy/girl sort of thing, now played around the park and quite a few blocks from home.

You were almost out of grammar school now. Neighborhood games no longer mattered. The boundaries had changed, among other things.

If you still called it Hide'n'Seek at this stage, it didn't matter if the game was ever played out to the end. It didn't matter if the streetlights ever went on, or someone was calling you home over the backyard fence far away from where you felt you really were.

For you had suddenly found something nature had been hiding from you for a long time. You had found love — first love, puppy love, as grownups chose to make light of it. And no matter the name, it was an old, old game of very mysterious rules. But one you were sure you would never lose.

CLP

Cicero

I return to Cicero often these days. I spent a childhood, a boyhood, and a young manhood here before moving away. I visit my parents, my friends, say hello to the few old neighbors who are still left on the block. I keep coming back to that particular stretch of Cermak Road that was the heart of the place to me, Cermak Road from Central to Lombard.

I come back to reestablish my identity with an ethnic culture, the Czechoslovaks. I come back to have roast pork, dumplings and sauerkraut at any one of the homey little Bohemian restaurants along the way. I come back for a beer at Klas' or Old Prague. I stop at the bakery shops, the butcher shops.

I stop at Tony the Shoemaker on 58th Avenue and swear at him, argue with him over prices and workmanship, joke with him the way I did 15 years ago.

People sometimes ask me about the bigotry in Cicero (as if Cicero bigots are any different from Oak Park bigots, Oak Brook bigots, or Kenilworth bigots). I'm not sure Tony the Shoemaker or any of the old hangers-on could even define it. If bigotry means they're afraid to let the "colored" in, then they are guilty of it.

In a way, I identify with the Ciceronians. If I had worked my tail off for family and shelter, and saved and saved and saved and if I had put most of my faith and imagination in the preservation of my property, then I too might fear the movement of the blacks. But since I have no direct investment in the old neighborhood, I can also afford to be as liberal as anybody who lives in Marina City or Kenilworth. I do not condone the violence, the underhandedness, the hate. But I can understand the mentality of fear.

When my family moved there, Cicero was the New West Side, the new Bohemian enclave. Many settled there to work at the huge Western Electric Company on Cermak and 48th. At one time or another, it seemed every Bohemian, Polish, and Yogoslav family had someone who "worked at the Western."

Though Capone was in power along the Chicago boundaries, Cicero had an aura of an early suburbia about it. The houses were mostly brick, solidly-built single dwellings, two-flats, and bungalows. The streets and alleys were spotless. Prairies and prairie lots still gave the whole scene a touch of the countryside. The Bohemians, all the Slavs, took tremendous pride in their homes, their backyards, gardens and fences.

These people went into a frenzy of housecleaning twice a year. I can remember my father taking the Venetian blinds apart to paint them — every damn slat! These people had backyards of flowers and vegetable gardens that seemed to burst into perfection with the mere wave of a garden hose. My image of the average Ciceronian is a man in his undershirt, old pants with the cuffs turned up above his ankles, standing quietly alone in his backyard, holding a hose waist high, gently watering his lawn with rainbows.

Yes, Capone ruled Cicero, but the average Ciceronian never saw, or pretended not to see, the women dance in the raw at the old 4811 Club on Cermak, never met a hooker, never entered the book joints on 25th Street or Cermak Road. And news of all the dark action was seldom acknowledged by the local paper, the Cicero Life. Even when it was, who cared? Not John Buchta, average Ciceronian, who had his own Cicero life to live.

Has anything changed?

Take some early morning shoppers, along Cermak Road, Mr. and Mrs. Tony Vesely, each with a hand on a paper shopping bag.

"I live here 54 years," says the man with an old Bohemian accent. "Was born in Czechoslovakia. Vork here at Ceco Steel. I like here. No move, no move anywhere else."

Says his wife: "Is okay, Cicero, but streets is all the time dirty now. Don't keep clean like used to." The blacks? "Is everywhere problem, no? I think black should live with black, and white should live with white. No problem then."

Local government? I ask. Both husband and wife throw up their hands in disgust. "Is all crooks. Everyone is crooks. I'm sorry to say I even voted for them," the woman confesses.

Cicero has always been "occupational territory" and the natives are seldom restless as long as their persons are secure and their property protected. It has always been. It's not that you can't fight City Hall; it's that you don't need to. City Hall has always known precisely how to cater to the Ciceronian mentality a silent force for good or evil, but mostly a silent force. Threats of fire, theft, chaos will be answered swiftly.

But since 1951 and the first attempt of a black bus driver and his family to settle on Lombard Avenue, the reputation of Cicero has grown uglier and uglier. First Capone, then the blackhater image, and then Martin Luther King. King's belief that "Cicero was to the North what Selma, Alabama was to the South." All of this "force" which brings no understanding among the natives, only fear and hate. Followed by a force of their own. And never out in the open. For Cicero is an alley fighter that strikes in the dark. When all the lights are out in City Hall.

Old Jim Jelinek hawks newspapers, and I can hardly believe he's around, toothless but still laughing and hollering and preaching.

Baseball's his main story. He's umped more neighborhood games than any man alive. "I used to play professional ball myself," he says. "For five years. I'm still umping. Got a game coming up next week. Lot a money riding on a game years ago. Two hundred bucks sometimes. And you know what? I was a pitcher. And you know something else? I was one of the best! You're goddam right I was? I had 3 pitches . . . like this," he demonstrates in the darkness of his stand. "And I'd deliver like this . . . that was my high one. Than I had a drop ball. But the best was my slow one, like this . . . then I pulled the string on it. The hoods backed one of our teams. I once struck out 42 guys in 15 innings."

The old man hawks a few more newspapers, talks a little Bohemian to his customers, and then I throw him a curve, a question about the problems of

Cicero, the blacks, the whole shebang ...

"Blacks? They're all over here. They work here. What the hell you gonna do? But they don't live here! There's no colored ... and there won't be. And if once they get in, that'll be it. I've lived here 56 years. A lot of good people live here. The police, the firemen ... they'll never let them in. You know what's gonna be the ruin of this country? Politicians and blacks!"

So it goes along Cermak. So what do you do? Play ball! I smile at the old ump.

What's there to lose? Ah, that's the real question. Everything, everything, when you're dealing with an ethnic culture that was born in poverty, weaned on the depression, physically, morally, financially strenghtened by the work of war and peace, and finally resurrected by property and cold hard cash in the bank. Their life savings is their only true religion.

A generation of Czechs, Poles, Yugoslavs, now in their 60's, 70's, 80's, with thousands of dollars safely banked in the savings and loans along Cermak Road, they are not about to let loose of what they think life is all about: security. And they are not about to let go of Cicero. Their sons and daughters might — in time, but right now the dike still stands, although the water is rising.

What other culture but the Bohemians bought their first house (perhaps a beautiful brick bungalow) and "saved" it by living in the basement? My own grandparents first did this in Chicago. All the chaos of living, all the entering and leaving, the eating, drinking, cooking, baking, visiting, washing, fighting, pinochle playing, loving and hating was done in the basement. The upstairs was a dustfree museum of unused furniture, clean white curtains, hand-worked doilies, Czechoslovakian crystal, thick soft carpets that you seldom walked upon without being ordered to "take your shoes off." Cicero was once filled with Bohemians who lived this way ... securing the house for some future event (perhaps the visit of a rich relative) which never seemed to happen.

Charles Zajic, president of the Western National Bank at 5801 W. Cermak, has been with the bank for 45 years. A neighborhood bank — like most of the others along Cermak, including the savings and loans — that was built upon a particular thrift.

"We've succeeded because of the ethnic groups here," he says. "The Bohemians are very thrifty. The Poles are the same. The Hollanders, too. We used to have a lot of them, but most of them got very rich and moved to Western Springs."

The young people? Are they as thrifty as their parents?

"No, I don't think so. The older folks used to deny themselves things. They always had the hard cash. They bank it. But the young don't mind going into debt over their ears. Cermak Road ... it's known as the Bohemian Wall

Street," Zajic continues. "From Cicero Avenue to Harlem there are three banks and I think there must be 11 or 13 savings and loans who have deposits of over a billion dollars."

Blacks? The question seems to haunt the heart of every Ciceronian. "Blacks have opened accounts here," says banker Zajic. "Most of them are ministers. And the minute they do, they ask for donations. I don't really know what the future holds for the town."

The way Zajic sees it, the older people are staying while the younger ones move west and northwest. Yet the vacuum is being filled by younger blue-collar workers from Chicago who are buying the older homes, remodeling them, and in most ways keeping up the property the way the old Ciceronians would like it.

Where the dike may give way, the weak spot, seems to be along the line, the Chicago border, Cicero Avenue, the Grant Works area — once heavily Italian — the whole northwest sector of the town. Southern whites are in this area already. They pose a threat, but not as big a threat as the blacks who once again "almost" moved into Cicero on W. 12th Place last spring.

But they didn't make it. The black family said that they didn't know the home they bought was in Cicero. They thought it was in Chicago. But Cicero reminded them with gas-filled bottles and shots in the dark.

"The area is well-secured," said Cicero's council president, John Karner, after the incendiary incident. "We've got to keep law and order."

"Does this mean integration?" someone asked Karner.

"I hope it doesn't mean that," he replied.

I drop in to see John the Real Estate Man along Cermak Road to check the housing business in my old town. John, a likeable young Italian, explains some of the problems and trends he's up against.

He's never been pressured by the blacks, but he's aware of how the Cicero image affects his business. He tells a potential buyer over the phone: "I've got a nice 6-room bungalow in Cicero ... "

"No, I don't want that," replies the customer. "I don't want to live in Cicero."

"Why are people put off the moment you say Cicero?" he wonders. Why indeed. "It must go back to Capone," or Martin Luther King. "The trend is going from Berwyn on west. People do want to move to Berwyn. Bungalows, they're hard to get. We have a saying in real estate that they're built like a fortress. And they can being close to $40,000, if they're in Berwyn.

"But I live in this town. I like it. I don't think Cicero hates the world. I think basically the people of Cicero are good and hard-working. We have the same problems as any other community. I don't think the people live in fear around here. If it happens, it happens. But I, for one, am proud to be here."

I have a boyhood friend, Joe Schweiger, of the Victor Shade Company in

Cicero, at 5810 W. Cermak. He went to work part-time at the first store in 1951, when he was in high school. Today he owns his own place. Joe is big enough now to hang on. "The banks," he claims, "are gettig bigger and bigger. All the little guys are going out of business. The banks are absorbing all the empty stores and turning them into parking lots."

Blacks don't seem to pose a threat to Joe. "Hell, they work here. There's a lot of them that come in my store. They get ripped off by Chicago merchants, but we charge them the same as anybody else. But you've got a strong real estate group here. They're against block-busting."

Boulevard Manor, on the south side of Cicero, in particular, seems to be holding its own. "I've been offered two times what I paid for my place, and it's only 13 years old," says Joe. "It's a good place to live. Some Bohemians, and a lot of Italians there. You know the Italians don't chintz when it comes to fixing up their houses; 35th Street's a good business area. And you know the Bohemian ... his home is his castle."

A late Saturday morning: I walk down Cermak, checking the window of Minarik's Bakery ... blueberry *bobovka*. 95c, pecan coffee cakes, *houska*. Outside the savings and loan, I watch a big black man with a cigar enter the place. Two grade school kids standing outside act like they never saw a black before and hold their noses as he passes by.

Inside the savings and loan, computers are humming and clicking, passbooks are flashing, coins are jingling, and at the teller's windows neighborhood savers are standing five and six deep, including the black man with a cigar in his mouth.

There are free coffee and cookies at the door. The marquee flashes an electronic message: DON'T DESPAIR ... IT'S SPRING REPAIR ... GET AN IMPROVEMENT LOAN ... HERE. The Bohemians are banking, and all's well with their world.

In the alleys, in the afternoon, kids are playing street hockey, basketball, baseball, the way I once did. Underneath the eave of an old garage a pair of young high school lovers kiss. Down still another alley, Joey the Peddler stops his red truck and holds up a bunch of bananas for a customer. In my own alley, a neighbor walks a dog and talks up the weather with another neighbor across the way.

As I go up the front stairs of my old home, another neighbor, Eleanore Simek, calls me from across the street.

"Are you still here?" she asks.

"I'm always here," I reply, "In and out."

"Remember when we used to sit on the front porch and sing?" she says.

"That was a long time ago,"

"Thirty years ago."

"God, that was a long time ago."

That evening, over dinner with my Aunt Millie and Uncle Joe, my parents keep talking about moving out, but they probably never will. My mother spent a good part of her life "working at the Western." My father spent over 48 years riding the Douglas Park El back and forth to the Continental Bank downtown. Cicero is his neighborhood. He can walk it. He'd be lost anywhere else.

Aunt Millie and Uncle Joe live in an apartment on 35th Street in Boulevard Manor. They've lived in Cicero for years. They like it. They don't want to go anywhere else. They both worked "at the Western." Says Uncle Joe, "It takes me five minutes to get to work. Why should I live anywhere else? Besides there's one savings and loan in the neighborhood, and two racetracks (Sportsmans's and Hawthorne). Where else could I get such a combination?"

And Aunt Millie tells about a neighbor across the alley who seems like the epitome of the Old Ciceronian. "You could set your watch by her every Sunday morning, between 9:30 and 10. She is out there washing her white picket fence. She picks up all the paper and junk in the alleys and gangways and fills up everybody's garbage can but her own. She likes to keep hers clean. Her and her dog. And she's always feeding the birds. Her yard is sometimes filled with bread for the birds."

"Tell him about the ceramic cat," says Uncle Joe.

"Every spring she takes her ladder and climbs to the top of the garage and puts the ceramic cat on the roof."

"Why?"

"To keep the birds from dirtying the garage roof. But she's been sick lately, and you can tell. The alley's a mess."

I step into this neighbor's spotless house for a minute. She's a heavily made-up but pretty woman in her 60's. She's not accustomed to welcoming strangers in her living room ... no Bohemian is.

"I pick up litter all the time. I don't like litter all around, so I keep it clean around the whole block. I pick up cans and paper and cigaret butts. And there's a stray dog nearby. I feed him too. And the birds. But the seed has gotten so high. And bread! I throw three slices of bread out there every morning."

As for shopping along Cermak Road. "The streets are so littered these days, and the sidewalks all broken up. I notice all that litter. I think everybody who walks should pick it up."

She folds her hands in her lap and thinks about Cicero for a while. "Oh, you hear that Cicero's such a bad place to live because of the gangsters, but I don't think the people pay too much attention to them There's no crime here that's committed by them. It's the colored coming in and doing the purse snatching, not the gangsters."

Crime, in other words, is OK as long as it doesn't get into the wrong hands.

"The local government is all grafters, I suppose, but they're good to the people. Our taxes are low, and our garbage pickup is free. The politicians are filling their pockets, I imagine, like always. But you can call the town hall if you want your trees trimmed and they're here within a week. I have a new sidewalk and I only paid half — the town paid the other half."

Walking the quiet streets late at night, I feel the neighborhood hasn't changed that much since I left. The streetcars are long gone, and I miss the sound of the bell signaling the passing of the L. I miss the gateman hanging up those red lanterns in the night.

"Remember when we used to sit on the front porch and sing?"

I remember and miss the voices and the sounds most of all. I miss the kids calling out their games in a summer night. I miss the sight of Bohemians in their basements at night, playing pinochle around the kitchen table. I miss the next-door neighbor, old man Cibulka the master bricklayer, who would sometimes take out his concertina and play those sad Bohemian songs well into the night — but only when he drank too much beer, only when he felt too sad.

"Are you still here?"

I'm always here. In and out.

I miss the heart of Cicero that an Al Capone never knew. And though I've just met her, I already miss this good Cicero woman picking up the litter around the neighborhood, feeding the birds, justifying her own life in the face of all those fears which keep Cicero alive and struggling.

Cereal

My earliest recollections around an oilcloth kitchen table center on the essence of cereal. I may have been a Pablum baby, but that doesn't matter. Farina, maybe once in a while. Oatmeal, hardly ever.

Corn Flakes. Kellogg's Corn Flakes. That's the real center of it. My inner and outer journeying through the universe of cereal began with Kellogg's Corn Flakes.

Breakfast at Grandpa Papp's centered around whatever he felt his body cried out for. One thing in my life I never saw my Grandpa Papp ever eat was a bowl of cereal.

Grandpa believed in eggs for breakfast, four to six fried eggs, thick slices of slab bacon, rye bread, butter and coffee . . . and as much homemade bakery as Grandma could get out of the oven. There was a particular ritual with the rye bread. After it had been heavily buttered, he would cut each piece into small rectangles and triangles.

Sometimes, when my mind grows weary of the cereal world, I indulge in a Grandpa Papp breakfast. These are special mornings of sun and blue sky. Mornings when you understand that you will live forever. After four fried eggs, bacon, triangled buttered rye bread, hot black, sweet coffee, I step outside with a smile in my stomach and look for somebody to kill.

Cereal, though, is a head food. It had to come out of the East. And the West, of course, never trusting the purity of anything, did what it has always been the nature of the West to do when faced with change: lessen the impact of the pure strain; make a commodity of it; capitalize on whatever the experience.

Corn flakes were good for you — and so I ate corn flakes for breakfast every morning. The literature on the box in those days was fairly mundane. There weren't many comic strips or giveaways at first, and certainly not Tony the Tiger. Just a picture of a green stalk of corn growing, is all I can see from this vantage point. And I never did comprehend how they made a corn flake out of a corn cob. But mysteries like these emanated from a place called Battle Creek, Michigan. And anyplace called Battle Creek had to be in command of things, as far as I could imagine.

The saving factor for corn flakes in those days was sugar. Without sugar, corn flakes, the whole cereal concept, was crap. That must be understood from the outset. I could no more eat a bowl of raw corn flakes than a dish of wood shavings.

We had three sugar bowls in the course of my life around the kitchen table. The first one belonged to a yellow set of Screeno prize dishes with a strawberry motif. It was a squatty sugar bowl with two big ears for handles and a lid with an ear of its own. It was an easy bowl to pass around. And it was even easier to knock all the ears off. The de-eared sugar bowl lasted for a good part of my youth and was always a topic of conversation — "Who the hell knocked the other ear off the sugar bowl?"

The second bowl was a fancy piece of red and clear Czech crystal with a World's Fair Silver Spoon. I never liked that sugar bowl. It had an air of smugness about it. You reached for another spoon of sugar from it, and the whole damn bowl seemed to back off and sigh, "Again? Now really ... isn't once enough?"

Furthermore, I was always forgetting to return the World's Fair Silver Spoon, becoming enamored of its size and depth as I was ladling sugar into my cereal and coffee, thickly caked from too many dips in the sugar bowl. (Perhaps they were trying to teach me table etiquet at the time. But I still have little regard for any spoon with the priority of its own bowl.)

The fancy Czech crystal sugal bowl, for some unexplained reason, was one day declared a family heirloom and reassigned to the nostalgia of the attic, where nothing is ever used again. The World's Fair Silver Spoon tarnishes somewhere under a heap of Japanese stainless steel spoons.

The last, and present, sugar bowl is some kind of metal container (once silver-plated) that my Mother had chrome-plated so the shine would last forever — and looks just like silver. It's a wide open comfortable bowl with a space notched out in the lid for a spoon, but no character whatsoever.

So corn flakes (and damn near everything else) needed a heap of sugar to make the world meaningful. And you could either sprinkle the sugar on the dry cereal first and then *add the milk, or pour the milk over the dry cereal first* and then add the sugar. There's a world of difference between the two rituals.

Those who sprinkle sugar on their corn flake first (as if they *knew*) are those unimaginative eaters of structured lives. They're the same ones who butter their bread *before* they eat rather than while they're eating. They're the same ones who play boundaries on all their pleasures rather than allowing their passions to determine all the sugar that is necessary.

Give me a man who knows precisely how much sugar he wants on his cereal, and I'll give you a man who has already bought cemetary lot and had the headstone inscribed with his name and date of birth.

So you add the milk to the corn flakes and then begin the sugar run. Back and forth, back and forth to the old sugar hole. Not enough this time, too much next time, so what? so what? It's good for you because it tastes so good. The flakes are crunchy soft, just right, and there's still half a bowl to go! How unsanitary to use the same spoon after putting it into your mouth!

Should I have another bowl of corn flakes and this time slice some banana in it? Why not? And lots of sugar. I got an uncle suffering from a touch of diabetes ... He's crazy ...

Final Corn Flake Conclusion: corn flakes, once milk fed, but for some reason left unattended at the bottom of the bowl, or the side of the bowl, or the top of the table, dry in time and stick stronger than Elmer's Glue. There is no way to resurrect an old corn flake. It is sometimes better to dispose of the cereal bowl than to scrape away stuck corn flakes.

Which brings me to the other world of cereals. I'm not sure of the exact date when my corn flake world crumbled away. But since this is not so much a history of cereal as a philosophical statement about cereal, suffice to say that at one point in my youth around the kitchen table I awoke to the discovery of three new boxes: Rice Krispies, Shredded Wheat, and Kix.

What joy! What incredible joy to come upon a bowlful of Rice Krispies in the morning. My ritual of milk and sugar remained the same. The taste difference was slight. But the sound! My God, the celestial sounds!

In the past I was accustomed to silence at the breakfast table. (Partly because both my parents worked, and I frequently ate breakfast alone.) There was the radio to turn on, if I so desired. And nothing else but the canary, who was rather stupid when it came to song.

But now, goddam it, the cereal talked! What's more, it even had names: Snap, Crackle, and Pop. Every morning I would run to the table and look for those three rascals in my cereal bowl. Now, what was old Snap up to today? That looks like Crackle over there. And where the hell could Pop be hiding this morning?

Finally I had some friends to join me around the breakfast table, as I sometimes marched around the breakfast table with good old Don McNeil and the Breakfast Club radio show. Good old Snap, Crackle, and Pop were there too. What a wonderful world of good guys right in my own cereal bowl.

Shredded Wheat I was forced to try once I had finished with the box of Rice Krispies. Shredded Wheat did little for my psyche. It was a visual thing with

Shredded Wheat Biscuits. I used to marvel how they looked like small pillows made of string and wire.

I did the milk and sugar thing to it. Nothing. The Shredded Wheat Biscuit refused to be transmogrified. I just could not whip it into any kind of meaningful shape. It sucked up the milk like crazy, and it was *still* dry. I could hardly tear it apart with a spoon.

Once I got a wad of it in my mouth, I remained unimpressed. I kept feeling I was eating an SOS pad.

For some reason, the box of Shredded Wheat had a picture of a waterfall either on the side or back. That's the thing I remember most from my Shredded Wheat Biscuit experience. I'm not sure of the connection with Niagara Falls. (Maybe Shreeded Wheat Biscuits grew there? Maybe they fell over the falls? Maybe if I ate enough Shredded Wheat I would see Niagara Falls someday?)

I remain an unconverted Shredded Wheat Biscuit man.

Kix ... ah, Kix. It was the name. That's all. The name. Kids love to kick. And Kix, for whatever reason, affected my animal energy. (I even thought Grandpa Papp might like Kix.) I could kick the goddamn kitchen table and chairs over a bowl of Kix. I could kick the canary till it would sing. I could go kick the hell out of my friends on the way to school this morning because I was filled to the top with three bowls of Kix.

Another weird thing, Kix was round! My God, what are these cereal people doing to me! Flakes, wire brad brans, rice, string, and now little round spheres you could just roll in your mouth like soft marbles. And the color! Kix weren't the blah color of most creals. Kix were yellow!

Well, I had a ball with Kix. I never became a true believer. But whenever I felt like fun, I'd fill me a bowl of Kix. Ma, I'm goin' out to kick some ass today!

The cereal world began growing faster than I. There was no way I could keep up. There were other worlds calling me, and it was with great reluctance that I gradually pushed myself away from the kitchen table. Away from all the wonders and new sensations the cereal people promised and frequently delivered.

I began to skip breakfast.

Oh, I had a round with Puffed Wheat shot from cannons. The cannon and the old white haired guy in the black hat fascinated me more than the weightless and almost spooky white cereal. (How tall was the old guy in the black hat? How come you could never see his hands and feet? What did he have to do with shooting cannons anyway?)

Raisin Bran was a descent into hell.

I never got into Wheaties, so in some small way I seem to have denied myself the champion feeling at breakfast.

The box-top gift thing hit the child's cereal world like the second coming of corn flakes (Frosted Flakes). And it's still going strong.

I will admit, though, that I'm still waiting for my Atomic Bomb Ring. I sent the money and the box top, and it's been almost 25 years now. I know the Cereal World People won't fail me.

The shape, the sound, the taste of cereal today borders on the bizarre. A psychedelic cereal world. Honey Combs, Lucky Charms, Apple Jacks, Sugar Smacks, and the whole monstrous world of Count Chocula, Franken Berries, Boo Berries ... Who would have thought it? Transylvania in Cerealdom! Surely we must be prepared for a Mafia Sugar Shot, an A-bomb Biscuit, a Linda Lovelace Cereal Lozenger fortified with Vitamin C. The sheer genius of the cereal people to instantize the cereal bowl for us future diabetics! No more going back and forth to the sugar bowl anymore. Now it's merely milk and magic time!

And so the body is once again satiated, but what of the spirit? Can a man be born and born again? (The East smiles enigmatically in its empty cereal bowl.)

The truth slowly begins to seep out. Cereal in the West is not what it seems to be. Negative nutritious. All fun and games, pomp and circumstance. Fortified with vitamins and all, Western man is going nowhere in the morning, burning up all kinds of energy he didn't necessarily receive in his Quisps — that beautiful, gay sounding cereal.

The cry from the West Coast (which is closest to the Far East) ... Man does not live by corn flakes alone. Man needs *natural* cereals!

Enter crunchy Granola.

And I did like the sound, the first time I filled the old cereal bowl with the silence of such natural cereal, all the potential energies for body and soul ... and no preservatives added. I forced myself to love it. "It's good for you!" I remembered by Grandmother's words. But lo, I could not stand my first trip with Granola. It was all a bowl of nuts and bolts. My jaws tired too easily and continued working things over even in my sleep.

And so what course does a man follow when he knows something isn't good for him? He continues in hot pursuit with a touch of the death-wish about him. An Evel Knievel of the cereal bowl

Pass the Frosted Flakes *and* the sugar bowl. I'm feeling especially down this morning. Diabetes, here I come. The trouble with Tony the Tiger is he has no balls.

But leave it to the transmigration of the cereal world people to arouse the dead souls and make converts of us all. Leave it to the West to outdo the East, package the product, low-key the music, and merely hum the crunchy Granola song. But this time around, call it Quaker's 100 per cent Natural Cereal.

We like the Quaker, the cameo calm assurance of the old white-haired gent on the box, in customary black hat and coat. We can trust him to our morning spirit. And if we're real Americans, there's nothing we can count on more than 100 per cent. As for "natural" cereal, that's where we're all at today, or supposed to be headed. Isn't it? To be natural. Be ourselves. Love me for what I am.

By God, I could live my whole life, this time and next time around, on one bowl after another of Quaker's 100 per cent Natural Cereal. Take it straight, right out of the box, by the handful. The land of milk and honey ...

America, you are what you eat. And the cereal people have finally discovered what's good for you, and still good for them ... more and more and more new natural brands to follow.

I eat a bowl of Quaker's 100 per cent Natural Cereal, and I stop the world. This is where it's at.

My Atomic Bomb Ring remains suspended in another galaxy.

I have conquered diabetes.

Even the old gray haired Quaker on the box looks a little serenely like my Grandpa, though I can't see what eggs and bacon violence he may still hold in his hands.

Shorty the Locksmith

He's a little man, about 5 feet high, and looks out over the counter at you with something close to disgust. You're not quite sure of him. "So vhat's your problem? You got bad keys? These are junk keys. Vhat butcher you go to, huh? You vant butcher work, you go to butcher in dime store. You vant a real key made, you go to a locksmith."

He talks a little like Myron Cohen, and his whole setting, at 5309 W. 25th Street in Cicero, resembles that of "The Pawnbroker." The dark walls behind him seem to drip keys in brushed metallic hues of silver and gold. Locks, too, are everywhere. Pairs of old handcuffs hang from above, gathering dust in a darkness of only gleams of reflected light.

"You vant to write a story about me? Who vants to read about a locksmith? Anyvays, you're too late. Somebody else vill do it. The undertaker. Next month I be 85 years old."

His real name is Julius Fischl, which comes as somewhat of a surprise. He's not supposed to be anyone else but Shorty the Locksmith, who has been in the same shop for 46 years and lives in the back with his wife, Edith. He came from Bohemia in 1912, and started out fixing phonographs. "There vas no locksmiths then," he explains. "Nobody locked anything. But later, there vas beginning vith the locks, you know?"

The window of his shop seems empty, though filled with faded cardboard signs for Yale locks. Nothing in the window or the sign above the door would ever compel a person to just step in and have a look around. Shorty's whole business mystique rests on one principle: You *need* him. Because he's a master locksmith (if there is such a title). Because there probably isn't a lock made that he can't get into, or a key that he can't duplicate.

"That is how is supposed to vork right now," he tells a man with a broken lock. "I don't see nothing different here. You can only put in one position, see? Vhat do you know about locks, huh? You think you know about locks? The most important thing, you know? To see vhere everything goes before you take apart! See, no experience."

He finds a container for the lock, and hands it back to the customer. "That'll be $2 for the box, and nothing for the experience."

There is hardly any light in the shop except for a little of the natural light creeping in from the doorway and window behind. The dusty, cream-colored walls, the tin-pressed ceiling, the few overhead fixtures, hanging unlit, the almost bare wooden floor, the glass and wooden counters mellowed with age . . . how many thousands of arms leaning into them, jingling a handful of keys or a broken lock for Shorty's close inspection? . . . everything speaks of long ago, and a craftsman whose main concern is solving metallic mysteries and letting the rest of the setting take care of itself with time.

The standing space for customers is small. About five people can occupy the area somewhat comfortably. There is a hot radiator near the door to lean against the warmth, while waiting. And in one corner there is a single seat from an old fashioned wooden school desk. People stand around, jingling keys in their hands, waiting, watching, listening to Shorty, who usually happens to be speaking to just about everyone at the moment.

"Yes, lady?" he addresses an older woman who has come all the way from Prospect Heights to have some keys made. "You need locks in Prospect Heights, lady? I thought there vas no crime in small towns."

"Oh, we have our troubles there too," she says.

"This key is no original, lady. Who made this junk?"

"Sure, it's the original. It's the one they gave me. It's the only one I have."

"Lady, lady ... You got one key here made by Mr. Voolvorth."

"Well, this one I know was made in a store. Some girl made it. What does a girl 15 know about making keys?"

"Nothing. You vant real keys made ... you go through a town, you look for a locksmith."

"But there aren't any around there. That's why I had to come all the way here from the suburbs."

"Lady, people come here a hundred, two hundred miles. Last week, a man from Florida. Vell, not just to see me. But I fix for him."

"I like this place, you know," she tells Shorty. "All those gold and silver keys hanging there so pretty. I like this better than a jewelry shop."

Shorty has not time for aesthetics. He finds the proper blank for her, moves over to his machinery along the wall beneath the keys, flicks on the little lamp above the whirling wheels, tightens the keys in place, and bears down to the business of grinding keys perfectly, to fit and last.

Another man enters in old, gray working clothes. His pants, his jacket, everything just hangs from him, even his glasses which rest far down on the bridge of his nose. As always, there are people you can never really tell about. Especially lock and key people ... Shorty's customers. He's come to have a few keys made. But he's got something else on his mind as well...

Who knows what set him off? Maybe it was merely watching old Shorty work so meticulously cutting a new set of keys. Suddenly the man is launched into a tirade concerning the spirit of this country.

Watching Shorty diligently at work, he seems to have less faith in the morality of others. "Everything is greed," he tells Shorty. "This country does not honor intelligence, only greed. That's why we are lost. Other civilizations created cultures ... music, art, poetry. But all we are interested in is money. Human intelligence means nothing! And a country based on greed is lost."

"But you know," adds Shorty, "the young peoples I am not so vorried about. They vill do something good, you vill see. Maybe not you or me vill live to see, but afters. I don't mean the bad vones you see on the TV. No. There are so many good vones you never hear. The 4-H kids ... good kids. No punks.

An old Italian has been waiting in line. He has been here before, it seems. Many times before, with the same problem of a key not fitting a lock. Shorty is a little angry with him because he is sure the key fits, but that the man is not turning it hard enough in the lock.

"This vay!" he hollers at the old Italian. "You see! Like this! Is no other vay. Now you can pull key out, now you cannot. See?"

The old Italian laughs and hollers back, "But I do that, Shorty, and no work! Still no work!"

"Vell, maybe you're too old. No push and turn hard enough. You need maybe new voman."

"Thas right," laughs the old Italian. "Voman with big ones like this! . . . AH, YA, YA . . . "

"Say, I gonna tell you," smiles Shorty. "I gonna have a sex operation."

"No," laughs the Italian, already doubling up with laughter.

"Yes, yes. I gonna have my brain moved from up here to down there."

And both of them break up in the laughter of old age. "You take this key home now, and push and you turn," he tells the old Italian. "It vork. I made it to vork."

"I know, I know is not the key," says the Italian. "I know you no make a bad key."

It is getting near lunchtime. Shorty's ailing wife, Edith, shuffles out from their place in the back to help clear the store of the remaining customers. She is Shorty's second wife, and he seems to have taught her the key business.

"My first wife got sick too," Shorty seems to explain to one and all. "Ah, lots of trouble I have. She vas with the cancer for 15 years."

Edith waits on one customer, recognizes by number that the key to be made is no longer manufactured, and is about to send the man on his way when Shorty overhears and advises the man to try another place on Cermak Road.

"I made so many of those keys, I've nothing left," he says as he joins his wife at the counter. "Is an old key. But maybe you still find blank somevhere."

"So vhat you make for lunch?" Shorty asks his wife.

"What do you want?"

"I vant nice big steak," he says.

"You don't have the teeth to eat a steak," she laughs.

"She vorks here," Shorty explains, "but I don't pay her nothing. I'm looking for a new voman. You know, I'd never marry an old voman again. Nothing older than 19."

Another customer enters, then another, then two more . . . keys jingling in their hands. Edith looks up at the clock . . . about 10 minutes to noon, while Shorty returns to the machines and his business of making keys.

First a car key for one man. "I like this key," says Shorty, whose whole personality, it seems, has been shaped by keys of inferior quality. "Is good key. I made vone like it last week for a $10,000 car."

"Well, this ain't no $10,000 car," says the man.

"This is good key, double-edged. They make specially for drunks, you know? Yes, you put in any vay, it vorks."

"Well, they made it for the right guy. How much I owe you?"

"How much you got?"

"Yeah, I wish I had your money."

"Yes, but I tell you. I have big problem. No place to put it all. I can't get no more shoeboxes."

A young girl moves forward with her problem, a new key to be made, and a car door lock that sticks.

"You ever lubricate that lock?" he asks.

"Never," he smiles.

"So vhat do you expect? Bring the car in front of store. I fix as soon as I can."

The girl fades away to the outside, and two other men press forward to the counter, one of them slightly beered up. The sober one hands Shorty the key. "Can you make one like that?" he asks.

"If Shorty can't make the key, throw it away," says the beered-up buddy. "Shorty can even make a key for an Edsel."

It is past noon. Edith puts the lunch sign on the door and locks a few of us in, while Shorty continues to grind away at a few remaining keys.

"I made this key a long time ago," he tells a young man.

"How do you know?"

"Years ago I used to stamp them. See, right here. This is my key."

The last customer leaves, the door locked behind him, and then two others appear, trying to get in. Edith has gone to the back to make lunch.

Time to call it quits? Forty-six years is a long time for a locksmith.

"I don't vant to retire and belong to the Honey Dew Club," says Shorty. "You know vhat is the Honey Dew club? Honey do this, honey do that ... Anyvays, I don't consider this a business. People come to see me as friends."

He glances up at the clock ... 12:20. He looks at the two people outside with a touch of scorn. He unlocks the door and lets in a few more friends, jingling keys in their hands.

Soda Pop

I'm maybe five years old, with an uncle leading me by the hand to a corner tavern. He holds the bar in both hands, nods to the bartender for a stein of beer, lifts me up and sets me down on the stool beside him. "Give the kid a glass of soda," he says.

A small glass is put in front of me, making all kinds of bubbly music: soda. I lift the cold glass in both hands, listen, taste the sweetness going down. Maybe it was root beer. Maybe it was Coke. For certain, it sure as hell beat the taste of milk.

I'm hooked on soft drink in a swallow.

This is the 1940's.

The world's at war. The '40s last a long, long time. Round, red and white Coke signs are everywhere ... over here and even over there. In a corner drugstore I sit at the marble counter of a soda fountain and watch a soda jerk mix me a Coke, hand it to me in a beautiful glass the shape of a vase with Coca-Cola written on it. Mmmmmmm, like liquid candy.

Roosevelt dies. America needs you, Harry Truman ... 30 seconds over Tokyo. I have sent to Kellogg's for my Atomic Bomb Ring. Victory gardens and street parties. There's a neighbor on our block wose son is a bombardier, and now he's coming home a hero.

Both going and coming from grammar school each day, I'm a bombardier. And during lunch hour, me and a fellow Flying Tiger pilot sneak off the school grounds for a short mission down the alley to the candy store, bombing garbage cans along the way with our paperbag lunches. We gladly sacrifice whatever it was we were supposed to eat plus all the wholesome milk Borden's Elsie the Cow could make for Twinkies. And a cold bottle of Coke.

The man in the store opens the top of the red and white Coke soda cooler, reaches in the cold water, and hands us two dripping bottles which gleam and flash in the sunlight. The Coke bottle has character. I don't know a thing about beauty or design at this age, but it's a bottle formed to feel beautiful in your slippery hands. Fixing the silver cap in the opener on the side of the cooler, I push firmly, force the cap off with a pop and a woosh (simultaneously catching it in my other hand), put the bottle to my lips, and rear back my head in exaltation — praise be the creator of cold Coke!

More riches. The bottle cap catcher is full. I dig in, fingertips scraping on the sharp edges, and fill both pockets for later deposit in cigar boxes of treasures at home. For I am a collector of soda caps.

Cokes never last long enough. The empty bottles, with a cast of green to them, diminish all too quickly. More nickels would make them full again. Life was sweet soda forever.

It was a phosphate phosphorescent world as the wonder of soda widened in our very midst. Aside from the color of Coke, there was the rollicking taste and feel of foamy root beer, and the whole carnival-aura sensations of grape, orange and strawberry soda.

And root beer was mosly one of a kind and drunk to the savage drum beat of DAD'S/OLD/FASH/IONED/ROOT/BEER (Oomph!) — DAD'S OLD/FASH/IONED/ROOT/BEER (Oomph!). But orange and strawberry and grape were something special. If you grew up in an ethnic neighborhood, you might get a swig of them at the local tavern, but more likely at the gatherings of families in celebration ... weddings and picnics.

Weddings inevitably meant good food, laughter, loud drunken relatives, polka dancing till 3 in the morning, and free soda for the kids — small glasses of bright orange soda till it was coming out of your ears. Once in a while, the unexplained magic of grape; but mostly orange which puckered your lips after the tenth glass and made the roof of your mouth itch. At this stage in my life, just the memory of those weddings fills me with an orangey gas. I haven't been able to drink orange soda since.

Strawberry soda ran rampant at picnics, a crazy colored clown of a soda. Soda with the taste of laughter and lollipops. My God, what will they conjure up next? Cherry, of course. Cherry! I can't take it anymore ... time to run the potato sack race, time to play softball, time to dance and play cards and sit under the cool trees and drink a bottle of cold soda. More strawberry soda, please ... and a glass of cherry ... till the tongue turns crimson and you have a mustache to match your Grandpa's, only yours is a funny red.

"If you don't stop drinking all that soda, you'll get sick!"

We got sick, year after year, though all the summer picnics. We never learned. Our stomachs, along with a mixture of sun, the woods, and good times, taught us otherwise. If you're young and thirsty, drink! (Preferably strawberry soda.)

Seven-up was also part of our soda syndrome, coming on strong in that mean little green bottle with the orange and white 7-Up sign. It, too, was a nice bottle to hold with a cap worth keeping. But I never met a kid at that time who had any kind of a passion for a soda he couldn't see. You poured it into a glass and it came out looking like water with bubbles. And the taste did not trigger anything in our bloodstreams. You did not yell, "Geronimo!" after a swig of 7-Up. You belched in a sort of sweet way, and your eyes watered.

For years 7-Up remained a soda (like ginger ale) for oldsters to practice their chemistry with. They took whiskey, added 7-Up and came up with a variation of the classic concoction called a highball. At weddings throughout the '40s there was beer, highballs and orange soda. Enough to keep the family happy for hours.

Candy stores, picnics, alleys or backyards, given more than one bored kid drinking too much soda, there were inevitably games. The sound of soda was phzzzzzz. And the sight, whatever the color, was distinguished by millions of tiny bubbles which lay secretly hidden, mesmerized within the liquid till the proper balance of power was executed. Till one kid stuck his thumb over the top, vigorously shook the bottle to a bubbly frenzy, aimed at the opponent's face, and fired by gingerly moving the thumb from the opening, just a fraction. The stream, the spray, the soda fight was on.

If you stuck an empty bottle under your upper lip, and blew carefully, you could imitate the sound of a ship or foghorn. If you stuck your thumb in and out the opening in a particular fashion, you could make a beatful popping sound. If you collected enough empty bottles by junking down the alleys, you could return them for 2 cents a piece and redeem all your soda virtues and vices interminably.

And I remember Kayo from that time. I still search for it periodically with a wistful eye in big food stores and one horse stops throughout the country, hoping somewhere a bottle of Kayo will emerge.

Irony of ironies, Kayo wasn't really soda at all. It was sold in thin, clear bottles that looked like soda (with a yellow cap). But Kayo was closer to chocolate milk than anything.

Kayo was sweet, it was chocolaty, it was smooth as cream. Part of the ritual of drinking Kayo was the dark chocolate which always seemed to settle in the bottom of the bottle. So you tipped the bottle upside down, checked the amount of chocolate gathered there shook it till the color was uniform, then opened the bottle for one of the rarest taste sensations known to boyhood.

And I remember Canfield's Cream soda. It, too, was clear like 7-Up, but the taste had to be something close to the divine. It was rare when a bottle of cream soda appeared in the refrigerator. Company must be coming. Maybe some long lost relative from the old country was going to pop up. To show him how well off you were, you'd hit him with a glass of cream soda. What a miraculous drink.

And there was Orange Crush. Though a surfeit of orange soda at weddings did not develop a sudden orange soda habit in my days, I occasionally found my body in wanting of an orange fix. And Orange Crush did it. Mainly it was a bottle thing. For Orange Crush came in the craziest bottle of them all; a brown, heavily ridged bottle that closely resembled a beer bottle. It was a real prize to hold and indulge in. Orange Crush drinkers were in a soda society of their own. They acted more grown up. They pretended they were drinking beer.

We were not the Pepsi Generation in the '40s, though we chanted the song: "Pepsi-Cola hits the spot/ 12 full ounces, that's a lot/ twice as much for a nickel too/ da . . . da . . . da . . . it's good for you!" I forget the last line but it was something like that. (I can still hear the Andrews Sisters singing it.)

Pepsi was around but it never dominated our neighborhood scene the way Coke did. And unknown ritualists that we were, Coke came first and so we stayed with it. Especially since things (like Twinkies) went better with it. Yet whatever we drank then (the '40s) we knew what we were — thirsty and thankful there was true soda on the scene.

The '50s found us moving from grammar school to high school, from punk-kid to teendom. From obnoxious, independent adolescent, to confused puppy-lover, to self-assured young adult. Our old standby, Coke, helped carry us through. This was a time of gentle Ike, fearful Joe McCarthy, the rock and roll of Bill Haley and the Comets, the jazz of Brubeck, the folk songs of Pete Seeger. Soda of all sorts of silenced us, made us spectators of the black-leather-jacket world of Brando and rebel James Dean, and the white-bucked wonderland of Pat Boone.

If we experimented or dared at all, it was with our soda. We sat with our saddle-shoed, cahsmered steady and unsteady sweethearts at those old fashioned soda fountains which were fast becoming extinct and ordered wild concoctions of cherry-cokes, vanilla-cokes, chocolate phosphates, and a drink some poet dreamed called a Green River. A lime drink that carried me time and again out of concrete Chicago and down some graceful flowing riverstream in a rustic countryside I could only imagine. I still wonder . . . do they make Green Rivers anymore?

As the world of soda fountains and soda jerks, technicolored sodas, Kayos, cherry-cokes, and Green Rivers slowly disappeared before our very eyes, we sat there softly unaware. Technology was on the march. Vending machines were fast replacing soda parlors. Old brands would disappear and new ones appear overnight, trying for a piece of the soda drinker's soul. (Everybody, it seemed, could make Coke — though nobody had a better bottle.) Royal Crown Cola came out of nowhere and stole my heart.

Rumors, too, began to fly: If you took a bottle of Coke or Pepsi and rubbed it on the bumper of a car, the chrome would come off! And if it did that to the chrome, imagine what it must do to your stomach! If you mixed Coke and aspirin, you could get high. Even worse, you could die! Holy Moses, our whole soda kingdom seemed threatened! Weren't there any good guys left? Any good times? Is this what growing up meant — curbing your thirsts?

But moving from the late '50s into the early '60s, somewhere in my travels, I met the good Dr. Pepper who saved my life and soda lust. The Dr. Pepper soda taste was unique. Something like cherry-coke, but even more. Oh, so much more. Dr. Pepper put me on the beam again. (Hell, it had to be good for you or why would a doctor put his name on it?)

Furthermore, the times were a-changin'. Didn't Hugh Hefner, himself, the father of the centerfold and the new sexual revolution, live and lust for Pepsi?

I began to do some serious soda drinking/thinking in this time. For one thing, I rediscovered Pepsi. Working summers on construction for my old boyhood buddy, John Cibulka, a bricklayer on his way to becoming a contracotr, I sweated and cursed and pushed those heavy-motha concrete soggy wheelbarrows up ramp after ramp. Filled the scaffolds with bricks, loaded and unloadeed platforms for foundations. And beer didn't keep me going, though it was available.

Pepsi pulled me through. There is no way imaginable to capture the self-renewal, the lusciousness of Pepsi pouring down your seared and anxious throat so cold it stops the heart momentarily. It became a soda for all season, like Dr. Pepper. In the cold of winter, I'd heart them up and add rum.

Yes, the world was changing. Kennedy was king, soda popped up everywhere in pop-top cans and bottles of almost grotesque dimensions. Even Coke came out with its own inimitable bottle shape in a size that was surreal.

And from the late '60s into the '70s, soda and surrealism seem almost one. Old soda bottles die, are destructably dead. and are replaced by cans that all feel and smell and look alike. No class ... no class whatsoever. Names like Squirt and Tab and Fresca corner the market. Mountain Dew, Shasta, Worms, what have you? What are these people trying to pull.

Unforgiveable of all crimes, sodas now seem manufactured for our own good health. More and more of them have a mission in mind. I speak now of that whole unstomachable medicinal soda branded "diet drink." That whole unspeakable philosophy of non-sweet!

Damn it, if you want to go on a diet, don't drink soda. Don't foist your fat frustrations on us chronic, real-sweet soda drinkers. Don't flood the stores with your woes and eventually replace us.

Join the Pepsi Generation! Things (all sorts of thing) do go better with Coke! For some, coke is more than Coke these days. It's the real thing. So sing the Dr. Pepper song until you believe. It's catchy, and you'll feel much better drinking and singing the time away.

And for a grand finale in our time of pop history and pop presidents, for a true testament of our non-speak post-Nixonian times (what's true? what's false?) try an UnCola! Yep, 7-Up is back, stronger than ever with Peter Max himself painting galaxies of a bubbling universe we'll never know ... where everything is what it's not. Here's to the UnCola. The Zen drink of our time, which is, of course, all time and no time ... at this point in time.

Man on the Moon

As the gentleman janitor for three apartment buildings in the neighborhood, Mr. V. is a busy man. Not so busy though, that he cannot find enough time in the day to engage in the old European art of café sitting. He has sat in sunny café's drinking brandy and coffee, reflecting upon the times, all over Europe and South America. Here in America, though, he must settle for less. He must settle for weak coffee, no booze, and a shiny vinyl booth buried far in the back of a restaurant busy with discount store businessmen, noisy with teenagers and rock.

Yet the old gentleman retains the common Prussian courtesy for a woman (in this case the waitress) or any one else who will join him for coffee and conversation. It's Mr. V.'s nature to always stand, tip his hat, and bow upon greeting someone. Then he will offer his hand and a pleasant smile. He seems entirely out of place.

He speaks six languages — Lithuanian, German, Russian, French, Spanish and English. English comes the hardest, for he has not been here long enough to truly master the sound and grammar.

He has been everything from a professional soldier in the old country, to a journalist in South America. Here, for the past 10 years, he has been busy janitoring — changing light bulbs, fixing faucets, shoveling snow. "Vat can I do else? Old man. Soon retire."

He laughs. Mr. V. is always laughing. Partly from nervousness, covering up his burden of the English language. And partly because he thinks what he says is funny. And sometimes it is, in a confusing way.

It would be easy to make fun of this gentle man. Easy to mock his style of language, his overly-mannered behavior, his obsequiousness. Easy to point a finger and say, "Can you imagine that guy, speaks six languages and does nothing but carry out garbage."

Perhaps because of this, Mr. V. is always ready for conversation. A man in such a position must have many stories to tell. Ah yes, Mr. V. has story after story. And no matter where a man listens to him begin, the end is sure to fall in Europe.

Lithuania is a long way from the neighborhood. But today man has almost touched the moon. A small world? Perhaps. But for Mr. V. the beginning was still Lithuania.

A beginning in one of those tiny countries that was always getting the hell knocked out of it by one major power or another. And so today Mr. V. pieces his story together from Lithuania to the moon and back. But the moon has nothing to do with it. Or does it?

This gentle man, a soldier? "Vy sure. Vas major in army. Vas expert pistol shot," and Mr. V. laughs and bows his head.

"Vhen Russian soldiers come in Lithuania, very bad. Like cannibals. No good. Eat like pigs. Drink, take women."

And the Germans?

"Ah, Germans different. Germans come in, no destroy nothing. All Lithuanian soldiers then be part of German army. Germans bring flowers, throw flowers, laugh, good time."

Never heard that story. Just a good-time army, huh?

"Ya no kill anyone."

What about the Jews?

"No many Jews in Lithuania. Small percent."

You mean after the goodtime German army got through with them.

"No many Jews. No camps, hahaha ... "

And you had to fight in the German army?

"Ah sure, sure, hahaha ... "

Mr. V. is on his third cup of coffee, lapping up an egg yolk with a crust of toast. He is old but still light years away from the theme of the story he tells. Enough of the Jews. Enough, enough ... but Mr. V. jumps a span of time and continues, head bowed, in whispers ...

"Look Jewish people today. Bomb planes, fight Arabs, fight all the time. Vatch the Jew."

Enough. Let's shoot for the moon.

"Ya, is good. But rocket, you know, rocket is Germany. All German. Von Braun, good, good, German head. V-2 vas the vay, hahaha ... "

Mr. V. checks his watch. He must get back to the building and fix a radiator. He stands, bows to the waitress, and kisses her hand. To the man in the booth who shared his conversation, he bows and signals goodbye like a policeman stopping traffic. Mr. V. steps outside, looking up and down the street for a Leader.

Softball

They were not playing softball in the prairie lots of my old Cicero neighborhood that summer evening. The prairies were all gone. The alleys were empty and so were the streets. They were not playing softball at Burnham School or the field at 16th and 59th Avenue. (Waco Field, it was sometimes called, for reasons nobody knew.)

There was only one place left. The community house on 16th and 57th, which was the home field in the early '50s for a gang of softball players who called themselves the Cicero Pirates.

How the team got its name remains a mystery — undoubtedly an intellectual outgrowth of a Saturday matinee at the Villas on Cermak Road. I doubt that we ever heard of *Treasure Island*. But we understood the style of piracy on the screen and knew if we were to become a softball team to be feared, we would have to be reckoned with as the Pirates.

The actual playing field was sandwiched between the community house on the north and the playground on the south. No matter how you looked at it, where you put the bases, it was not a real ball field. If you played on the west end of it (as the Pirates always did), the right fielder would have to position himself over the playground fence, on top of the slide, to make the game meaningful. A hit over the right field fence was homer, or course. An easy one for a lefty, and batters usually aimed for it. Left and center were deep enough, the left fielder had to look both ways before crossing 56th Court in pursuit of a fly ball.

At this time in an old softballer's life, I was happy to discover the game still being played in a field as familiar as a Clincher softball. Around the community house kids milled in small camaraderies waiting for the game to begin, leaning on their bikes, lagging pennies on the sidewalk or just punching each other for the hell of it.

A bunch of players around high school age, in green and white uniforms marked Central Pizza 656-0766, laughed and swore and moved the big ball around the infield, waiting for the rest of the team to show up. They came in dribbles. Two guys in a car, one guy walking, another dropped off by a friend. They sat down on the sidelines and put on their spikes. A small cheer went up as each new player appeared. ... "Hey, hey, get a load of who's here!"

Get a load of that green and white.

They looked sharp in their uniforms. Softball teams always did. For a young kid, there was always that unexplainable excitement in coming across a ball game on a sunny summer evening, and it was the circus colors of the uniforms that caught your attention. Red and whites, blues and golds, yellows and blacks, purples, maroons ...

The Cicero Pirates never had uniforms. They had jackets instead.

Black and white.

Even now when I think of the singular soft satin beauty of the Pirate jacket my feelings begin to well up in me. For a beauty-starved kid growing up in a neighborhood of hard textures — broken gangways, concrete alleys, asphalt and brick streets — there was little to compare with it, not even the average backyard with standard red and white peonies.

Most of the Pirate jacket was made of this black, silky-satiny material that glistened even in the dark. Down both sleeves ran a wild band of white. On the back of the jacket was enscrawled and woven and sewed in beautiful Palmer penmanship, the word "Pirates," which kind of swept away over the right shoulder. And in front, right over the heart, was an emblem, a visage, words fail me ... a pirate's head! Hat, patch, red bandanna and all. People didn't have to just read we were the Pirates. They could see it!

And for the *piece de resistance* (a phrase no pirate ever uttered), the jacket was reversible. And when the ball game was all over, and the sun was just going down over the roofs of the Bohemian bungalows on 57th Avenue, and the Pirates had lost another ball game, and your girl was holding your jacket on the first base line, and it was time now for the team to break up, for the guys to take off for night-time sports, for you to walk your girl home and buy her some ice cream, you took the jacket from her like some sacred vestment, swiftly turned it inside out, and there it was like magic — a zebra skin jacket that would melt the heart of any sore loser.

There was no other decoration on the zebra skin, just wave upon wave of soft black and white stripes. Other teams might get the girls by the color of their uniforms, their style on the field, their swing of the bat. But the Pirates had a baseball jacket that wouldn't quit.

We wore them all the time, in or out of season. To school, to church, to work and probably even to bed. We may have been unheralded in the field, but the neighborhood knew when a Pirate walked the streets. Little kids, dogs, even the sidewalks trembled a little.

Other teams had sponsors for their uniforms, usually a tavern or funeral home to pick up the tab. No one would sponsor the Cicero Pirates. No one. Not a one of us reflected the innocence of Jack Armstrong, the All-American Boy. We didn't have a guy in the bunch who could touch the heart of a tavernkeeper. The only guy with freckles and red hair was a wild bricklayer, John Cibulka, who came on like a Bohemian Zorba, and looked at least 10 years beyond his sweet 16. You wouldn't send Cib to the corner tavern to hustle up a sponsor. Cib wouldn't come out again.

We had to find a racket to pay for our jackets. We were forced into private enterprise. Maybe we were all potential Horatio Algers or Junior Achievers and never knew it. More likely we instictively understood that life was a gamble, like a ball game; you win or you lose. After all, our "heredity and environment" was made up of church bingos, tavern slot machines, summer carnivals of dice and big wheels and friendly family pokers games in the basement. Besides, we didn't know "Cicero" meant a famous Roman orator.

Dick Neufeldt, our sometimes shortstop, gave us lessons on playing the game to win. Everything was worth a gamble to him. He always walked around with a deck of cards in his Levis, just in case. As a result, the Pirates probably played more poker than softball. The odds just weren't with us on the field unless we stacked the deck.

So how do you get a couple of hundred dollars for baseball jackets? You raffle off a portable radio and sell chances for a nickel or dime. And who will buy a chance from a potential Pirate on a portable radio they can't see and probably doesn't even exist? Just about anybody as long as the chance book looks legal and the price is right.

Men and women are born gamblers. Neufeldt understood this. Blackjack was his game. He always dealt. He understood the odds and seldom lost.

We made enough money to outfit 10 softball teams. And a portable radio was bought and actually raffled off. (I think Neufeldt won it.) So finally the Pirates looked like a team and were ready to take the field — any way they could get it.

"What time does the game start?" I asked one of the players for Central Pizza.

"About 10 minutes," he said.

"Where's the other team?"

"We're not playing here, just practicing."

"Then where's the game?"

"I'm not sure, Hawthorne, I think."

"Over the bridge, you mean?"

"Yeah, I guess so."

Over the bridge was not Pirate territory. I don't know who used to play there. The only time a Pirate went over the 52nd Street bridge was to visit the racetrack with Neufeldt, our trusty guide. "I got a great parlay," he'd say. "We can make the last three races. How much dough you got on you?"

The Hawthorne field on 29th Place was big enough to hold four regulation softball games. There were six teams practicing and I could see the green and white uniforms of Central Pizza off in the distance. But then red jerseys caught my eye —BILL'S SERVICE 25th & Central STANDARD JIM'S SERVICE 31st & Laramie. What a name! — no magic of the "Pirates" about it. But what really stopped me was sitting on the grass in the lotus position, tossing a softball lightly in the air like a crystal ball. A genuine hippie wearing a BILL'S SERVICE ball shirt!

Did this cat really play the game? He did. Somebody said, "Andy, warm up," and the hip got up from the grass and moved into the pitcher's box.

A startled member of the opposing team was heard to say: "Hey, will you look at their pitcher! Keds, a bandanna in his hair, beard and all! He ain't for real, he ain't for real!"

Flower child, I said to myself, you better have some real magic because these guys are going to kill you.

The other team, call Jack & Bill's, had no uniform and for this reason reminded me of the chaotic spectacle of the Pirates on the field — a pair of old Levis, a hand-me-down pair of somebody's too long or too short baseball pants; a T-shirt, a sport shirt, or no shirt at all; gym shoes, dress shoes, spikes if you were lucky. The players seemed a bit older than the others, more the young married set, a little less determined to win.

As often happens in softball, the teams were ready but the ump was nowhere to be found. Ours was usually the last to arrive. His excuse, if any, was, "I had to see a man about a horse," which was probably the truth.

When he finally showed up, the scorekeepers exchanged lineups and the ump marked the foul lines, stepped off the bases and called for the game to begin. I could hardly hear him say, "Play ball."

The game, I have to say, was pretty dull and there was only a handful of fans. The two pitchers, they alone, possessed whatever style, whatever life, was left in the old ball game.

Andy the hippie was a sight to behold. Less for his flowing locks, his beard, his bandanna, his kiddie Keds, than for his delivery. Obviously the rules of softball had changed since the Pirates played, because this guy seemed to make balk after balk. He'd stand there reverently giving the ball an old Hare Krishna chant, then reach back to give the Clincher a little fire, then stop dead at the point of delivery, meditate for a moment, and gently lob the ball over the plate like a soft kiss.

The men of Jack & Bill's seemed to find relevance in his come-together offerings for they pounded the hell out of every one. The score was 7 to 0 in their favor in the first inning. The kind of lopsided score that often happens in softball, especially when the Pirates played. But you didn't play or watch a softball game expecting to see a pitchers' duel or a brilliant play on the field. Softball was every man's chance to be a hero, hit a home run, show a little power in play. It was a neighborhood folk game for kids approaching manhood. Your style was in whatever imagination you could let loose.

One thing that happened as the game moved through slow motion at the Hawthorne field that night was that both teams came a little more to life vocally. Players began to talk it up, saying the same things the Pirates said, the same things softballers everywhere will continue to chant come hippie or high water: "Run it out! Run it out!" "Let's go, guys, let's go! Let's get some runs!" "Nobody out! Nobody out!" "Keep 'em on the ground!" "Who's up?" "Come on, George, pick it out! Wait for yours." "Come on, Paulie, shoot it out there hard, lotta holes out there, lotta holes!"

Jack & Bill's pitcher was a heavy set guy named Jerry, who wore a bandanna around his head, perhaps in deference to his counterpart. Jerry, too, was all style. He would wind up in a wild underhand motion, arch his head out at the batter as if he was going to bite him, pretend he was about to let the ball go like a shot, then hold up and pass it back and forth slowly between his legs.

But it was all show. Only the pitcher seemed to have any control of the game. Yet it was obvious that he was throwing a soft object so big that it had to be hit. So the batters knocked the hell out of it and seemed surprised to discover just where it went in the field.

The balks continued to puzzle me. "Fakes" the players called them. And a pitcher was entitled to only three. It's no telling what the Pirates would have been able to do with the mystery of the fake. Neufeldt probably would have taken side bets on which one of the three possible fakes would be real.

Jack & Bill's led, 10 to 4, in the fifth inning, and it was getting harder and harder for me to concentrate on the game. I kept seeing the Cicero Pirates out there.

Nobody knows how many Pirates there were. There weren't any regulars. To be truthful, you didn't even need our jacket to be considered a Pirate. If you happened to be hanging around the field and the Pirates were shorthanded, never mind if you weren't so hot on softball, never mind if you were 40 years old and your wife was having another baby, never mind what the other team said about rules. Get out there and play. You're a Pirate!

Some of our finest players were drafted from the ranks of the spectators. Who could forget Chuck Suchy? Suchy, who drove a beer truck part time, was the height of any two Pirates and had hands that seemd useless, they were so big. You sent Suchy up to bat when, usually by plain thievery, every base had a Pirate on it. You tallied up another four runs before he even laid the bat on the ball. Softball, to the Pirates, was always a flexible game. You could shape the excitement, even the outcome, any way you wanted ... if guys like Suchy were around.

"Hey, he's not batting again!" someone on the other side would protest. "He was just up!"

"That was last time," said Suchy with all the sincerity of Long John Silver. And no one would disagree. The ump was too occupied with finding a horse on the scratch sheet.

Where have you gone, Chuck Suchy? Where are you, Pee Wee, the Pirates' sometimes red hot third baseman? Where's Fat Eddy Spaghetti, the catcher who always had brilliant blasphemies for the ump, the ice cream boy and stray dogs?

Where's Bob Baroni, the guy who got all the girls, the only guy who played in Saturday night dress clothes every night? What's Cib up to these days? Where's little Jimmie Vlasty, that Bohemian comedian? Where are the big Mengler brothers who spelled disaster for pitchers? Where are you, Neufeldt, and what are the odds today?

Whatever happened to Cooks, our official jester, the only Pirate who never played ball?

What about Schweiger? What about T. K., whose father was a doctor? Our "rich kid," as we referred to him on the team. Lanky, lefty, T. K. who just happened by in the Doc's Caddy and was pressed into action at the plate. Winner on a team of losers, T. K. would connect with a mush ball that plopped in the right field playground and seemed to lie there in agony. Home run. Automatic.

"Who's he? Where'd he come from?" the opposition asked.

"He's a Pirate. And his old man's a doctor. So just play ball and quit crying."

And where are all the Pirates whose names I can't even remember? Those who played for an inning, a hit, an out, maybe an entire season? What's the score? Who's up? How many down? And what the hell happened to all those jackets?

The score was tied, 12 to 12 at the top of the eighth at Hawthorne. Because the ump had been late this was the only game still going in the heavy twilight.

Across the street in the quiet of this old Cicero neighborhood, old men still stood in their undershirts carefully watering their lawns with a garden hose. A few people sat on the front steps. Children were called home for the night.

The ball game could go on forever, though it ended shortly, 19 to 13 in favor of the older guys on Jack & Bill's.

There was some debate as to which team should keep the softball, a few cheers for the winners, and one pat on the back. There were some misgivings on the part of the losers, but no one to put the blame on. The Pirates would have cursed each other out for hours.

Time, it seemed, had caught up with both teams.

Mostly they both broke up as soon as the game was over. Mostly the younger guys banded together in twos and threes and sped off to whatever night games the hour still offered them ... just as the Pirates had. Mostly the older guys climbed into their cars or walked home alone.

For softball was the last gathering of the guys. It was the final game. Before the odds were against you. And the team was scattered for good.

The Garlic Eaters

Picture an Italian . . . you've got it. The language sings in the ears, the hands swoop like swallows . . . tomatoes, green peppers, melons, grapes, oranges, garlic and an armload of red, red roses. A heritage of the senses. And that's how it should not be forgotten.

In one way or another, no matter what your last name was or where you lived around Chicago, the Italians got to you. There was just more romance to their life-style than any 10 ethnic groups stuck together.

And I can't forget that smell of garlic. Nor the time I rode a streetcar as a small boy with my grandmother. The old, mustachio next to her reeked of some sensational smell. "Garlic," whispered my grandmother . . . Italiano."

I have relived this story a thousand times. My father-in-law to this day tells almost the same tale at the mere breath of garlic in his food. "It's good for the heart," I tell him. "I remember going to work in the morning," he says, "and the whole streetcar used to smell of garlic." You can change streetcars, even get off and walk, but you can't get away from it.

Eventually I moved from Chicago to one of the greatest concentrations of Czech speaking people and Slavic culture in any suburban area — Cicero. A neat little community of hard working people, named after a Roman orator and put on the map by an Italian gunman, Al Capone.

Kids elsewhere played cowboys and Indians, we played G-men and Al Capone. After all, he was a neighbor, lived just down a few streets . . . just another local kid who made good.

Cicero is not exactly proud of its reputation but has learned to live with it. And I have yet to hear a Ciceronian completely disown the Capone image. It's a little trump card kept up the sleeve in the face of cold anonymity.

"Where you from?" asked a fishmonger in broken English one cold morning in Bergen, Norway. "Cicero," I stammered out. He picked up the biggest fish I ever saw, held it under his arm like a tommy gun, and killed me with laughter.

The anti-black reputation is a rather recent one for Cicero. I remember the first incident of a black family trying to move into an apartment house on Lombard Avenue, in 1951. I was there, in the prairie across the street, when the rocks began flying, when the rumors ran rampant. And I hated the threat of change as much as my neighbor. This was even before the days of civil rights, Martin Luther King, Malcolm X, black power and open housing. All this was to come later. And Cicero's main reaction, then and now, would be to tighten its fist.

Times change, but Cicero clings to what it has, and what it thinks is best for it. It's a question of values, of course. And to the ethnic minorities — the Czech, the Pole, the Yugoslav, the Italian — it's the value of their own property which they respect most of all. You have only to step into their house, their basement, their yard to see what pride of home means to them. And so they judge a man very simply, by outward appearances: Show me the kind of house you keep, and I'll tell you whether or not you can be my neighbor.

So, go tell the old Italian growing tomatoes and green peppers in his back yard that integration is the only human solution to his neighborhood. Or go tell the Bohemian carefully manicuring the lawn around his two-flat that he has to rent an apartment to blacks. But don't expect him to listen to you — ever. "Do you know what my old neighborhood (the near West Side of Chicago) looks like today?" they ask. "Well, that's not going to happen here."

And what of the Italian connection in problems such as these? Well, there's a secret, almost unmentionable pride in keeping the Italian in Cicero. It goes back to Al Capone, perhaps, and all that his reputation connotes. For in the dark side of the heart of most Ciceronians is the firm conviction that blacks will never dare move into Cicero as long as the Italians are around. Ask any old Bohemian on any bench along Cermak Road, and he will say, "The Mafia will never let the niggers in."

It's the same old story most Ciceronians bring home and relate with relish from all parts of the world. All friends of the family; a powerful calling card old Uncle Al left us.

A neighborhood had its divisions in that day, as all neighborhoods do. And Italians for the most part inhabited the northeast sector of Cicero known as Grant Works. They filtered in there from Taylor Street and other parts of Chicago, and in time slowly filtered out along 12th Street and into other parts of Cicero and Berwyn and Riverside and into Elmwood Park and further west into Melrose Park, where they seem to predominate today. ("Melrosa Park," so the ethnic joke goes.)

Grant Works, through, was alive with Italians . . . with backyards of flowers and vegetables, with men in sleeveless undershirts (today, fashionably dubbed "tank tops") hanging over fences. They puffed those terrible black cigars, *Parogi* ("Dago ropes," we called them).

The women were big, bosomy, aproned, with rich black hair pulled back in knots, and always a few gray wiry strands sticking out here and there. They stood forever on front steps or in gangways, hands on their hips, with little kids hanging onto their knees. Mama Mia . . . a fierce looking woman, frequently twice the size of her man, and with a heart five times bigger than both of them.

What a sad world it would be without "them," whoever "they" happen to be, depending on who you are and where you're at. You find humor in a people or a place or a custom probably because you love it, because you envy it, because you see yourself. The Polish have never been able to understand this. If you come from a culture that can't be laughed at at times, then there can't be a hell of a lot of it worth living, worth saving. How does it go these days? . . . "Nothing's funny in America anymore."

"My son's going to that new Italian university."

"Which one is that?"

"What's-a-matta-you!"

Or . . . "I've got an Italian refrigerator."

"What's that?"

"An ice-a-box."

An Italian told me both of those.

"Mama Mia, that's-a-spicy-meatball," was the best show on television once. It spoke to the bellies and heartburns of all people.

I forged my young manhood on hot pizza and Italian sausage sandwiches in the '50s at one of the first Italian restaurants in our neighborhood, the Central Snack Shop & Pizzeria, 16th and Central in Cicero.

We met there as a group of guys, hung on there through most of the night (and years), mixed there with the girls (eventually married some of them) and nourished ourselves and our senses with the smell of hot beef, sausage, oregano, tomato, and the hot sensation of mozzarella melting and often burning the roof of the mouth.

And there was once a wild and happy kid, a part-time member of the gang, whose only name we ever knew was Dago Lou . . . Dago Lou and his electric blue pants.

You don't forget communication with the hands and arms. I still find myself using it unconsciously in anger or humor, and suddenly recall I'm still alive and maybe a kid at heart. It goes like this. You see . . . the old arm feels as strong as ever.

The Italians connections just keep coming. I surprise myself the more I dwell on the matter. As young men, seriously going steady, perhaps about to be married, we took our women to the most continental, the most romantic restaurant we could find and afford — the Italian Village on Monroe, down in the Loop. This had to be Italy ... the good smells, the intimate dining, the darkness, and ah, the red wine. "Pass the Chianti, please ... and more garlic bread."

In college I roomed for a semester with an Italian barber named Enzo Berti. He became a schoolteacher. And, if I know Enzo, he's probably still cutting hair on the side.

The best man at my wedding was a guy named Jim Ascareggi (whose father was a barber in Cicero near Grant Works) who introduced me to Italian opera. Ascareggi was one of those guys who went around whistling the entire score from "Tosca." He used to hop on a plane and fly to Dallas for the night just to hear Maria Callas sing Bellini's "Norma." (Bellini? My God, how can I forget! The Cafe Bellini on Rush Street! The most civilized coffee shop ever to hit crude Chicago, only to go down in flames a few years later and never return.)

When I began to teach, I introduced the Italian life to young people via some of Sandburg's Chicago poems, then Moravia's stories, Silone's novels. My department head at Lyons Township High School in LaGrange turned out to be an unknown (to me) Italian from Cicero by the name of Aldo Mungai. Another Italiano alive to the fingertips, always gesturing in grand sweeps of imaginative expression, a considerate listener, a lover of Dante, a perfect paisano who understood the value in giving a man the full freedom to teach.

We talked of Grant Works, his neighborhood and, at times, his father, his grandfather, the dances, the celebrations, the game of *boche*, Dao Red wine, and how much of all this was dying ... a way of life his children and mine would never see, let alone ever share in conversation, punctuated in sweeping gestures by an Aldo Mungai. Powdered garlic in scent-tight tins instead of a string of crisp white bulbs hanging from the rafters, spreading the message of fire through the sense of smell.

The Italians have spread all over the old neighborhood now, across the street, down the block, the next alley over. They're mingled and married to Bohemians, Poles, Slavs of all sorts. Bakeries, butcher shops, restaurants along Cermak Road reflect the times, the mixture. All for the better, I guess, though one would like to contain the pure for old-time's sake. Even the old parish of St. Francis of Rome, once ours is now theirs.

And I live mostly and too much in the country now, far away from that time and place. I'm hidden in the middle of a fresh green woods with hardly anybody in sight but a few dour Swedes scattered here and there ... and there's no smell to the cooking. There's hardly an Italian name in the 30-page phone book.

Except for down the road about a mile where a young couple bought a farm shortly after we settled in. "Till is his name," so the rural grapevine went. "He looks like an Italian," reported a nervous old watchdog with more than a hint of dismay.

"There goes the whole north 40," I smiled in jest, though she missed the true excitement in my voice.

And so the Divine Comedy does not end. The connection continues. Till is his name indeed (formerly, Tiritilli) and we build a friendship week after week, month after month, on a past that goes back to Taylor Street and the whole Italian lifestyle ... a couple of Chicago outcasts in Dairyland.

We practice our hand gestures at the cold and monotonous gray skies, and use all the foul street talk with great gusto. We sit on an imaginary stoop in a green landscape of pure air, fantastic sunsets, and wonder (in winter) just what the hell we're doing here, why we've been assigned to purgatory, when the Chicago-Mediterranean's more our style.

"You know what the hell I've got a taste for?" says Till, pushing aside a bland Swedish meatball. "A Dago beef sandwich with lots of gravy and green peppers!"

I nod my approval and pick up the scent of garlic.

Carnival Time

Carnival time in my neighborhood was a special time that always came at the end of summer. For over a week, we lived a night life of spinning lights, popcorn, hot dogs, potato pancakes, and champion cries of "Look what I won!" And when the Ferris Wheel was at last dismantled we knew that everything that was worth anything was all over — summer, baseball, bicycles, and staying out late till the streetlights went on. School was about to begin.

But not until the carnival was over. At least, not until then.

Ours was a church carnival, and like so many other carnivals that have come and gone in Chicago, it was always held on the gravel lot next to the school. We knew approximately the opening night, but we were never sure of when the trucks would come; when the men would begin to build our world of tents and wheels.

We were always caught by surprise. (Did they come with the trucks late at night? Or so early in the morning that we were still in bed?) One of us would finally spot them — probably the guy who worked an early morning paper route, and then he would tell us, "They're here! The trucks! The carnival, they're putting it up.

And so we'd go on our bikes to watch them, to run through the dusty grounds, to pester the carnival men with questions like, "What kind of rides you going to put up?" and "Do you have a Tilt-A-Whirl?", all the while knowing full well there would be the same rides as last year and the year before: one Merry-Go-Round and one Ferris Wheel. On the gravel lot where we had fought and played ball and Red Rover, right there by home plate, stood the beginnings of a gigantic wheel of silver. And there in the outfield, a restaurant tent, a Merry-Go-Round, and a Bingo booth. A whole village of rusty colored canvas tents was built in only two or three days of miracles.

The hero of our carnival grounds was the Ferris Wheel Man. Bare chested, a greasy motorcycle cap angled on the back of his head, tattoos of snakes and hearts all over his arms and swearing (a language we were just beginning to learn), he would grab the long lever with one arm and in an instant send the great wheel up and over and around and around. He would slow it down momentarily, squinting up to its heights near the sun, checking cables, making sure of a smooth, steady motion. And then he would hook in the red and green numbered seats; spacing them, giving them a little swing with his foot before sending them up on their way, watching them sway out in descent till the wheel was full and ready to turn.

He ignored our begging for free rides — except when we got too close to the wheel, and then he ordered us to get the hell out of the way if we know what's good for us. The girls got the free rides, not us.

On opening night, we paraded down the long neighborhood blocks with a gang of seven or eight guys, always picking up a few more on the way. Our pockets were heavy with change begged from parents, uncles, aunts, and grandparents. When we got to the grounds, the sun was still out. Only a few booths were opened; the rides stood still, not a carnival man in sight.

So we would walk around and around the grounds, each time discovering something new: another booth about to open, more carnival workers arriving, the Merry-Go-Round beginning to move, more people filling the grounds, darkness, and finally the colored lights going on all over like soft fireworks.

Our money was spent fast on just three things: the Ferris Wheel (riding way up in the night, bragging at the highest point that we could see the neon green and red Western Electric sign miles and miles away above the tree tops and buildings); the restaurant booth (hot dog and soda, hot dog and soda, hot dog and soda); and knocking down a pyramid of wooden milk bottles with a ball ("Three for a dime, Nine for a quarter").

Running out of money early in the evening (sometimes in less than an hour) was a nightly disaster, which grew worse each succeeding night, since there was never as much money around as the first night of the carnival.

We would try borrowing from each other, but that seldom worked. So then we would comb the carnival grounds for lost money, for colored tickets to the Ferris Wheel that the man had accidentally forgotten to tear. And if we had only a nickel, that we had found or saved, there was always a chance to survive; to gamble it away on "Over & Under."

One night I built up my last nickel to five dollars! And other nights, many other nights, the dice rolled wrong, and a big hand picked up my last Buffalo.

That was the Old Carnival of tents (the awnings bellied with rain water after a summer shower); of gambling (Over & Under, the Big Dice Wheel, Slot Machines, Hooligan, and Bingo); of liquor (cold beer on tap, a shot on the side); of useless prizes (Kewpie Dolls, Cub pennants, colored paper leis to harness the neck in wreaths of victory, and canes with skull handles); of booths where the best prizes were an Indian blanket, a flashlight, or maybe a lamp. Booths of birds, goldfish, and even once (only once) a booth with live chickens. (How many years ago was it that one of the guys, Fat Eddie-spaghetti, won a black-and-white feathered chicken? The laughter of carrying it all around the carnival grounds. The horror of his mother giving it the ax in the basement the next morning.) And rides — always the Ferris Wheel, always the Merry-Go-Round. ("What kind of rides they got this year?" "Same old stuff." "Why can't they ever get a Tilt-A-Whirl or maybe an Octopus?")

Carnival Time in my neighborhood still comes at the end of summer, just before school starts. It's held in the same lot — now paved with asphalt. The rides: still the Ferris Wheel, the Merry-Go-Round — with some talk of maybe a Swingin' Gym next year. There are fewer tents. Instead, the booths are long white trailers pulled up by trucks, unhitched at precise locations marked on the asphalt, and readily opened wide for business.

Liquor and gambling, in their purest forms, have long passed from the carnival scene. (No chance now for a kid down to his last nickel.) They still play Bingo, only now they call it Cities, or Nations, or something. The numbered spinning wheels, which clicked and clicked and clicked past the black numbers while you breathlessly held on, have been replaced by glass bowls of long numbered tickets (202009) which hold few surprises.

The prizes have changed for the better. Practical. Expensive. Electric blankets, transistor radios, pole lamps, patio furniture, and much too that is practical, passive, plastic. Great prizes for grownups; useless for kids.

But I will go again at carnival time; and I will bring a small boy. The Merry-Go-Round will greet us; for who, after all, would dare change the ageless motion of silent wooden horses with their mission for the young.

And we will ride the Ferris Wheel; going higher and higher; rocking to a stop as each red-and-green numbered seat is emptied and filled; coming to a halt at the very top; looking out over tree tops and buildings; searching for the neon Western Electric sign miles and miles away.

Tony the Shoemaker

He's a tall, somewhat sleepy-looking guy. Hair neatly combed back, dry and straw-like. He has always looked the same, though years and years have passed.

Tony Zubrickas, in green work clothes and blue apron, is simply a neighborhood shoemaker. Nothing less, but maybe more.

Tony, at 2139 S. 58th Avenue, took over the shop in April of 1949 from old Frank Margolle. Margolle was a venerable, Walt Disney kind of shoemaker with a twinkle in his eye, a pipe in his mouth, and a back slightly bent from too many years at the bench.

Old Margolle was old then when I passed by his shop more than 20 years ago or went inside to watch him work that fantastic, long green machine of buffers and grinders and wheels that whirred on into the night even after the switch was turned off. Yet old Margolle still lives. I saw him just yesterday shoveling snow in front of his house, on the corner of the block where I once lived, only a few blocks from the shop. He's in his nineties, pushing 100. Maybe old shoemakers never die or even fade away.

And Tony is on the brink of becoming a legendary, old fashioned shoemaker himself, if he hangs in there long enough and continues to fix a few shoes and entertain anyone who has a few minutes to share. Since the trade itself is bordering on legend, all Tony has to do is grow a little older, a little grayer, put on some round spectacles, and begin shuffling around with a handful of nails in his mouth, sounding off about life and things in general. But he has always done that.

That's what I liked about Tony the shoemaker when I was in high school and found it difficult to vent my emotions at home. I'd go to the shoemaker instead and tell him off.

"Why the hell don't you work for a living like everybody else?" I'd yell at him to get his dander up. "All you do is stare out that window all day or listen to polka music on the radio. Get to work!"

"Why? Just to be the richest stiff in the cemetery like all the other Bohemians?" he'd answer with a straight face, followed almost immediately with a quick smile and a laugh.

Through the years his place has become a hangout for neighborhood society, kids all the way through retirees. My own father still manages to spend a part of a Saturday afternoon at the shop. It gradually became the thing to do among my friends and family to never pass by Tony's without stopping in and giving him hell for a few minutes. He needed it. We needed him.

Maybe a shoemaker is more than a shoemaker . . . if he's a good shoemaker. As he was saying yesterday, when I banged on his window before going in (and he acknowledged the greeting with an old fashioned gesture): "I'll take the good old days anytime. You can have this. Then I would sit in the front stoop and watch all the people going by to the 'L'. I'd talk to them. They'd wave. It's been pretty good around this neighborhood."

"Have you seen old Margolle?" I asked him.

"Once in a while he stops in if he needs some glue or something. Naw, he doesn't miss it. Fifty years in this racket is a long time. If I could get out, I would."

"Yeah, but then you'd have to work."

"Wise guy. Why should I work? Anyway, with all this machinery, like this auto-soler here for heels and stuff, I can get the work out much faster. But they got so damn much machinery on the market now, you don't know what to get . . . if you could afford it. Nowadays you'd need about $10,000 to get a shop started."

"So it's a good life, isn't it, you lousy shoemaker?"

"You should talk! When the hell you going to work for a living like everybody else? Your father was in here the other day and said you're traveling again. Some guys got it made."

"Yeah, like shoemakers."

"You can see how much I'm doing right now, can't you? Not a helluva lot. People think you're making a fortune during the summer. Then in winter if you make expenses you're doing damn good. There ain't a shoemaker left to the east of me for some ways. This is one business you just make a living at. You don't get rich."

"That's because people have stopped walking."

"Yeah. Most of my traffic now is people going to the bus. But at least people are buying better shoes now than they used to. In the last few years people have finally wised up and stopped buying all that cheap crap at the big discount stores. You can't do nothing with those shoes except throw them away."

"What's a good day ... when you feel like working?"

"A good day would be when I run through about 15, 20 pairs of heels and 5 or 10 pairs of soles and heels. That's if I feel like working. But lately I've been pushing through like nothing, now that I'm getting older. I do a lot of waiting service, too. Haven't refused anybody yet for a pair of soles and heels."

"What about all the time you waste shooting the bull with all your old cronies?"

"Oh, that don't count. This place has become kind of a refuge for them."

There is one old guy, Joe, sitting in a chair against the wall at the moment. Tony sometimes joins his visitor in the next chair and the two of them sit there in reverie. Joe is 86, and in Tony's damn near every day. First he stands at the counter and watches Tony and looks out the window, then when he gets tired of that he takes a chair and waits for customers and friends to come in.

"I think I'll go see Bill," he says and shuffles out to visit the barber next door.

"Don't hurry back," Tony yells after him with a smile.

"You need an apprentice," I tell him. "Come to think of it, I've never heard of an apprentice shoemaker. 'My son's studying to become a great shoemaker' sounds strange."

"Not many replacements in this racket. They had a couple of schools for shoemaking ... I think there's one left in Texas. This is a dying trade if you come right down to it. I used to teach a guy some years ago. I taught him everything I know. He stayed in this racket about six years, got an ulcer, and went back to tool-and-die-making. I told him not to get into shoemaking unless he really wants to suffer.

"When you come right down to it, age is against me. I got into this racket at 33. Hell, I was having bad luck then. I used to drive a truck before. I went to shoe school after I got out of service, a place on Belmont. It's too late for me to do anything else. I've been here 23 years. I'll stay with this. There's really no retirement age to it. There are guys 75, 80, still in the business. I don't intend to stay that long. I hope."

Another old-timer comes into the shop, Jack, a few years younger than Joe, and the precinct captain from the other side of Cermak. Jack, too, seems engrossed in times past. "Joe and me used to work together. I think I built the biggest die in the world at the old Harvester plant. It weighed 10 tons and stamped out a manure spreader all in one piece. Everything changes."

Joe returns from his visit with the barber and takes up his position at the counter to man the window-watch for passers-by. Jack stands and stares against the radiator. Tony sits up straight in a chair. It's a bad day for shoemaking.

"On days like this," says Tony, "if I see one person come in for a pair of heels I wonder what the hell's wrong with him."

Another old man walks past the shop, raps on the window, and yells at Tony: "Throw those guys out. Their time is up."

It's a bad day for shoemaking, but maybe a good day to be inside the shop with Tony and friends, waiting out the winter, waiting out the time.

"Yeah," says Tony. "Come winter these Bohemians put their boots on and that's it till April."

Playing the Horses

It is a summer afternoon and I am a grown man standing outside the fence at Sportsman's Park in Cicero with a bunch of other little kids, and I am hooked once on just the sight of horses.

The first horse I ever saw was owned by my Grandfather on a farm in Three Oaks, Michigan. I forget its name, but it was the biggest animal I had ever seen. It was supposed to pull a plow to help my Grandma till the land, while my Grandpa went back to Chicago to find a job to keep both Grandma and the farm going. That horse was a loser and so was the farm.

I saw the horse run only once. My Grandfather came back one Saturday and decided to harness the horse so Grandma could rake some hay, as soon as she finished baking and making butter.

He got part of the strappings over the horse's head, got both his hands tied and twisted somewhere under the horse's belly, screamed and cursed so loud in Hungarian that the horse reared, knocked my Grandfather down, and took off in something like a gallop, stomping through the small vineyard and into a far field of corn.

That was the first horse I ever saw fade from a home stretch. Grandpa swore he would kill the sonofabitch the next time it came near the house. You see, Grandpa didn't like to lose either.

And that night at the kitchen table Grandma dealt him still another terrible blow with the pinochle cards. And then he accused her of cheating. And then she stood up and threw the whole deck at him plus a handful of hard bunco dice as well. Me and the horse watched from the window.

But back in Cicero there were thoroughbreds, real horses that ran because they were supposed to. And there was Hawthorne and there was Sportsman's. And somewhere south over that marvelous old 52nd Street bridge, high above all the railroad tracks, the smoke and steel and rust of the industrial West Side, you slowly descended upon a kingdom of color and horses forever known as "the track." And as kids we'd stand at the fence watching the track, waiting for the miracle of 10 sweat-shiny horses come thundering at you in the stretch, into the turn. You could feel the concrete sidewalk shake.

To have great horse races, you must have great horse players, said Walt Whitman.

Mine was not a family of great horse players and I never met a genuine horse player until I came across a neighborhood legend, Levi Luke, who was hooked on horses at an early age and wore Levis, only Levis, when everyone else was already moving into electric blue pegged pants.

Levi was a gamlbin' man. He loved country music, worshipped Hank Snow, and could be usually heard humming "The Streets of Laredo." He was almost 10 years older than the rest of us, but was always a kid and a cowboy at heart.

I think the first bet I ever put on a horse was placed with Levi around the confines of the local Community House. Since we were always broke, Levi became our buddy and our bookie. He taught us how gambling could be a way out.

First it was poker, then it was horses. It didn't really matter how you played the game, but whether you won or lost. You always won a little and lost a lot. Except for Luke. Who, according to his carefully kept records, was always a little ahead.

"I'm in front about $15 on poker this year and about $35 on the horses," he would say. "Listen, I got a good parlay for the 6th, 7th, and 8th at Hawthorne," he'd suggest to us. "Give me a buck a piece and I'll drive you to the track and we can watch 'em come in. And I won't charge for the gas, either."

Luke was always a fair-minded guy that way. If you wanted to do anything with him, you had to learn to pay the price ... especially a ride in his '36 Dodge, 4-door sedan, which we came rolling up to the gates in after the 6th race, when they let us in for free.

From the outset I could sense something was wrong, and I was not cut out to be a horse player for life. Once I got in the track, once I stood near the people at the windows, then moved with them into the grandstand and finally up against the fence, once I saw the truth and beauty of 10 thundering horses and their bobbing jockeys in satin electirc shirts come into the wire, I couldn't care less where my money was riding or if it would ever add up.

I was a poet who didn't know it. And I had to lose a hell of a lot before the revelation of where the real action was, and why winning didn't matter.

Along with the track, Levi taught me the layout of a bookie joint as well. We'd usually go there on Saturday afternoons with his pop. Other fathers abandoned their kids at the local show or let them run in the alleys. Only Levi's pop believed in a kind of open classroom, a storefront school. You want to teach a kid arithmetic? You want to teach him the value of money? Take him to a bookie joint on a Saturday afternoon.

I tagged along. I needed all the help I could get in arithmetic, and I loved to see the action of numbers inside the book joint . . . the way results were posted above the bookmakers' cage, how much and how fast money passed hands for a ticket, how everybody in there was a sitting, pacing, brooding, solitary computer.

And the neatest thing of all for me was the mystery of "where did they hide the book joint today?" Behind the candy store? The drug store? The barber shop?

I mean, here were all these ordinary people on the street shopping, visiting with neighbors, buying newspapers, doing the things ordinary people ordinarily do. And you sort of mix in with them, become part of it all, and then kind of nonchalantly walk up to a side door, stand there a few seconds to be checked out through a two-way mirror or a slight crevice, and then suddenly dissapear.

And now you're inside, and it's like another country. Bright lights, smoke, food, a blackjack game in one corner, dice in another. And an incredible number of people, even old grandmothers in house slippers peering into racing forms a few inches from their noses.

Though time has passed, though book joints as they once were are gone, though Levi has relocated farther west and we are almost strangers, though I haven't placed a bet in 10 years . . . the subject is still horses as I stand outside the fence of Sportsman's this bright afternoon and watch the trainers walk the horses. The grandstand is beginning to fill up.

I find my place in the steady stream of horse players and make my way toward the entrance gate. Prices have changed, but not much. Clubhouse, $2.75 (I've never made that scene), Grandstand, $1.50 (here I come) Medicare, 50¢ (what a nice way to treat an old horse player).

I have no hot tips, no particular horse in mind. I'm here because of a vague rememberance of things past; I'm here because horses are running.

To reacquaint myself, I load up on a turf edition of a newspaper, a scratch sheet, and 'The Official Program of Sportsman's Park . . . Welcome to the Afternoon Show', 35¢.

I watch the program man playing an old con game with the guy ahead of me who has put up 50¢ for the program and is still waiting for change, while the program man turns quickly to another sale.

"Hey, I gave you half a buck."

"What?"

"Half a buck. Where's my change?"

"Oh, yeah. Thing's happen, you know. They happen."

"Yeah, yeah, yeah ... "

I gave the program man exactly 35¢, and smiled at him knowingly.

Inside the grandstand, underneath, in and around and against the windows, the tote board, the pillars, the hot dog stands, I remember and feel once again, what it means to mingle with the 'people'—the incredible assortment of men and women for whom playing horses is the whole way of life.

You work in an office with people — but they are not "the people."

Or you live in a suburb with people — but they are not "the people."

Or you attend a party or a church or a club — but they are not always "the people."

"The people" are to be found in train stations, bus depots, huge sporting events, old neighborhoods, city streets, and racetracks.

I don't know what it all is that separates them from the rest of us, except that maybe they have lost a little more, and they show it.

They show it in faces that reflect the triumph and tragedy of blowing a whole paycheck on Lady Luck. They show it in clothes that don't matter to anybody as long as clothes cover what's supposed to be covered; they show it in gestures, in speech that is laced with what poets once called "the common tongue." (Months later I would tell a class of young writers ... "You want to find people? Go to the racetrack.")

There is a man standing next to me wearing a torn black raincoat and white painter's cap; a black woman goes by with a mink cape, a crazy green hat, and a quarter ton of costume jewelry; there is a man in gray work pants and a sharkskin vest with a gold watch; there is a young woman in a 1940-type skirt pushing a baby stoller, holding another baby in one arm, carrying another inside of her, and grasping a pink tip sheet while angling for a place in line outside the daily double window.

At 10 minutes to post time (2 p.m.), I hear a great trumpet play that exciting call to attention that is forever in the hearts of all horseplayers. You want to know what a little music can do for the soul of man? Go to the racetrack. Watch the people storm to the windows at the mere sound of a horn.

I even find myself responding unconsciously, moving toward the windows. The daily double... now how would Levi play this, I wonder? I have won only one double in my life, and that was with his coaching. We split $22 bucks about five ways, as I recall.

I look for the easy way out and check the tipsters in the newspaper, the scratch sheet. Favorites—everybody's picking "the horses most likely to succeed" — with little odds. I play it safe. I decide to go with the favorites, Help's Here in the 1st and Chess Town in the 2nd, and pick up some easy dough for openers. 8 to 5 on Help, 7 to 2 on Chess. At $2, you can't lose—but you can't win much either.

Standing in line, one place from the window, I am suddenly struck by that inexplicable hot flash horse players best describe as a "hunch." Quickly glancing at the charts for maybe the 2,000th time, I decide to swing with Barbeulah in the 1st, because my wife's name is Barbara and because the jockey's name is Macbeth and I like the Shakespearean overtone, and Table's Girl in the 2nd, because that's a hell of a name for a horse.

I find a seat in the grandstand, clutching my winning ticket, and groove to the sound of the announcement... "THE HORSES ARE AT THE POST... THEY'RE OFF!" Wow! That even beats "Ladies and gentlemen, the President of the United States."

Mob psychology ... people poetry ... mass movement ... what do you call it? For an instant, as the horses break from the post, there is monumental silence in the air, about as lasting as a horse's smile. And if you're up in the grandstands without binoculars, the numbers of horses, the colors of the jockeys, all is a blur.

After the first bend, the people begin to rise in place. Some of them begin to filter in droves out of the stands and toward the fence. The announcer sounds like, "BESCK BRDFT RDHETD STWORTY!" And before you know it, the horses are rounding the final turn and there's this symphony of horse players, such a crescendo of voices as the people become alive, electric to the fingertips, arms flailing, swearing, cheering, cursing, words of 'the people' pouring out in a poetic passion that originates somewhere from the source of the billfold ...

"Bust 'em baby, bust 'em ... "

And I have surreal visions of a shiny black horse falling into pieces all over the track.

And the instant the first horse cracks across the wire, the tumult subsides like the click of a switch, save for a large chorus of sighs, a dirge of Ohhhhhh'ssssss for the poor losers.

The winners are posted on the tote board, and there is the sudden realization that I too should have joined the sad chorus of losers. Help's Here was 1st and paid $4.40. My dear Barbeulah stumbled in 9th. And for that jockey, "Macbeth," I mumble to myself, "Avaunt! and quit my sight! Let the earth hide thee! Thy bones are marrowless, the blood is cold; thou hast no speculation in those eyes which thou dost glare with!"

So it's back to the charts, back to the tipsters, the program notes, the gossip around the hot dog stands, the little bits of info eavesdropped here and there for the next 20 minutes or so.

I could play Table's Girl to win again. But I'm through with her after Barbeulah let me down. And if I don't play her, she'll probably win since I had her on the double; therefore, I'll psych them all out and go for seconds, go for place. What the hell, second best is good enough for me.

Studying the charts, I conclude that Bet Jay Be is a good gamble to run second in the second race . . . "Showing much promise; fits the company," says the scratch sheet. Kay Wells picked the horse to win, somebody else to show. Perfect, Bet Jay Be will place. I put a big 2 bucks to place and go back to the stands.

But there is no way to describe the confusion that goes on in a horse player's mind. There is never any peace. One is constantly hounded by the question, "What if?"

I decide that I'm not satisfied with seconds. I want firsts! And who has almost everybody picked to run 1st and 2nd? Table's Girl. So I run back to the windows and smack down another two bucks to win.

There. Now I'm satisfied . . . although I'm wondering about a horse named Might Mr. A . Nope, it's Table's Girl and Bet Jay Be.

"THE HORSES ARE NEARING THE POST . . . THEY'RE AT THE POST . . . THEY'RE OFF!"

They're back already. Valiant Call comes in first and pays $23.40, Chess Town, second, paying $4.80. "Who the hell is Valiant Call?," you want to scream with the rest of the losers lined up along the fence. Where did he come from? And who said he could win? What does the scratch say . . . "Horse is dropping down in class . . . Had speed at Centennial: dull local area." And what the hell is that supposed to mean?

A vicious circle begins spinning in a horse player's head . . . names, numbers, remorse for what you should have done but did not do. Tabler's Girl! Whatever happened to old Table's Girl, everybody's favorite? She came in third from last.

By the third race, if you're still in a position to wager, you begin to feel sorry for yourself. You begin to feel what it will be like to go home in a few more races without enough money to buy the evening paper.

So the third race takes on the drama of now or never. A sense of recklessness seizes you, and you go for the whole ball of wax. $10 on Flemish Prince to win. 3 to 1 odds, you can't go wrong. Everybody's picked him. He's a "Track Special" on the sheet. "Hit stride in last; right back again," they say. If ever a horse is destined to be a winner, it's Flemish Prince. Besides, he's carrying my very lucky number, 3.

I'm one of the first to place my bet. I have plenty of time. I have a hot dog, a beer; I mingle with the masses. Sitting on the steps, tuned in to the whole racing scene, I hear a man mumbling to the man beside him, "I just ain't makin' the right decisions." What a stroke of philosophical insight! And you don't get that in books. You feel it at the track.

I move to the empty grandstands and absorb a little more of the beauty of racetracks. I watch the ducks in the pond, the flowers, the green grass. A racetrack is prettier that a bull ring, makes more sense than most stadiums. There's more contact with the natural.

"Do you remember what No. 4 paid in the last race?" a woman on her knees asks me. "I had the ticket but lost it."

"You're lucky, lady. I'm trying to forget that race."

I move down to the fence to be closer, hoping to help bring Flemish Prince on in, and I notice for the first time a remarkable absence of young people at the track. No teen-agers at all. Some 20-and 30-year olds. But 40 on up seems to be the racing crowd.

And long hairs, it dawns on me, except for a couple of old men who probably can't afford a haircut, I'm the only one with hair over his ears.

Horse racing, I surmise, must not be part of the Consciousness III crowd. Yet I wonder why? Surely there must be some old vibrations here for the young to tune into. The spirit of horses, of horse players must mean something.

I stand next to a group of old, hard losers and listen to them peel off veritable folklore of racing.

"New York horses? Anytime one comes out here, I play him. And I bet I win three-quarters of the time. Chicago horses ain't doin' crap. The Illinois breeding ain't no damn good. New York horses, California horses will beat the hell out of them anytime."

"You must remember J. Boucher?" says another. "Chip-a-Munk won eight in a row when this was a half-mile track, wire-to-wire, remember that? Remember Boucher, the world's worst jockey? He just hung on, that was all."

"Yeah, he took the inside rail and kept there. He could a won by 20 lengths."

"Boucher, he won eight in a row, and I never heard of him again."

"What's your horse?" I ask.

"Mystic Light."

At the sound of the music, I return to the fence. I've got big money riding on this race.

"AND THEY'RE OFF! ... "

Flemish Prince I can't see, but I can feel he is leading the pack right from the gate. The horses flash by, and I try to register the order of numbers ... where the hell is 3? There goes 3 ... he'll never catch up.

In the back stretch I hear Everetts Sassy out in front, and a cluster of horses consisting of Good Luck Baby, Stylish Bim, and even The Redeemer. Flemish Prince, I presume, must have run into a moat.

Across the finish wire it's Stylish Bim, first; the Redeemer, second, and Everetts Sassy ... no ... it's a photo for third. The announcer explains,

"Photo for show between Everetts Sassy and Mystic Light."

Flemish Prince came in 10th!

The 4th Race is off, and I don't care who the hell wins. I'm sitting this one out. I'm down to my last buck anyway, and couldn't place a bet if I felt like it. So I'm back at the fence trying to tune into a different perspective.

Hell, I'm no gambler, just like my Grandfather was no farmer. Levi Luke, now there was a gambler. Or my Grandma with a pinochle deck, there was a dealer who kept a firm hold on the odds. Or this black guy next to me, screaming at the horses ...

"Come on number 6 ... bring that 6 on down here! ... It ain't the horse, it's the driver ... He afraid he gonna have an accident ... Jesus, look! Three horses pass him by! GET ON 'EM, MAN, GET ON 'EM! ... THE STICK! THE STICK! ... AHhhh, hell! ... Damn, damn ... You see that? That horse want to run. Ain't nothin a matter with that horse. There just ain't no damn driver ... "

You have to have that involvement to be a real horse player. You have to learn to lose screaming it out of your guts.

Glancing at the program for the fifth race, I am brought back to my own lifestlye, and settle again for the pure poetry of just plain horses, and the people.

The poetry in names alone is enough for me to tip my hat to all the unknown poets somewhere out there in the racing world. I sit out the fifth, sixth and seventh races, too, and delight, instead, on the connotations of Sorb's Lark, Dancing Wolf, and Howlin' Wind. Who said there's no culture at the track?

By God, in the 6th there's a horse called April Poppy and another, June White. And in the 7th, how about the image of Jungle Eagle or Amar Amber?

The line-up for the 8th reads like a poem by Gertrude Stein: Me Carla, Oh Camile, Black Wine, Upsie, Kitchs Knee, Nowata, Mad Hatter ...

Flashing on the Truth of the Hunch once again, sounding out those old vibrations, smiling the inner smile, I pretend to play the 8th Race and pick Oh Camile aross the board (for old time movie sake) and Mad Hatter across the board (for Alice and all the wonderlands), and then with something of the style of a true horse player, I leave the track without even caring to see the race run.

I'm sure of the outcome. What's more, I've even covered myself with Mad Hatter. There's something heady in knowing you're a different kind of winner.

Later in the evening. I check the morning editions of the newspapers. Oh Camile paid $29.60, $10.40. $5.00 Mad Hatter, $4.40, $3.00.

Sometimes to win is not to play the game.

In Praise of Sausage

Sausage may be the truest link between old country and new, between past and present. Sausage can make you stuck in time; just a whiff of garlic can bring it all back. Even now I can taste the prazsky (Bohemian salami) in the refrigerator. I know it's there, and it's almost lunch, and it begs to be eaten. Sausage can speak to one's gut.

I remember my mother cutting off the end (it was really the beginning) of a prazsky and handing it to me by the string so I could sink my child-size front teeth into the red, garlicky meat. "Don't eat the skin!" was the only admonition. And I went after the sausage like a tiny animal till there was nothing left but string and empty casing. All my insides cried out for more. Sausage has this appeal to the animal instinct. Souffle for the gourmet, sausage for me.

Sausage is home. A liver-sausage sandwich in your lunch bucket for school. A salami sandwich on rye in a brown paper bag for the job. And a plate of cold cuts on the kitchen table every Sunday evening.

Cold cuts at our house on a Sunday evening meant liver sausage, summer sausage, and sometimes sulc, a jellied head cheese. In the fall, and through much of the winter, there was always another Bohemian specialty, jaternice.

Jaternice. It takes childhood, boyhood, and young manhood to acquire a true taste for them, and it's best to have Bohemian grandparents to break you in. Whatever the interminglings and strange marriages of other sausages (what country doesn't make some type of an Italian salami these days?), nobody makes jaternice but the Bohemians.

And no two men, not even Bohemians, will ever agree on the taste sensation of any one sausage. You can bite into the greatest Polish in the world and somebody eating the same sausage right next to you will bitch about there being too much garlic — and somebody else, not enough. Never trust any man's opinion on sausage.

An ethnic-American history of sausage has to begin with hot dogs, of course. The wiener, the frankfurter, the Berliner of Germany, and now the sausage of our democracy.

Give a small child his first raw hot dog to hold onto, to munch, and you give him his first lesson in the civility of sausage. If you were lucky enough to be reared in an ethnic neighborhood, the butcher broke you in. He saw you staring through the meat cases at all the blood and guts of his butchery, so artfully arranged, and he snapped off a hot dog to counsel you in the carnivorous ways of man.

That's the first link, the best beginning, simplicity in sausages. Some never proceed beyond the realm of Oscar Mayer and Smoky Links. Others, sausage savants and sages, begin to journey by bites and slices into and through the sausages of many countries, never quite fulfilled — which is reason enough for their journey.

The Bohemian moves from the hot dogs of his favorite butcher to prazsky at an early age. In between, and along the way, he may be given many courses in klobasy (cream sausage), butchta (veal loaf), debrecinky (small, highly seasoned sausages), cerbulaty (fat, garlic sausage), sulc, and jaternice, black or white.

But prazsky is the old standby, a sausage for all seasons. Open any Bohemian refrigerator or check the rafters in the basement, and you'll find a hunk of prazsky. It's one of the basic ingrediants in the Czech's Life Force.

And the best prazsky, according to a recent poll conducted by the author in such traditional Czech stongholds as Cicero, Berwyn, 26th Street, Riverside, and La Grange, comes out of the Crawford Sausage Company (since 1925) at 2310 S. Pulaski. They make a prazsky called Daisy Brand and distribute it in many stores throughout the city, especially in the basic Bohemian neighborhoods.

How to describe prazsky? Blushing pink slices, garlic, aftertaste. Thick hunks of it on Bohemian rye with butter, washed down with beer. The fresher the prazsky the better. Too many days in the refrigerator and it loses much of its spicy impact. You want to be able to eat a prazsky sandwich, breathe heavily on somebody, and watch his eyes water. That's fresh!

I go to the people who make prazsky for the particulars. To George Horna, who has been associated with the Crawford Sausage Company for 41 years — deliveryman, sausagemaker, and now a retired executive vice president.

He explains how seven men, most of them butchers (including my Uncle Bill Burda's father) organized the company to make sausage primarily for the Czechs then living in the Lawndale area.

"Hot dogs, ham, bacon, minced ham, prazsky," he explains, "we made it all for the Lawndale area." And what about prazsky? Where did the name come from?

Prague, he supposes. "Then it was changed to prazsky because it was easier to pronounce. Our main thing was quality. The best meat.

"Beef and pork go into it. Salt, pepper, a little sugar, garlic ... We use all natural spices. I can't tell you all that goes into it. Some of it's secret." Sausagemakers and their secrets; worse than mushroom hunters.

"Sausagemaking has changed, though. You remember how you used to see the diced hunks of fat in the prazsky? Now that's all gone The people got fat-conscious. But what they don't realize is that's the way suasage has to be made. The fat adds to the flavor and taste.

"Texture's another thing. How much pork? How much beef? Too much beef and it's tough. Too much pork and it's too sloppy. We do everything by hand ... still the old way. Meat is not the same every day. When you work it in your hands, you know what the meat needs. You know it in your hands. Machines don't tell you this."

Crawford Sausage, according to Horna, makes more than 40 kinds of sausage. "But our best sellers are still hot dogs and prazsky. And we are the only ones with veal sausage that's really veal sausage."

As for Polish sausage, Bohemian style: "We make our meat a little coarser. We want it to be seen. When you cut that slice, it's got to be shown that there's good meat in there. And garlic and a little more pepper for the Poles."

Later, the scent of paprika is all around as I meet one of the best sausage-makers in the city: Frank Szalai of the European Sausage House, 4361 N. Lincoln. Hungarian to the heart, Frank can wax symphonic over sausage. His whole being, his expressions, gestures exude a sense of sausage.

There are three brothers in the business, Joe, Steve and Frank, who smiles and says, "I am here 17 years after the Revolution. I was carpenter ... many things before making sausage."

Frank's specialty is a Hungarian salami called hertz. Now, truthfully, it takes a real sausage freak to find much difference among salamis. They are fine-tasting and desirable, but they all look alike to me. Yet each sausage-maker will cling to the secret of his salami as if it were a birthright.

"Frank," I say. "Cut it straight. What really makes Hungarian salami so different from Italian or any other salami?"

"Ahhhhh!" he smiles as if he has caught me in an obvious error of logic. "We use the paprika!"

Frank beheads a fresh Hungarian salami for my inspection. It's a rich maroon and rather slippery-looking, as salami should be — and there, inter-mingled, the orange-red heart and soul of Hungary: paprika. Its contribution to the taste is soon apparent and readily appreciated.

Frank Szalai's life seems intertwined with sausage. The meat cases, the counters, the hooks are full of them. His butcher shop is mostly a sausage shop. Big, fat, thin, long, short, fresh, cooked, dry, with names that border on mystery.

He will give a new customer a taste of anything that looks interesting: a csabai going for $3.20 a pound; something else, quite delicious, called cserkasz, which he says means "boy scout"; gyulai (dry) named for a city in Hungary.

There's also debreceni, which brings me back the Bohemian debrecinky. Where did it all begin? Each country, it would seem, has forever been trying and tasting and stealing sausage secrets from each other.

Frank makes a smoked liver sausage called bagcskai, which means, he thinks, "smallish liver." And he makes a coarse liver sausage the likes of which I have never seen or tasted anywhere else; you can actually see the pieces of meat.

Moving back to the debreceni, Frank shows me how the Hungarians eat them. They look about the size of a man's finger, something similar to a small thuringer.

"You eat with horseradish," he says. "Just like this ... horseradish, mustard, sauerkraut. Sometimes parties ... maybe Hungarian freedom fighters, we eat debreceni. In Europe, they serve by train station, you now. Americans some people watch the television and eat debreceni ... break off like this, eat. No?"

There is also head cheese; his finest, he says. Made of pork tongues and pork snouts. "Look here—hurka," he exclaims, pointing to a sausage that looks like a small horse collar. "Made with rice and blood in natural hog casing. A tradition in Hungary, in wintertime when people kill the pigs. Family have party in the evening after all the jobs over."

Ah, finally. The true beginning of prazsky and hurka and liverwurst and whatever.

"They butcher pigs in the fall, in the winter, and they make the sausages and keep till the summertime. They smoked the meat. No refrigeration, see? Every farmer was, then, a sausagemaker. You used the lard for cooking, the bacon to eat ... all different things, and some people like the heart. But every family, a different taste of sausage."

But what's the secret, really, of sausagemaking?

"Spice," he smiles. "Spice is the main difference. And the different kinds of meat. Good sausage is 100 per cent pork. Is different, different country. I can't eat the Italian sausage. They use the rosemary leaves; the Hungarian people can't eat this!" he pounds his fist vehemently.

"Oh, garlic we use. We like that. That's very important. Our customers ask, Is homemade?' Yes. Sixty-five per cent of the business is sausage.

"I can show you the meat we use ... everything the best. The meat is so fresh, is beautiful. Look," he picks up a jowl thick with red paprika. "Such a beautiful jowl. Is called abalt szalonna ... just a little cooked.

"Red paprika is from Hungary," he points to the cans and packages of imported red pepper. "Almost 95 per cent of every Hungarian meal has paprika. Used almost every day. And you know, is really good for you. The paprika has the vitamins. Yes, scientists say, vitamin C."

We move to the cooler, where the sausagemaker goes into rapture over the beauty and blood of his meat, and to the smokehouse, where only natural hickory is burnt. "Nothing artificial, nothing!" he slams his fist.

Finally he opens another cooler door, and we enter a large room, the kingdom of Hungarian salami. A forest of salami ... hundreds and hundreds of them hanging in various stages of curing, some ripe with mold, getting harder and stronger and tastier every day.

"Salami maybe needs 12 to 16 week before we start selling in the store," Frank says.

Is that another secret than? The aging?

"Just the spicing is *different*," he pounds his hand again. "Salami last long, long time. Forever," he smiles.

But just when you've eaten one kind of sausage and thought it the best you've ever tasted, you discover yet another summit in the distance. Usinger's in Milwaukee, for instance. Perhaps the Valhalla of sausagedom.

Usinger's Famous Sausages, made in Milwaukee since 1880, come from an old six-story building at 1030 N. Third St., and a good part of the country beats a path to that door. "America's Finest Sausage" is the slogan, busy little elves the symbol.

Usinger's goes back to Grandfather Fred, who came to Milwaukee from Germany in 1880 with all the recipes he would ever need to become a millionaire in the art of wurst within 50 years.

Entering the first-floor factory store, open to the public, I am immediately surprised by the 1890 atmosphere, the glass and marble counters, and the sound of German crackling above the ranks of sausage, which are assembled and readied at every perimeter.

I head behind the counter for the office and a briefing with Robert Siebecker, not a sausagemaker but a serious student of sausagery, part of Usinger's wonderful world of sausage people.

I am given a white butcher's coat and a funny yellow hat that says USINGER'S FAMOUS SAUSAGES, which makes me "official," government approved and inspected, and welcomed.

Doors open ... and I am overwhelmed. The Usinger forces in white coats and funny little caps blending the meat, stuffing the sausages, trucking them around the floors and into the smokehouses, busy, busy, busy.

The production, the efficiency, the machinery, the carts and racks of sausages are so staggering that no question seems quite adequate. I'm back to a civilian's concern of how large the army . . . just how much sausage is at their command?

"We don't like to give out any definite figures," says Siebecker, "but well over 100,000 pounds a week."

Usinger's employs about 150 hard-working sausage people, and you sense that they know what they are about. Traditionally, Usinger's takes care of them. "We feed all our employees two meals a day — platters of sausages at 9:30 a.m. and noon," explains Seibecker. "There is very little turnover. When they leave Usinger's, they retire."

Sausage . . . so many different kinds. "About 75 varieties," says Siebecker. Thumbing through Usinger's Sausage Manual later, I pinpoint the particulars: Blood pudding (Long nosed sausage) . . . made with only beef blood . . . bits of cured ham fat are generously interlaced throughout. Tongue blood sausage . . . very popular . . . only tender, select, young pork tongues are used. Braunschweiger liver sausage . . . this delicately seasoned, natural-casing sausage is nationally famous . . . only large sweet Bermuda onions are used, not onion powder . . . a light smoke adds that finishing touch of perfection. . . .

The list of sausages march on and on: goose-liver sausage, bockwurst, brat-wurst, knackwurst, strassburger, schwartenmagen, mortadella, pastroma, German-style salami, landjaeger — the old German "hunter" sausage, to be carried in the pockets while hunting. . . .

"This is our all-beef summer sausage," Siebecker says, pointing to a rack of a couple hundred dark red ones, hanging there in glory. "Everybody's on this beef kick. We're making more all-beef products than ever before."

We inspect the huge smoking chambers, where the aroma of burning hickory wafts sublime, the fire pit on one floor, the racks of sausages hanging above on the next.

He describes the braunschweiger liver sausage as their No. 1 best seller (I taste it later and know he speaks the truth), and then launches into the subject of casings.

"Natural hog casings on the braunschweiger . . . expensive. The casing alone now costs us $1.55. Pretty soon you're going to start throwing the sausage away and eat the goddman casing. Now this casing here," he explains, "is called a beef bung cap. It's like an appendix. One end is naturally closed.

"Here's tongue blood sausage. We have more tongue than blood, not like most companies. Also, a link blood sausage — one of those dying items. Not too many people left who enjoy this anymore. We used to make more than 100 varieties, but as the people who want them die off, we slowly discontinue making them.

"Old ethnics eat more sausage than anybody. Young Americans eat more hot dogs. We get the kids when they're older, more affluent. Usually some ethnic introduces them to sausage."

As for all the economy talk in America: "You can eat a one-pound steak, but you can't eat 10 wieners. You get what you pay for; no shrinkage in sausage."

Usinger's sausage is never too far away. "Chicago is our No. 2 market," says Siebecker. "Stop & Shop (in the Loop) is our biggest single outlet in the country. We even ship to Japan ... mainly braunschweiger and all-beef summer sausage. Liberace has our sausage shipped to him. Danny Kaye's been here. And Mayor Daley ordered from us."

I turn in my white uniform and funny yellow hot and prepare my retreat to Chicago, but I have to ask about Usinger's elves.

"The German tradition," Siebecker smiles. "The elves are the sausage-makers in Germany. The Irish have their leprechauns, the Germans have their elves."

There are no elves or leprechauns in my old neighborhood back in Cicero. But Bohemian sausagemakers, cooking, grinding, and stuffing the old world wonders down in their basements, are just as elusive and nearly as legendary these days.

I remember once seeing Old Man Pardus, oh, so many years ago, down in his basement making sausages one night. There was always something secretive about the operation. As with the winemakers, it seemed, no one was supposed to know just what magic these oldtimers were up to each fall, down there in the night.

Now Pardus is gone; perhaps everyone now buys his jaternice from the local butcher. And then I remember Jerry Kachlic, the milkman, who lives a few doors away from my folks. He's still a young man in a way, not even close to the rank of an old-timer. How could I have forgotten? Didn't he bring some of his jaternice to my folks a few years ago, and didn't I eat and enjoy them?

Jaternice. The Bohemian Jet, some local poet has tagged it. The Bohemian Banana, others call it. But neither is an adequate description. It's a cooked sausage, less than a foot long, about the girth of a wheelbarrow handle, with the two ends tied to sticks. It comes as either black, jeleta (blood and barley), or white, jaternice.

Grandparents and fat uncles tell scary tales about just exactly *what* goes into jaternice for good reason: more for the fat uncles to eat.

"You know what my Grandpa says jaternice are made of? Pig's ears! Pig's eyes! Pig's brains! Pig's snout and tail and blood and everything ... uuuhhhggggg!"

But if a kid has any guts, he usually comes back to his dish of jaternice in young manhood and lives to heap praises upon it. Moreover, he forces it down his own son's throat, all the while telling him, "Pig's ears are good for you ... Pig snouts are the food of the Bohemian gods!"

What you do is fry them in a pan. You listen to them sputter and spurt, and you swear, maybe, when the casing cracks open and all the stuffing oozes out. But if you're a Czech jaternice lover to the heart, you take a singular delight in watching all the stuffing pile up in the pan for additional frying.

Then you scrape the whole mess on a plate, butter up some homemade rye, open a bottle of beer, and enjoy, enjoy. The peak of the jaternice taste sensation comes after most of the casing has been squished empty with the edge of a fork. Then you raise first one, then the other end of the sausage, holding the sticks in your fingers, and put whatever is left of the end of the casing between your teeth and draw it all out to nothingness.

And now I'm back on my old block, sitting with Jerry Kachlic and his wife at their kitchen table and reliving the wonder of it.

Why does he continue to pursue the art of homemade jaternice when butchers up and down Cermak Road have plenty? Jerry states it all very simply: "I can't eat that junk.

"I use a whole pig head," he explains. "I have the butcher cut it in half ... no eyes, no brain, though; mainly the snout and tongue. And I use the lungs, heart, liver. After the head is cooked, we debone it and grind it to whatever consistency we want.

"You see, it all depends on what kind or grade of sausage you want. Superior, medium, or just a mud-run. By putting extra tongue, extra heart in it, you make a richer sausage. Most of the butchers make a mud-run. The fatter the product, the more soup (leftover juices from cooking the pig's head) and bread you put in. The bread absorbs the fat and the soup, and that gives you the weight. The butchers are heavy on the soup, heavy on the bread, and that brings up the weight. Spice? Ah, that goes by taste."

Sausagemaking was something his father did: "Once a year Pa would go out and buy a head. And we would all make sausage."

The son makes Polish sausage too, pork sausage, and even Italian sausage. But his heart seems to lie with jaternice.

"I can make from one head to five heads," he says. For spice, aside from secret ingredients, "I use salt, pepper, garlic, onion, and marjoram. I start the night before, cleaning all the casings. Sanitation is very important. I'm up at 4 in the morning, and everything's cooked by 10. Then there's the grinding, cooking, preparing bread and spices, adding the bread. All this is blending ... very important. The more blending you do, the better your sausage ... but always holding back a little, because you can always add spice to your sausage ... but you can't take away. Then you skim your soup and add that to the mixture.

"After that I'll take and stuff one. Just one. And then find someone to try it on, preferably someone who don't drink. So you get an old baba (old lady ... grandmother) from the neighborhood and you ask her to try it. 'How is it, baba? Too much salt? Too much marjoram?' Well, maybe more marjoram, she says. So I go back and add more marjoram. You can almost never add enough marjoram. I can make 500 pieces in one day. By 6 o'clock, we're cleaning up."

So the neighborhood sausagemaker lives on, sharing with friends, neighbors, relatives, walking into a local tavern with a pound of homemade sausage under his arm and saying, "Okay, boys, try some of this." And it's all gone before a man can reach for seconds.

The Savings and Loan

The return of the prodigal son

I was spent, back on Cermak Road, my arm outstretched, my pockets empty, paying homage of sorts to the life force of a neighborhood (especially this neighborhood) — the Savings and Loan.

Up and down Cermak Road they stretched (not to mention the side streets and general area), temples raised by and for the Preservation of Thrift. Temples of glass, alloys, and marble that glinted in the sun. Temples that electronically flashed the time, weather, and saving messages for the multitudes that flocked to the doors with passbooks in hand, free gifts in mind, compounding their interest.

There are 16 Savings and Loan Associations in the Cicero-Berwyn area with assets of $1,231, 109,604, as of December 31, 1975. Not to mention five banks whose assets are not included in the total.

You may laugh about the ethnics, tell Polish, Bohemian, and Italian jokes till the cows come home, but when the chickens come home to roost, the ethnics will be still sitting on their bundles. My private history of Savings and Loans goes back to these people. For one thing, their folk art of saving has always eluded me.

And here I was, a grown man, still in search of the total, the source. Clutching a damn near blank passbook in hand, I mixed with the multitudes wending their various ways toward Central Federal Savings, or Olympic, Lincoln, Ridgeland, or the first Bohemian skyscraper, Clyde, and headed for the one I grew up with: Mid America Federal Savings and Loan, which in my memory always stood on the corner of 59th Avenue and Cermak, across from the funeral home with the fancy bushes that were trimmed in wave upon wave. (I don't know what it is about money and death, but I must have been attracted to them early in my life.)

The early days

I missed the Depression. But others have never let me forget it, from the day I first clutched a precious penny in my hand with instructions to "save it for when the Depression comes." Throughout my childhood I thought the Depression was either a bogeyman waiting for me in the closet or else a sad, distant uncle who would save his silence and Sunday afternoons for me, sitting in the corner (facing it) with his stein of beer.

I don't know when the passion to put it away is supposed to begin, growing up in the American way. WASPS, I hear, are sometimes born in bank accounts and wrapped in trust funds. Ethnics, too, fierce savers, often anoint their newborn with a savings account at the local Building and Loan. All I know is that the passion somehow passed me by.

I never filled a toy bank (a jar, a bottle, a can) to overflowing in my life. And whether it was locked or just plugged, the sound of coins jingling in there was pure music to a non-saving soul. A penny in hand was worth two dimes in the bank, any time.

I understood the meaning, the stark reality of something and nothing. (Now the bank was heavy, now the bank was light.) But for some reason I was born with a deficit when it came to the desire, means, meaning of saving money. I can't blame it on heredity (my father was a banker) or environment (I grew up Bohemian). So it must be a birth defect, a psychic aberration. Saving was just not in my stars. Leo, a sun sign, must have burned a hole in my pocket.

Growing up and down

From the West Side of Chicago, where I was unacquainted with savings institutions along 26th Street from Lawndale to Pulaski, I moved to Cicero, where they sang the Bohemian National Anthem upon rising each morning:

Oh give me a home
From the Building and Loan
Where my wife makes Knedliks *all day ...*

I was surrounded by a neighborhood of savers. Not only Bohemians, but all the ethnics: Poles, Hungarians, Yugoslavs, Lithuanians, Germans, Italians, Irish ... And not only money. Bottles, boxes, old newspapers, old nails, string, bags, rubber bands, pencil stubs, what have you. The ethnics saved everything because somewhere in their Old World blood they understood, though seldom expressed, that *everything* had value. Their basements and attics contained treasures they could never part with. Only dust and dirt were worthless. And Bohemians, especially, never gave either a chance to settle.

Saving was ingrained in the head, heart, hands of every neighborhood kid growing up ethnic. Should a hint of seduction take place at the local candy store, immediately the bogeyman of the Depression would cast a deadly shadow upon our souls, our too eager hands. "Just wait till the Depression comes, and you're standing in a bread line or selling apples on the corner ..."

It was then that I began to feel the religious significance of saving, the morality of a rainy day. Hell was the Depression. Heaven was money everlasting, a great big Building and Loan in the sky. If you saved, you were good. If you wasted, you were bad. (Only later in life, when I became a writer, did I really sort it out and discover that Hell was just being broke and that writers were permanently assigned to that territory.)

All my friends saved pennies, nickles, dimes, quarters, half dollars, and silver dollars. When their bottles and boxes and banks were full, they lugged them down to the nearest Savings and Loan and made a deposit. (What's a deposit? I was learning a whole new lingo.) And all they had to show for 50 pounds of pennies was a little book with a record of their savings. What's more, they swore to me, that same money they put away would earn more money by just being there, and they would keep getting more and more money till some day they would be rich and own a two flat or an apartment building!

Didn't mean a thing to me. Incomprehensibly, I was way ahead of my time, already living in the now. I had money in my *pocket*, where it seemed to have an immediate effect and did some good.

Being broke, though, did make a difference. When you turned to one of your boyhood buddies and said, "Listen pal, how about loaning me two cents?" and he said, "Sure, with interest, three extra cents a day," it was a whole new world. (What's interest?) I was getting an education (not to mention a screwing), and I didn't like the net result at all. I mean, what shall it profit a man? But the philosophy came later.

"I hope the Depression gets you!" I threatened him till he ran home crying, looking over his shoulder.

Young manhood

I understood that one had to work for a living. That made sense. Money didn't grow on trees, as my father often reminded me. (That and the Depression were certain truths.) I even took occasional stabs as saving a few dollars. And with the first experience of a check — pay to the order of ... me! — I was overwhelmed at the prospect of a young man's earning power. Why, where did it all come from? Who needed all of this?

Save it! I was reminded. Save it for a car, save it for college, save it for marriage, save it for a rainy day. Remember the Depression. I even began picking up things in the alley — broken chairs, old wire — and bringing them home, in search of my heritage.

I started to stash extra cash in my dresser drawer and eventually made the Saturday morning pilgrimage to the savings shrines down Cermak, where Building and Loans beckoned everywhere. I went to the closest, Cicero Federal Savings and Loan, as it was then called, and I began an on-and-off romance with the place that would last for close to 20 years. But I never did fall into Savings as a Way of Life.

Instead, I've remained a student and an observer of the scene, standing many a Saturday morning in Mid America Savings and Loan (as it's been called since 1961 — the name Cicero was perhaps a bad investment), drinking my free cup of coffee, nibbling my free cookies, studying the blankets to be given away (if only I could come up with a $300 deposit), and watching the incredible scene of savers, believers, salting it away for those rainy days. And wondering why, why and where I went wrong. Me, the only man in line clutching a withdrawal slip. (Immediately I was considered suspect by my countrymen, for, after all, I held the wrong *color* slip in my hand! I was not contributing. I was taking!) Surrounded by depositors, maybe a hundred strong, with a consciousness keyed for compound interest . . . immortality.

The search for the saver's pathway to dividend and the divine

If I blew it in childhood, young manhood, and even in my very genes, the answer had to lie somewhere outside myself. My Old boyhood buddies now owned their own businesses, their own two flats. Their old bottle-of-pennies accounts had accrued not only interest at an ever-growing rate of increased interest compounded as fast as you could blink your eye, but their very pass-books had begotten passbooks from many Savings and Loans in the neighborhood.

I was determined to get to the bottom of it. To probe the saver's soul.

Philosphy, religion, wisdom, what have you. A penny saved is a penny earned . . . penny wise and pound foolish . . . as a man sows, so shall he reap . . .

I consulted Sophocles who told me: "For money, you would sell your soul." And I agreed with him. I consulted Emerson who told me: "The world is his who has the money to go over it." And I found him knowing. But how do I get my assets up? John Heywood told me: "The rolling stone gathereth no mosse," but I already knew that. There's never been any mosse under my feete.

And what do you say, Mr. Somerville? " 'Tis ready money that makes the man." Yes. And you, Mr. Dumas? "Business? It's quite simple. It's other people's money." Ah, but you, Mr. O. Henry of the surprise endings, sitting there surprised in the hoosegow, charged with bank fraud? "You can't appreciate home till you've left it, money till it's spent, your wife till she's joined a woman's club, nor Old Glory till you see it hanging on a broomstick on the shanty of a consul in a foreign town."

Sam Butler seemed closest to the truth: "All progress is based upon a universal innate desire on the part of every organism to live beyond its income."

Yet, in the end, I was still found wanting. So, banking on the words of Barrie — "poets are people who despise money except what you need for today" — I retreated to the source.

The source

It still stands on the corner of 59th and Cermak across the funeral home. But Mid America Savings and Loan has gone through a number of transformations. I remember it as just a small stone building, on its present site since November 1939, when its assets were $1,568,296.82. The building has grown up, down, and sideways since then. Its assets were $284,293,999 at the end of 1975. With little help from me.

Putting all savings philosophies and homilies in reserve for a moment, I step into the office of the man who may know what the Saving Way is all about. I shake hands with Mr. Hugo Koranda, a saver himself from way back, a Bohemian by blood, and now chairman of the board of Mid America, where he began as a member of the legal staff in 1949. (Whereas some ambitious parents of the past might wish the Presidency upon their sons, in our neighborhood, to become a Hugo Koranda, a head of a Savings and Loan, would be the ultimate.)

Hugo is a dapper-looking Bohemian, in good physical shape, with a ready smile, a firm handshake, and a good eye for all kinds of figures. (It was always a pleasure to do business with the women tellers at his windows.) "We're about five million dollars ahead in savings this month," he says without my even asking or understanding. "Even on a day when money was tight, we would gain close to $100,000."

But I am in search of more vital statistics this morning. And Hugo may hold many of the answers, much of the meaning. He, along with his assistant vice-president, Vlasta Sneberger, and the other fine members of his staff, may help provide the balance sheet of the savings mystique.

According to Hugo, and the history of Mid America Savings and Loan, it all began one day in 1921 at Bohumil Brousek's saloon at 5820 West 22nd Street. A group of local citizens, over a game of cards and beer, came up with the idea of setting up a Building and Loan Association. Soon after, 14 of the regulars from Brousek's saloon pledged $1,000 each to get hold of a state charter and opened the first Delnik Building and Loan Association.

April 6, 1922, marked the beginning of the Savings and Loan boom for this group with assets of $14,000. Meetings were held every Thursday evening in the Brousek saloon to take in payments for the (savings and loan) the members had joined. After each meeting the receipts were counted and checked with the passbook, then a loan committee was appointed from the board of directors to inspect and appraise the homes that had applications on hand for loans. One year later, assets had increased to $15,000.

Delnik changed meeting places in and around Cermak Road for the next few years. By 1929, it had $161,000 in assets. And then came the bogeyman — the Depression. "The withdrawals were greater than the receipts, and members who so desired could withdraw just a portion of their savings each week. No member lost a penny." In 1932, the Federal Home Loan Bank came through, and Delnik made plans to federalize. In 1934 it received its charter. The name was then changed to Cicero Federal Savings and Loan Association. And, in 1939, they moved to the present site, assets still growing out of those old saloon days at Bohumil Brousek's.

Hugo and I talk about some of the current customs celebrated at Mid America today which make the place unique and a part of its neighborhood. His heart and feelings open wide to his people, to all his savers, as he describes the scene on Senior Citizen's Day.

"When Social Security checks come ... the third of the month ... these people are standing in the street waiting for the mailman. And then they flood this place. You get 75-, 80-year-old people coming in. You hear about people who can't save, and here these people come in. Not only do they live on that money, they save it! They're old, but they're still saving it. It's so much a part of them."

And, on dividend days, Richard Scalzo, vice-president and treasurer interjects, "Most of our customers come in on a quarterly basis to have their interest compounded. Last week, there were lines and lines for the dividend payments. We ran crazy here up to the 17th of the month. It began on the third. We must have run eight to nine deep at every window, 19 windows in all. Every desk had a customer transaction going."

"They came here for a better life," explains Hugo in reference to the Bohemians, but it's true of others as well. "Not so much for themselves, but for their families. The first thing they wanted was a school. Next they believed in owning property.

"Sure there are a lot of jokes about their frugality, which is all right. It's a wholesome characteristic to make fun of. You've heard about the Bohemian credit card? Cash! The Czechs are very much a family-oriented people. The father's not playing golf all day. Grandparents open an account for a new grandchild. Giving a savings account for a present is a very common thing with them. They remember the Depression."

Vlasta Sneberger, the beautiful secretary and assistant vice-president who fled from behind the Iron Curtain, adds, "It's the feeling of security ... a home of their own. It generates pride in a person."

The Depression. I try to get a handle on it from Hugo's point of view. "Right in the midst of it," he explains, "the home-loans act started. The people were still saving. But during the war, when the people began to work, then they really began to save. And once the war was over, you had the big building boom. People wanted to own their own homes. We couldn't just take in savings, we had to have an intelligent plan to invest them."

But the saver, I ask. Who is he? How does he get that way? Have times changed? "The younger generation . . . well, they've got more money to spend. Not quite as thrifty as their parents. But the habit of saving hasn't changed drastically.

"Take the affluent suburbs. There you have the sophisticted saver. The fella who knows all about the bond market, buying on the margin. Those guys, a lot of talk. Their kids *know* they're going to college. Those are the guys who want the higher loans and pay them off slowly . . . maybe 20 percent down on $80,000. The Czechs will put 50 percent down. What's more, they're very anxious to pay it off. They always want to know if they can pay more each month. We almost never have had a foreclosure in Cicero, Berwyn, or Brookfield. But we get them in the more affluent suburbs."

Hugo Koranda, it's plain to see, is a firm believer in a penny saved is a penny earned. It's in his blood. He recalls that as a high school student in LaGrange, he once gave a speech in class on the subject of saving. "I had a savings account when I was 15 or 16 years old, in 1930. I used to mow the lawns of the kids I went to school with. Well, I remember kids raising their hands during my speech. 'Where do you get these savings?' they asked. They didn't have any idea. I told them that my grandparent's had opened an account for me when I was a little kid. And that I'd added a dollar here and there. The teacher asked me how much I had in savings. Four hundred dollars, I said. They couldn't believe it. This was a revelation. I saved money!"

Speaking of his efforts at higher education and of his law degree, Koranda admits, "For a Bohemian, this was very good. I was getting into a classier group. I began to see how other people lived. I went on to law school school, became president of my class, but when you come in with a name like mine, you don't come well introduced. It's hard to get there if your name is more than two syllables. But now I no longer need those guys, that kind of life.

"Listen, I'm always fighting for the Bohemians. I remind those other guys that the money they have to borrow for their homes comes from these people's savings. They're unhappy, most of those guys. It's hard to please their kids. They move from college to college . . . they're unhappy. Now, I drink, don't get me wrong. But so many of those guys *have* to drink.

"The Bohemians seem happier. I think what they want out of life is different — a good life for their kids. The other guys are always busy with other ventures. They don't have a family unit, so they're in trouble."

Mid America and most of the other savings and loans and banks in the area
understand the security consciousness of the ethnics and cater to it. Koranda
speaks their language, literally and figuratively, and frequently sits at a desk
right out front talking to the people, listening to them. "We got a lot of people
who come and use it like a meeting ground. A lot of the old ladies. It's like a
carry-over from the old saloon days."

Early in the game, Mid America became famous for giving things away.
And nothing touches the heart of an ethnic more than something for nothing.
"We must have started it in 1952. We started giving away pen and pencil sets
for a \$25 deposit. Now we give them away free! Now the gifts are different,
and the depositors are different."

It was Koranda himself who began the free coffee and kolacky for his savers
years ago. "I used to sit out there like a receptionist. Once in a while, people
would come in and say, 'Gee, it would be nice to have a cup of coffee!'"

So he started with the coffee and then added the free kolacky, but
eventually dropped the kolacky for cookies. "One hundred dozen kolacky
would go like nothing. It became too costly, too hard to handle." Even now,
with free cookies, Koranda admits, "There are some people who abuse it
really badly . . . some people fill up shopping bags full. That's why we have to
have a monitor now."

There is a community room, too, with complete facilities, seating 200
people. Mid America allows local organizations to use the room free of
charge. It is filled, almost every day, by groups such as the Club Myjava, the
Medinah Seniors, the Lyra Czech Singing Society, and the Greek-American
Ladies Auxiliary. And all of this in the neighborhood spirit of giving — and
saving.

"We used to give away dishes. By God, did those things go over —
flashlights, blankets. Now the give-away business has become very
sophisticated. Not just a flashlight, now it has to be a TV, a discount on the
thing, I mean. People call you and say, 'Are you giving anything away?'"

But how wealthy are these savings-conscious creatures? I wonder out loud.
These people whom I cannot identify. "The Bohemians have a lot of money,"
admits Koranda. "We have many old-timers with more than \$50,000, \$60,000
in their accounts." (I whimper — too loudly it seems. But Koranda keeps
pouring it on.)

"Mid America has never missed a divident payment." (I can't even compute
the interest on \$50,000, but I suspect I could live on it.) "We have close to
50,000 savings accounts, 10,500 loan accounts . . . " (I don't care, Hugo.) One
question, though: What about all those thrifty Bohemians who transfer funds
from one savings and loan to anoher merely to get their hands on the free
gifts? With some of these neighborhood Rockefellers, it's become more
popular than pinochle.

But Hugo doesn't blink an eye. "The bulk of savers who have $20,000 or more in one account have accounts all over the place," which doesn't help my saver's ego one bit.

The source has proved my inevitable downfall. I can't even repent. I'm about ready to take a handful of free matches and go home when Hugo introduces me to one of the old pillars of the temple, Mr. Charles Zelibor, 81, vice-president and part of the organization for 45 years. He doesn't smile. A rough and tough realist of the hard-earned dollar, Zelibor exudes pragmatism with every breath. He has no solution, but he lays it all out for me in past and future shock.

"It's a different type of person now. This is the second family now, and we're getting into the age of the third family. The number two families were getting money too easy. Their folks gave them everything: 'You gotta have it since we didn't.' And when the number two families go out and buy, they pay three times as much. They want everything they see, the best. But somebody has to pay for it. And who has to, but the number three families. And how are they going to pay for it if they're living off unemployment and welfare? The third families are now going into high school. They won't be as good savers. They won't have it. They figure it's easy. Whenever they get a dollar, they will spend it."

I'm a saver out of time, out of place, that's all. History absolves me. For I must be the second family, in the eyes of Zarathustra Zelibor. Or else I am the third family, ahead of my time — the unethnicized saver. Here today, gone tomorrow . . . and may the blessing of Artemus Ward shine upon us: "Let us all be happy and live within our means, even if we have to borrow the money to do it with."

Joey the Peddler

At 5 a.m. Joe Shelfo, a peddler since the age of 9, pulls his red fruit and vegetable truck out of a garage behind his home in Westchester and heads for the Randolph Street Market to load up for a Saturday run through the streets and alleys of the western suburbs. "Here comes Joey" is painted across the front of the truck.

It's cold. It's dark. The truck's heater screams and grinds in the agony of another frosty morning. Joe cusses it out, coughs to the very depths of his insides, lights a cigaret, and hunches over the wheel.

Smells of fruits and vegetables hang inside the dark truck. Tangerines, grapefruits, tomatoes, lettuce, broccoli, corn, crowd his mind. What's the price today? How much a pound? A case? A crate? Randolph Market beware, here comes Joey looking for a price, peddling his heart out.

Joe's neck bothers him, his back bothers him, he keeps driving. "I go for acupunch," he explains. "One more year then I'll move to Arizona, if I can talk the wife into it."

Shades of a peddler's American Dream: Arizona and the hot sun. Yet it's hard to imagine a retired peddler. And as Joe begins to shape his day you realize that peddlers, like poets, define their lives with such intensity that dying is their only retirement.

He pulls into the blue darkness of a closed market and backs his truck in front of Stryker's Wholesale Groceries, 938 Randolph. The old man and the son will be there to open the joint soon enough.

"Come on, let's get some coffee," says Joe.

Mitchell's Restaurant across the street is open. There's an old fashioned bar up front and a coffee counter in the back. It's a quiet scene, a clean, well-lighted place with a somewhat sleepy-eyed counterman pouring coffee and dishing doughnuts to the handful of men waiting for the market to open. The atmosphere is imbued with the silence and light of a Hopper painting and the scene itself, so reminiscent of the once famous marketplace of Paris, Les Halles.

Hyman the wholesaler takes a seat near Joe, talks sports, politics, economics, the way of the modern-day world ... "It looks bad." He's a benevolent man with a kind sense of humor. "Let's give the Jew the shaft," is his favorite expression in describing his life as a wholesaler in the Randolph markets. "Well, Joe, you going to service all the ladies again today?" he kids. "Yeah, everyday," smiles Joe. "They're all waitin' for me out there."

Joe goes up to the cash register to pay the tab, burrowing deep into his ped- · dler's pockets heavily weighted in coins, fishing through a handful of change for the exact amount. "There's the bank," kids Hyman. "Like a slot machine."

"I got diarrhea in dimes," laughs Joe.

Across the street, old man Stryker carries out bushels of pears, apples, oranges, setting up a neat display for buyers like Joe to check over, handle, haggle, either to buy or look elsewhere for a better deal.

"Got any tangerines?" Joe asks Stryker's son.

"Yeah," he moves back and opens a crate. Joe runs his hands through the tangerines, squeezes a few, closes the crate and opens a new one himself.

"What's the matter with these?" says Stryker's son, a little teed off.

"They're uglier than me," says Joe, closing the second crate, pointing to yet a third, unopened, and saying, "Gimme that one." Stryker's son shakes his head in disgust.

From Stryker's, where he keeps his truck parked till he's ready to leave, Joe walks over to Damore where he checks out the eggs, cookies, toiletries, whatever he thinks he can peddle today or the next day.

"I got some detergent," a clerk tells Joe.

"How much?"

"Six bucks a case ... $1.25 ... you can sell it for $1.50."

"Parade? ... I never heard of this crap."

"What the hell's the difference, Joe. It's all the same."

"Got any dog food?"

"Not today."

"What's the name of that crap?"

"*Parade*."

"Gimme a case."

A few doors down from Damore's, Joe moves into a larger fruit and vegetable wholesaler, C & S. A certain sense of history goes along with this place. The old man, Gus Siero, started Joe in the peddling business. "He gave me my first load of oranges in 1932," says Joe.

The language, now, the humor, the give and take, the whole lifestyle and reality of a peddler on market street gets rough and tumble now to the point where it's mostly unprintable. And what a shame. What a great sense of life these men exhibit.

"Did you say a buck for this broccoli? says Joe Shelfo to another Joe, a clean, heavy-set, gray haired and tough looking handler of produce. "It smells like _____."

"Go on and get it out of my _____ hair," says Joe the handler. "I knew I was gonna get _____ when I saw you."

"Got any corn?"

"Beautiful stuff. I got four crates for you."

"Let me see the garbage. Have any cheap tomatoes?"

"Yeah, in the drugstore, you cheap Dago."

Joe Shelfo feels a few ears of corn, tears off some leaves, smells the kernels. By all indications, it is beautiful corn. "Here, squeeze this awhile," says Joe the handler.

"How much on the corn?"

"Two-fifty a case. You can't miss."

"I'll take three."

"Take four, for crissake."

"Tomatoes ... how much? " asks Shelfo, breaking into a hacking cough once again.

"Ten for 30," says Joe. "You're coughing better. Die, you sonofabitch, die."

Shelfo keeps moving around the produce, feeling, touching, haggling. He's back to the broccoli and cauliflower. "You know who's gonna eat this?" he says to me. "That Great Dane across the alley from your father's. Yeah," he explains to Joe and others who are laughing. "That sonofabitch is this big and eats broccoli and cauliflower, whole heads of it."

Sam, the manager, comes from behind the desk and starts pricing and writing up Joe's order. "OK," he says, "Now let me sell you something where I can make some money."

Joe the handler yells "artichokes" to Shelfo, which seems to arouse some bitter memories on Shelfo's part. "You bastard you. I'm still crappin' them artichokes!"

Sam, trying to hustle some bananas on Joe. "That's a beautiful box." Says Joe, "You're still trying to make up for that corn, ain't you?"

"I gotta make enough for $600 a month rent, don't I?"

"Go buy that junk from Stryker," interrupts Joe the handler.

"How the lettuce?" counters Shelfo.

"Beautiful, Joe. Beautiful. You never saw lettuce like this."

"Gimme a crate."

Another man begins to load Joe's order on a truck while he pays Sam in cash. "Come on" he says to me. "Let's go see the Jew."

Hyman Sherman, Wholesaler of Marc's Miscellaneous Mart, dog food, paper, brooms, cockroach powder, toilet paper, is feeding his cats. Hyman, still steeped in the dark economics of the day, shakes his head wearily to Joe and exclaims, "Joe, I don't now what it's gonna be. I can't get this, I can't get that. Look at my mop department!"

Hyman muses over a dusty case of cockroach powder that he can't sell. (Joe still has a case on the truck he can't get rid of.) "I know, I know, Joe . . . true. Who the hell wants to mess with that, scraping it on with a brush, especially today, in a world of spray . . . pssst. Let's give the Jew the shaft," wails Hyman.

"But the Jew always ends up on top the Dago," reflects Joe.

"Jew, Dago . . . it all equalizes, Joe. What's the difference? We all got to get up in the morning, we all got to go to work. You know, I wonder about those guys in Washington . . . the thievery, the trickery, the deceit in the hearts of those men. I tell you, Joe, you wonder how they can ever go home at night and knock off a piece."

"They can't," says Joe. "They can't."

By 7:30, Joe's through buying. By 8, he's ready to roll. The truck has been loaded. Stryker's son stands by and studies all the produce Joe has bought from C & S. He's hot because Joe didn't buy more from him today. "What did you pay for those tomatoes?" he asks.

"Ten for 30," ($10 for 30 pounds) says Joe.

"Crap," says Stryker. "Let me see the slip, show me the slip!"

Joe does. He's paid $9.50 for 30.

"You call those tomatoes?" shouts Stryker. "Next time park your truck down there."

Joe is unmoved by all the dramatics. Monday morning he will park the truck again at Strykers. And maybe Monday morning he will get a better deal there than at C & S.

"If you buy off only one house, then they take advantage of you. The trouble with those guys (Strykers) is they're so goddam jealous."

Pulling onto the Eisenhower Expressway now, heading west to Cicero, to his brother Tony's house (also a peddler) where he will split the morning's produce, take on some soda pop, and talk peddler talk while waiting for the breadman, Joe reflects on the fine art of peddling.

"Years ago you could peddle maybe $700, $800 a day. No more. Now my biggest day, maybe $200. What hurt was when the chains came in. What hurts is all the sales with them coupons. You're supposed to sell it like they do, their price. And you can't. You just can't."

Joe compensates for this by buying fresh produce every day and providing a kind of old-fashioned door-to-door service. He concentrates primarily on the same customers who have been buying from him for years. He's not looking for any new customers, not at this stage in his life. He doesn't feel he has to hustle that hard anymore. He considers a $3 sale average, $15 to $20 a blessing.

He and his brother Tony split up the Cicero territory. "From 57th to Austin, my brother takes care of that, and I go on the other side." They alternate these patterns on various days and seldom stray beyond their established routes." 'Why don't you come here? Why don't you go there?' people ask. We don't even go into Berwyn. We've got enough right here."

Joe backs up onto Tony's driveway in south Cicero, while his brother pulls his truck out alongside Joe's and then the two of them, silently, mechanically, go through the routine of sorting the stuff, putting it in place in the trucks.

The three crates of corn (which Joe feels he had made a good deal on for $2.50 a crate) finally breaks the silence between the two men. "This stuff'll be five bucks next week," Joe tells Tony.

"How much soda you want?" asks Tony. "Gimme two case of large, one small," answers Joe.

"How much for the tomatoes?" asks Tony. "Nine and a half for 30," says Joe. "I paid 8 for 20," says Tony.

While Tony loads his truck, Joe begins building a display of fruits and vegetables down the center aisle of his truck. Starting with a box of cucumbers, he builds a terrace, steps after step, of peppers, apples, string beans, cauliflower, broccoli, pears, grapes, bananas. Both sides of the truck are shelved with rows of opened wooden boxes, strapped in to prevent them from spilling around turns and over bumps.

Aside from fruits and vegetables, Joe will cram the truck with almost anything he thinks will sell — cookies, bread sticks, dog food, toilet paper, cheese, eggs, noodles, sardines, Italian bread, canned goods of all sorts, even pots and pans. A string bag of garlic hangs from one side of the truck, a half a hunk of fresh salami hangs from the other.

Once the trucks are ready, the two brothers go inside the house to wait for the breadman. Tony's wife serves them coffee, cookies and plenty of chit-chat.

The talk around the kitchen table is Italian talk, in a way — talk of food, family celebrations, sons, daughters, and grandchildren, of which both the peddlers are proud, each comparing notes of bravado and laughter of as far as the relative toughness of their grandsons is concerned, flashing photographs and telling tales.

Ernie, Tony's young helper, comes in while Tony is discussing the plight of the modern peddler. "You can't yell out anymore, the way you used to in the old days. Now everybody's so damn touchy. You can't holler, you can't blow the horn. Too much noise, they say. They'll call the cops."

"I blow the damn horn anyway," says Joe.

"So do I," says Tony.

"And women nowadays," continues Tony. "First of all, none of them are home anymore during the day. They're all out working for crissake. And they don't cook the way they used to. They don't know about vegetables."

The breadman is late, and Joe weants to get going. "The hell with him. It's 9 o'clock already. I'm going. I got enough bread for today anyway."

So finally Joe is on the street, heading for his first stop. "I work from 9 to maybe 3 or 4. I don't push anymore. Yesterday was so bad, I went home at noon and didn't even make a regular stop in Riverside. I had two heart attacks, so now if I sell, OK. If not, hell with it. I've got some customers buying from me for over 40 years. I figure around 80 stops all together on this route."

He starts at 57th Avenue and 14th, parking in front of the house, going up the steps to service an old couple, an old customer. He comes back a few moments later shaking his head in disbelief. "The old guy died," he says. "Just a couple a days ago the old guy died, and I never knew it."

A red-headed woman from across the street appears at the back of the truck, and Joe stands there, above and before her, in a classic peddler's stance. He's a small man, hunched over a bit, right hand in the pocket jingling change. He waits for the customer to look over the produce, shifting a small black fedora up and down on his head. His motions are quick and direct, confined mostly to the immediate space at hand ... bending down for potatoes, reaching over for bread, backstepping to a hanging scale, bagging the goods in short, fast shots, whipping out a little notebook from his back pocket as he tallies the sale.

"I got some good corn," he tells her. "I wish they would eat it," she answers. Together they discuss the sudden death of the old man. "You never know," says Joe. "You never know ... I got some beautiful lettuce ... cheese? ... sweet potatoes?"

"The cauliflower looks good, Joe. I just wish they would eat it ..."

The talk turns from cold weather to Arizona. "It was 95 there the other day," says the redhead. "Yeah, well next year that's where I'm gonna be," says Joe. "Gee, I wish I could say that," says the redhead. "Come on with me, says Joe." "My wife don't want to go."

In a few minutes, Joe has filled a large bag of produce for her. "Seven dollars, eight cents," he says. "Thanks, Joe. See you next week." "So long, sweetheart."

Leaving the back doors open, Joe makes his way down the center aisle, hops into the seat, starts the truck, and moves out to the next stop. "Isn't that something, that guy dying like that all of a sudden? I just saw him a few days ago."

Pulling up in front of another house, blowing the horn, waiting for some sign of life, another woman descends the front steps and walks to the back of the truck. "How much are the potatoes, Joe?"

Joe waves to the woman's child in the front window of the house. He hangs up his scale again, plunks in the potatoes, two handfuls at a time, and begins weighting, figuring, peddling.

Another woman's face appears at the back of the truck. "How are you, young lady?" asks Joe. "Hi, Joe, pretty good." While Joe is hustling the fruits and vegetables, the women converse about housework. Joe flashes some bacon in front of one of the women. "How much?" "Dollar and a quarter," he says. "Give me one." Joe pushing corn now . . . "beautiful stuff from Florida" . . . apples, bananas, tangerines, bagging it. making another sale.

"That's $3.66," he says to another woman. "Did Dolores tell you I went back to work part-time?" says the woman. "Yeah, 10 to 2. I had to get out of the house or it would drive me nuts. Well, have a nice weekend," she tells Joe. "By the way, how are you feeling?"

"I'm gettin' some acupunch," he tells her.

"Does it work?"

"It helps," he says.

Back in the driver's seat and moving again, Joe waxes a little bit sentimental. "That's what makes this business so nice, when you got people that's concerned about your health."

In the alleys now, blowing the horn again, waiting for his true-blue customers. A heavy-set woman comes out the back porch, through the yard. "How are you, Joe?"

"Good. Real good," he coughs.

"I want some potatoes . . . And don't slip me those big ones."

"You sound like my wife," he says, opening up that beautiful box of lettuce, holding a big head before her.

"How much?"

"Forty-five cents."

"What! And how come Dominick's is selling it for 15 cents a head?"

"That's brown lettuce. This is beautiful," says Joe, sliding into another coughing jag.

"Throw it away already, will you," she tells him.

"I got good corn, baby," he replies.

"Yeah, but you know what it does to me," says the woman, running her hands through a box of pears. "Are these the same lousy Michigan ones you had last week?"

"No, these are New York pears."

The woman breaks into a laugh, "Joe, you're so full of bull. Gimme 6 pounds. And gimme some toilet paper."

"Shhh . . ." says Joe. "You're supposed to whisper that."

"How's your wife? She's still heavy, huh?"

"Yeah."

"Me too. We ought to go someplace and have our mouths wired shut. We don't move enough, Joe. That's our trouble."

When you've been peddling most of your life, you know the stops by heart. You know what certain people want, you understand the whole back-alley way of life. "This alley alone, I used to be able to sell $150, $200," says Joe, "You got to make 15 per cent" he claims. "If you ain't makin 15 per cent, you're hurtin."

He makes another regular stop and begins peeling corn. "This one here wants corn, but I got to peel it for her. If she wasn't such a good customer, I wouldn't bother. But she doesn't care what she pays as long as I give her the best."

Joe returns from the house with a batch of letters to mail. "Yeah, you do all of these things for some of the people. Another one back there had me fix her bell one day. Another one always wants me to carry her garbage out. I tell you, there's a lot of characters on this route."

You see a somewhat different kind of people in the peddler's daily world of back alleys and back yards. Not quite the same swift and sure people of the supermarkets, with shopping carts piled high. These seem a friendly, more neighborly type of people. Some hurting, very hard, for enough cash to buy a few pounds of potatoes. Others, like my own father, more inclined to keep the personal contact, the faith of the old peddler going . . . listening, as he does, for Joe's horn around noon every Saturday, then putting on his coat, and going out into the alley to drop $4 or $5 on stuff he very likely doesn't need. In a way, keeping alive that kind of street talk and bartering that once flourished in all the neighborhoods of Chicago.

"Fifteen dollars even," says Joe. "Thanks, baby."

"Yeah, this was a damn good business 15, 16 years ago," says Joe, starting up the truck once again. "The chains weren't too big then. Now the housewife shops once a week, and I'm just a fill in. I'll be losing that one soon," he says, referring to another customer down the line. "That's the only time I lose a customer, when they move. Or when they die."

Once in awhile he makes notations on a piece of cardboard behind the driver's seat. Joe's private accounting service. How many customers does he carry on the cuff?

"Around 12 to 15. One pays me a little each week, another one $15 or $20 whenever she has something. I got another Fats on the cuff. I don't even know her name. But I know she'll never cheat me. 'If anything should ever happen to you, Joe,' she says, 'I'll be sure that your wife gets whatever I owe you.' There's one customer owes me over $100 for the past two years, plus a few more bills in bad checks. She's supposed to come into some money soon. I got another one that owes me over $50 for the past 10 years. I'll never see that. But I'd rather hold onto these people then lose them for customers. At least they buy a little something from me each week."

"This alley, your Dad's alley," says Joe, "is worth $50 or $60 in the summer, if they all come out."

My Dad does come out, along with two or three neighbors. And they talk again about weather, work, and each other's health. "Hey," says Joe to me on an inside joke, "Should we sell your Dad some of that cockaroach powder?"

A few doors down, the owner of the Great Dane awaits Joe's approach. "Now watch me get rid of all that broccoli," smiles Joe. And he does.

The fine art of peddling takes on still another level as Joe, early in the afternoon, parks the truck near a corner tavern and goes in for a beer. The regulars recognize him immediately with a shout and a wave. The talk is mostly tavern talk, women, sports, work and dirty jokes. In five minutes Joe has more free beers before him than he cares to handle. Everyone considers him a personal friend and wants to buy him a drink.

"Can you cash a check for me, Joe?" "Sure."

"Hey, I'm throwing a party tonight. Stop by if you can, Joe." "Sure."

"Hey, Joe. You wanna buy a watch?" Joe looks it over. "Naw ... junk."

Through it all there's a subtle kind of peddling going on on Joe's part. Just when he's about to leave, the whole picture comes into focus. It begins with someone at the bar saying, "Hey, Joe. Before you go, got any tomatoes on the truck?" "Sure." "What kind of grapefruits you got, Joe?" "Good ones. Come on take a look."

And so it begins, a regular procession to the truck. Joe, a kind of pied piper of peddling. Men, women, even the barmaid putting on coats, going out to the truck. Joe, a few steps ahead, hopping onto the back of the truck, taking his classic peddler's stance. "Wait," says one guy. "I'm gonna call the old lady and see what else she needs."

"Corn?" replies another guy to Joe's soft sell. "How can I eat corn when I got no teeth?"

Joe pulls slowly away from the corner tavern scene, smiling, feeling good inside. All the corn is gone. He has just peddled a bundle — of fresh groceries. Only a few more stops down the alleys near Central and then it's over to the local gas station to fill up before going home.

Whenever a peddler stops, people suddenly congregate, looking, touching, asking, wanting to buy. He's at the gas pump and some guy's pounding on the back door. "You got any apples?" he says. "How much? How much this? How much that?"

Inside the station, more people hound him. "Have you got any tangerines on the truck, Joe? What do the pears look like?"

Someone else wants to know if Joe can get him a good deal on a record player. The gas station man sells Joe a stuffed doll for $2, while an old woman, hustling handmade dolls herself, berates Joe for not buying one of her dolls.

The world, it seems, is full of peddlers. We've all got it in us. Everybody's got something to hustle. Joe just happens to be a professional at it. He sees no stigma to the name.

"The only time I get insulted is when I go to a wedding or a wake and they introduce me as the peddler. 'What are you peddling,' they always ask. I tell 'em dope."

It's almost 4 in the afternoon as Joe starts up the truck, coughs up another mean streak, lights a cigaret, and heads for home. It was a good day for peddling, with only one regret. "I should a bought that other case of corn for $2.50," he says. "Next week it'll be $5. You want to be a peddler, you got to know how much to buy and when to buy."

Sokol: The Flying Czech

It was the rings I was after more than anything. Looking up at them at the old Sokol Slavsky gym in Cicero, I felt they floated down from the heavens, teasing the small, anxious hands of a kid who was sure that once he grasped them, he would fly!

Being a Sokol was part of growing up good and healthy and Czech in the old neighborhood. You didn't ask why you had to go to Sokol and do all kinds of jumping around in unison while somebody shouted at you in Czech — any more than you asked why you had to learn to play the accordian, eat tripe soup, take off your shoes at the door, or visit the relatives every Sunday. You did it.

And it was never a question of needing more exercise. As any neighborhood kid of nine or ten knows, all the hours of the day (and on into the night) were hours of physical combat: every sport in season, plus the daily running, jumping, chasing, and fighting. The streets, prairie lots, and alleys were our gymnasiums.

No, Sokol had nothing to do with the need for physical exercise. This is what I tell myself as I walk down the quiet streets of my old neighborhood more than 20 years later, a grown man, carrying myself toward the old gym with as much poise, balance, and pride as a slightly out-of-shape Czech can muster. Visions of the rings still out of reach . . . the Olympics, Olga Korbut, Nadia Comaneci . . . flying in my head.

Because Sokol (which I didn't entirely understand at the time) was a chance to instill a touch of grace in one's physical bearing. Grace, and a sense of tradition in a Bohemian kid (quickly growing up American) who was trying desperately, perhaps, to rid himself of all the old-fashioned traditions, lest he be mistaken for some kind of greenhorn.

Letí Sokol (one of the songs went), *Pêkný Pták / Letí vzhuru do oblak* (Fly, you Sokol, fly on high/ Fly up in the deep-blue sky).

Beating it up the steps of the old C.S.A. building (Czechoslovak Society of America), which holds the Sokol Slavsky Gym, 2138 South 61st Court, I am held back momentarily by a cloud of memories that are more important than the old gym, the exercises, even the rings themselves. For up these stairs and to the right, my grandparents once lived in a small apartment. My grandfather was in charge of the maintenance of the building in the 1950s. What's more, I once delivered newspapers to the old-timers living in the rooms upstairs, on the other side.

At the top of the steps, some doors. And, stepping inside the gym, I am overwhelmed once more by the sudden surprise of a room so large, so secretly hidden, it seems, behind closed doors.

A bit dark, but a true *old* gymnasium in sound, smell, even texture. The shiny brick walls, the wooden floor, the apparatus scattered about: parallel bars, horses, wall bars, horizontal bar ... and way up there in the darkness, my white rings, glowing like celestial objects in the Sokol Slavsky sky.

Sokol means falcon in English, symbol of strength and independence, a high-flying guardian of its own domain (read "country"). The symbol is important to people who take pride in their heritage and are willing to defend it.

Bringing it all back down to earth, Sokol is based on the theory that only physically fit, mentally alert, and culturally well-developed citizens can form a healthy, secure nation. In this country about 10,000 adults and 50,000 children and juniors actively participate in American Sokol Organization gymnastics, and the Czech Catholic Union Sokol, the Polish Falcons of America, the Slovak Gymnastic Union, and other groups bring the membership close to 250,000. There are such organizations in a dozen countries.

This is boys' and men's night (Tuesdays and Fridays) at the Sokol Slavsky Gym, with the first class of boys, ages six to nine, meeting from five to 6:15 p.m. (There is also a tots class — boys and girls, ages four to five — meeting on Mondays and Thursdays from four to five p.m. And girls and women's classes, the same days, later hours.)

Grabbing an empty folding chair along the wall, trying to remember how it used to be when I was on this very gym floor, I meet Joe Placek, 24, the Central District men's director. He leads me through some of the ins and outs of the Sokol organization.

"The tots program is mostly games," says Joe. "They do start working at gymnastics, though — simple tricks, just to get used to it. They're popular at shows, one boy pulling up his pants, ancther waving to his parents."

The first class of boys (six to nine), however, gets into it a little more. "They begin with simple apparatus," he explains. "We take the rings, lower them to shoulder height. We teach them to pull over, lock their toes in the ring, hang upside down, which is called the bird's nest. They seem to like that. Also, they work tumbling forward rolls. They don't do too much on the parallel bars or the horizontal bar. They work walking on the beam, forward and backward. They will do some vaulting, using the buck, the small one. They might also use the long horses, going over sideways, using the springboard."

It all goes back to Prague, 1862, and Dr. Miroslav Tyrš, the immortal founder. Tyrš was a philosopher, aesthete, art critic, and leader who looked upon ancient Greece as a model. After centuries under the tyranny of the Hapsburg reign, there was great interest in preserving the Czech language and culture, and Tyrš created the drills and exercises, devoting most of his life to the Sokol plan.

"Our first and overall task," he said, "rests in the premise that, before any other demands, we must preserve our nation in that general vigor that does not allow a nation to die, in that steady and fresh strength, in that physical and moral health that will not let any decay set in, an with that, no stagnation, that worst, even criminal action perpetrated upon nations."

By 1939, with a membership of more than a million, the organization was disbanded by the Nazis. It was reactivated after World War Two only to be shut down by the Communists a few years later. Today the organization as such no longer exists in its homeland; other gymnastic and sporting groups have taken over the former Sokol property.

As Tyrš wrote: "None, even the most glorious past, but the most active robust presence, shall guarantee our full future existence .... It is the cause that counts! It is mankind that matters! Alone, one is nothing — together, everything!"

Sokol Slavsky is one of eight active units that make up the Central District of the American Sokol Organization. Its national office is at 6426 West Cermak Road in Berwyn. Six of these units are in the west suburban area; the others are in Milwaukee and St. Louis. The first Sokol organization in America was established in St. Louis in 1865 by Czech exiles who had been forced to flee their homeland.

Sokol Slavsky, still alive before my eyes at the moment, was organized on February 20, 1890, in the DeKoven Street area of Chicago, moving to 18th and May streets in 1908, and in 1923 to Cicero. Two years later, its members built the present gym, only to lose it in the Depression. The C.S.A. then bought the building; recently it was sold to Olympic Savings and Loan across the street.

One mystery remains: the name Slavsky. Not a person, not a place, and, according to Ed Halik, president of the Central District and a member of Sokol Slavsky for more than 50 years, "It's something I'm still trying to track down. The closest I've come is a derivative of the word *slava*, which means glory."

The second class of boys (ages ten to 13) takes the floor now, and, judging by their size and attitude, this was probably my group years ago. They begin warm-up calisthenics, to music, and . . . yes, yes, . . . this is the way it was. We stood there, rank and file, 30 of us or more, following the instructor's movements. We held little black dumbbells in our hands and did each movement to count. It was all fun, and funny.

The funny part was that we counted crisply in Czech: *jeden* (1), *dva* (2), *tři* (3), *čtyř* (4), *pět* (5) *šest* (6) *sedm* (7), *osm* (8), exaggerating both the sound and our muscle-building movements. (Later on, in college, in life, I would become the hit of the party when, our of boredom, I would jump up and begin counting out my Sokol exercises in Czech: *jeden! dva! tři! čtyři!* It's in the blood.)

"All the calisthenics is done to music, done to count," explains Joe Placek as we watch the boys go through their routine. "They have it memorized. This dril is called *Prostna*, is roughly six minutes long, and is done to ethnic music. All the Sokols do the same one. In the Slet [the national exhibition of Sokols held every four years, the last five or six of them at Morton West in Berwyn], the entire field is filled with more than 1,000 people doing the same thing. That's when it really looks nice. Each group uses it [*Prostna*]. It's a good warm-up. You finish one of these, and you're sweating pretty well."

Sokol Slavsky class membership today consists of about 150 boys and 150 girls, plus 30 adults — a total of about 300 active members. "The adults you get more when you are working on calisthenics," says Joe. "For the old, it gets tougher. Generally, we lose those going out of the junior group [14 to 18]. They go on to college, some get married. Very seldom do they come back."

My eyes return to the action in the gym as a I spy a familiar friend, the pommel horse, pushed into place. The side, or pommell, horse has two handles that are grasped by the flying Sokols as they maneuver or vault over the horse. The pommels can be removed for vaulting the entire length of the horse, and the height of the horse can be adjusted.

"What they're running now is the squat through," explains Joe, an instructor who likes to work with the six-through nine-year-olds. "They run, their hands toward the horse; their legs bent, and they pass through their hands."

Ah, yes . . . vaulting the horse. I remember it well.

Each year, Sokol Slavsky has an exhibition at Morton East High School, in the Hapac Gymnasium. In my time, they were held at the Cicero Stadium. I made only one exhibition, but it was memorable.

There was a long line of us, all decked out in Sokol uniforms, preparing to vault the long horse, end to end. The stands were packed. And there was, no doubt, beauty in number, poetry in motion, as each Sokol dashed toward the horse, vaulting with precision and poise. Three or four kids ahead of me, though, was a childhood buddy, big Bill Kucera, who loped. Bill missed his step just as he was about to vault, running hell-bent into the horse, letting out an exaggerated scream, holding himself, while we proceeded to ram into him like sheep led to slaughter.

To Joe Placek, though, "the Sokol style tries to encompass everything. To develop strength, agility, grace. Each apparatus is designed to develop a different part of the body. When the boys work the parallel bars, that's a strength exercise. The side horse too is a strength apparatus, but it also requires grace because you've got to swing your entire body. On a high scissors cut on the side horse, you're judged on how high your hips are, mostly.

"The balancing beam is more for grace. It doesn't require strength; really more agility, coordination. I personally consider it one of the most difficult for boys and girls to do. If you'll notice, the boys are now doing a head spring on the short horse. You place your hands and and head on the horse, the edge toward you, and you extend your body straight up and then go over."

Confession: I never got that far along in strength, agility, or grace. I kept seeing Kucera crashing into that damn horse. I kept up with my *jeden, dva, tři,* and cut classes regularly. I kept my silent love affair going with those rings (which, for some reason, they wouldn't let me near), waiting, waiting, for the day the instructor would release them in my hands. Bird's nest, hell. I wanted to fly on the very first leap!

Joe Placek says, "The kids will go to whatever Sokol is closest to them. Anyone can join. Sometimes I'll take a class unit to show my grandmother, who has been in Sokol 50 years, and she'll go down the list and be amazed. 'Oh, here's one Bohemian name,' she'll say. Almost all nationalities are represented — whoever's in the neighborhood.

"We do try to keep some of the Czech heritage alive by keeping the class members aware of the history of Sokol. Each Sokol has an officer known as an educational director. He'll come down to the class and explain what Sokol is, where it came from. The boys, actually, are curious. Some of the instructors still use various Czech words in the exercises. And generally the instructor ends each class by saying, Nazdar! (On to victory ... good health ... happiness). And the class replies, Nazdar!"

How old is an old Sokol? "We do have a man in Berwyn, Vaclav Zenisek, who's around 70. Mostly he comes for the calisthenics, but occasionally he'll work out on the parallel bars. There's a fellow here at Slavsky who is 60 and still works out regularly, and several members in their 50s who are still active."

Still, Sokol seems to speak mostly to the young, and it has had its problems. Joe says that membership has leveled off.

"The late sixties was really a bad time for us, keeping the high-school kids, college, and young adult. But now they've started to come back. The Olympics helped considerably; Olga and Nadia attracted the girls. We have two boys now from Sokol Omaha who are considered possibilities for the Olympics. No one has ever made it to the Olympics from our area.

"Sokol, you see, really doesn't work for the advanced gymnast. The philosophy is for the masses. We don't have the instruction for someone who is really good; what we're trying for now is an extra class taught by a college coach. We try to keep it all on a level where everyone can participate, everyone can be successful."

Are there bad gymnasts? "Sure, there are always boys who are overweight or totally uncoordinated. We try to work with them. There have been occasions when we've worked with kids who are retarded. We have one boy now, Frank Flosman, with a deformed hand ... and he is something. He will do anything, try anything, and he will get terribly offended if you try to help him."

The junior boys now take the floor (14 to 18), and Frank Flosman is among them. This is the smallest group (only four of them this evening), as Joe sees it, because of the high school age. "They get involved in sports at school ... they discover what girls are ..."

The junior boys work hard. They move admirably; old Miroslav Tyrš would be proud of them. Frank Flosman shows incredible drive, and John Satek, Jr., excellent form. Young Satek, says Joe, has won a number of outside meets run by the United States Gymnastic Federation: "Floor exercises are his tops."

His father, John Satek, Sr., 46, is president of Sokol Slavsky and the instructor for this junior class of boys. Seeing the stocky Satek, Sr., in shorts, putting the boys through their paces, there is no question of who is in charge. He marches his class in close-order drill, regular army style: "About face! ... Forward march! ... To the rear, march! ... Left flank, march! ... Class halt!" It's the smallest army of Sokols in the world, but I wouldn't want to tangle with Sergeant Satek and his platoon on the field.

With father and son now out on the floor, a clue to Sokol strength (and survival) becomes more evident: individual, family, language, neighborhood, country — some of the inner forces.

The senior Satek is now running the boys through some vaulting. "Watch the position of the body here," he shouts at his own kids going through a layout, squat vault. Next, tumbling, the mats lined up down the floor and Satek right along the edge, studying every step and turn: "This is a preparatory move," he says. "You don't go up and go 'oops!'" One kid into a roll, but losing it. "You end up like this," demonstrates Satek, "and get going like this.

No! No! No! It's up! Up! About like that . . . yeah, that's it . . . now you got it!"

In John Satek, Sr., we get a little closer to the essence of Sokol today. He is what it's all about. All the connections, past, present, future, are working in him. He approaches me with what seems to be a tough and imposing attitude at first. I'm afraid he may have me vaulting the side horse if I'm not careful, or that he may send me up on the rings to see what I can do.

"I've been in Sokol since the sixth grade," he explains. "I became a senior member in 1949. Then physical director. I've been president about six years now. I've lived in Cicero all my life. Married a gal from the neighborhood, 19th and 57th. I'm a printer. Sokol is something that gets in your blood. I like to work with kids; I like to watch them develop. Some people like to work in churches. For me, it's Sokol. I think you need something as a diversion from your work. This is it.

"I've never been in a steambath, don't know anything about the Y.M.C.A. Teaching, though, drains me. Most of my exercise now comes from working with kids. I'm a department manager at work. I'm drained from that. I'm actually not much of a physical person, but this works for me.

"I've got one son in this class, one in another, also two girls and my wife in the women's class. There are six of us involved in Sokol."

I am relieved to learn that Satek was no Sokol enthusiast from the beginning either, though he did hang in there while I flew the coop. "When I started here, it was one of those deals where my mother had to drag me in by the ear. I fought it tooth and nail. But I started to enjoy it. I got my 25-year pin. You actually become a member when you join the senior class."

Along about nine o'clock at night the senior group of men quietly takes the floor. The seniors, only eight of them tonight, range in age from 19 (Art Placek, Joe's brother) to 57 — a man named Elmer Jezek.

Their instructor, Dick Ptacek, is leading them through the warm-up exercises (*Prostna*), which were written, or in a sense choreographed, by Dick and his daughter Lynne.

Their timing is perfect, their movement close to ballet: turning in a circle . . . arms out . . . to the side . . . above . . . stepping into formation . . . down on one knee . . .

"It makes a picture," says John Satek, Sr. "When you view it from above, all in order, everyone in uniform, it's quite a thing. The men's movements are as masculine as possible; the women's, as free and feminine as possible. It's a matter of trying to achieve perfection. The object of the whole game is to have everybody doing it as if they were one."

The Sokols, then, are still trying to keep it together, in their own way: tradition, family, country. Catch Elmer Jezek there, the oldest, dressed like a veritable circus strong man — long red tights, white suspenders stretched over a bare chest — moving with majesty. A fearless old falcon indeed, keeping it alive, working up an honest sweat for perfection and Sokol oneness.

"We hope it doesn't disappear," confesses John Satek, Sr. "I remember classes in the forties — 60 or 70 in a class. Now, if you draw 30, that's something. We have to hope that we instill in young people like my son the spirit to take over. We're getting old. As long as the young people take an interest, the Sokol Organization will continue."

The dancelike movements of the *Prostna* continue as the instructor joins the ranks, every movement memorized years ago. The senior Sokols now kneeling, now raising their arms, now tossing their heads back toward the heavens in a gesture of praise.

The Local Show

As a child he went to the movies himself. He ran down all the Saturday afternoon alleys that emptied, eventually. onto Cermak Road and the neighborhood show.

Sometimes along the way, he would call over the backyard fence ... "Oh, O Eddie! Eeeeeeee!" and Fat Eddie would answer, "I can't come out," or "I'll meet you there."

And so he would run alone all the way to the show, sit in the front by himself, eat Milk Duds and popcorn, and wait for the lights to go out, the trumpets to blast, the curtains to open; the horses, the planes, the gunfire to begin. Until ...

THE END. And he was putting on his jacket. Finding his aviator's cap. Walking through the soft lobby of red carpets, dark mirrors, funeral lights. Studying the night outside the heavy glass doors of the show, wondering how it was he always came in sunlight and went home in darkness. And why, so often, the rain had come while he was inside, or sometimes the snow.

Yet night, rain, or snow only increased the excitement because in a few seconds he had a mission over Tokyo. So he sped out of the show, the strap of his aviator's cap flapping, and jumped into the cockpit of the P-38. Cermak Road was his bright runway as he took off and headed for the dark alleys and the Japs.

His arms were stretched to the point of pain as he dived and banked and circled and climbed and banked again — against garage doors, garbage cans, fences.

Fat-Jap-Eddie (always lagging behind) was hit again and again ... "aaaaaaaBuuookissk!" till he crashed into his backyard And even then,

Eddie's house was bombed for good measure, and the P-38, decorated with hundreds of tiny Jap flags, sped off victoriously for the home base, through the back yard, up the back porch, into the kitchen ...

"Where the hell have you been? Your supper's cold!"

A little later in years, he still went to the movies himself. The same neighborhood show, but different movies — if there were any movies at all.

He would sit with a bunch of guys in the middle of the show, and they would wait for a bunch of girls. And they would talk and play games and bum money from each other and the girls would laugh and scream till eventually the usher came with his flashlight and threw everybody out.

Around that time too, he would find himself breaking away from the gang more and more to quietly sit in the back of the show with a girl who was waiting there for him. The war movie, the serial, the western were still exciting, but what he had beside him was even more fascinating, as he slowly inched his arm around the back of the seat.

He began to understand the cowboy who gave up his horse for a dance hall girl and a quiet ranch near the mountains. Even Lois Lane made sense for a superman.

He seldom goes alone to the movies these days. When he goes, he takes the woman and together they see "films," which she doesn't particularly enjoy. She prefers movies because, like liquor they help soften the daily world of screaming children, housework, bills, and a moody husband.

But he prefers films — foreign, and lately, underground. He prefers these because one night on the northside of Chicago he was watching *Wild Strawberries* or *Rashomon* or *The Bicycle Thief* and he saw suddenly that they were making films about him.

And now a few Americans have learned to sharpen the focus on the inside of themselves, and they are showing *Who's Afraid of Virginia Woolf?* and *The Graduate* and *Bonnie and Clyde*, and they are telling stories about him.

And so he remains constantly alive — excited and depressed — about all this that goes on in his darkness. And although he no longer flies home down the alleys in his P-38, he has remembered how to put his arm slowly around the back of the seat next to him — to keep himself together for whatever waits on the other side of the screen.

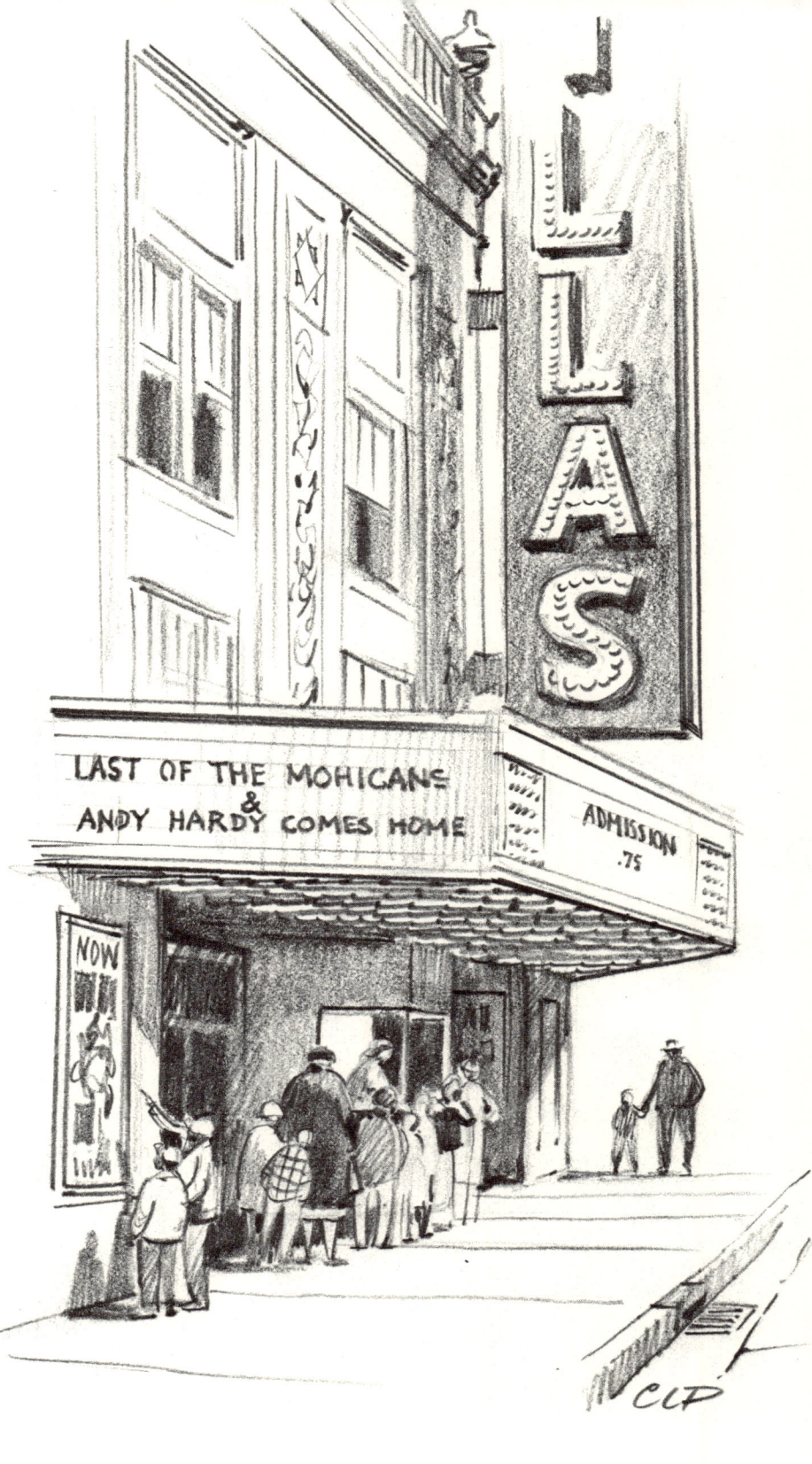

The Houby Hunt

HUMORING THE HOUBY HABIT

The Houby and the Bohemian are one. It's metaphysics and mushrooms from the outset. Pick up a Bohemian, and you're likely to find him gingerly guarding a mushroom under his foot. There must be a history to it.

The Irish have their shamrocks, the Germans their hops, the Italians their pasta, the Polish their perogi, but the ethnic symbol of the houby is reserved and revered among the Bohemians.

And when ethnic cultures begin to make jokes about the particular habits of other ethnic cultures, they then define that particular culture in such a way that being a Bohemian or a Pole does make a difference. And no one has more jokes told about him than the Bohemian (except maybe the Pole). What's more, the Bohemian can take a joke ... and just as likely tell one about his own people.

"Hear the one about the Bohemian version of Russian roulette? You put five good mushrooms in a paper bag and one poisoned one."

HUNTING THE HOUBY HUNTER

They live all around the city, but especially in the Bohemian enclaves around 26th Street and Pulaski, and the suburbs of Cicero, Berwyn, Riverside, and Brookfield. Most of the old hunters can still be found in those environs, with Cicero/Berwyn probably their heaviest stronghold.

They're difficult to identify (the very man in front of you at the bakery may be a houby hunter in disguise) unless you catch sight of one stealthily leaving the basement for the garage early in the fall, carrying a bushel basket, a knife, and maybe even a houby stick.

NARROWING THE FIELD TO THE FAMILY

Unfortunately, I did not come from a family of houby hunters. We ate them in soup, in gravy, on the side, and my grandmother undoubtedly hunted them in the Old Country and peformed a certain magic with them in her basement kitchen on Cermak Road, but time (my growing up, her growing older) kept us from ever getting into a study of this folklore. And worst of all, her time was up when I wanted her most and felt ready to join the hunt.

Everybody in the neighborhood, in the family, of course knows somebody who hunts houby. The problem is trying to pin an old master houby hunter down. You think you have the lead on someone, but then he kind of laughs you down like he's ashamed to admit he's part of the Old World underground ... "Oh well, I used to hunt them, yes. Sometimes I still do. I'll let you know, maybe, if I go out. I looked around last week in the woods, and there don't seem to be too many houby this year."

So I turn to my mother. "Ma," I say, "keep an eye open for a dyed-in-the-woods houby hunter." Ma corners people, works the phone over for a couple of days, and then comes up (through a friend of a friend) with an old Boehmian couple in Berwyn who still hunt. The only trouble is, it's the wrong time of year (spring), and they speak only Boehmian, and ... "And what?" I plead. And they're afraid. "Afraid of what? I'm not going to run and hide their houby baskets!" They're old and afraid, that's all.

So who do you turn to next? Mother in law.

She comes up with a vacuum cleaner man in Riverside and a house painter in Berwyn. But the house painter's hunting grounds are too far away and the vacuum cleaner man, in the end, fails to give me the nod.

September is approaching. Mushroom time is ripe. And I am a young hunter waiting in the basement with an empty basket, and not a single houby hunter's footsteps to follow.

THE HOUBY KING

It's become an annual thing in September, along Cermak Road in Cicero and Berwyn. Says the Berwyn Life newspaper, "The second annual Cermak Road Business Association's Houby Festival will open with a mammoth parade at 10 a.m. to run from Central Avenue to Oak Park Avenue."

On the eve of the festival, I check for houby hunters along Cermak. They are building a float in the garage for tomorrow's parade. And there are hunters in the group, all right; one man informs on another who is wearing a hat with a big plastic mushroom sticking out of the top. But the guy in the hat laughs, cracks a few jokes, and then disappears.

I go hunting for him in the basement, where a group of women are rehearsing their clown routines, and find him standing near the door with a stick.

His name is Earl Baumruck, and he's some kind of self-declared Houby King (say the boys back in the garage), but he's not interested in my desire to hunt.

I give him my number. "Yeah," he says, "We'll see, we'll see." Then he shows me the stick. "Know what this is? A houby stick. If you're going to be a houby hunter, the first thing you got to have is a houby stick." And that's about all the wisdom I get from the Houby King.

THE HOUBY PARADE

On a Saturday morning in Cicero, in late September, I awake to find that it is raining hard on the houby hunters' parade. I stay home.

My father goes anyway and later he comes home all wet. "How was the parade?" I ask him. "It was a shame you didn't go," he says. "The Black Horse Troop was there and everything."

A SEARCH FOR THE SOURCE

It is now October. I have maybe eight people hard at the task of bagging a houby hunter for me. I'm getting desperate. Soon the season will be over.

In times of confusion, a man frequently turns for guidance to some great source (oracle? icon? church? friend?) for peace, contemplation, and direction. And a Bohemian does not have to go far, only a few steps down to his basement wher his harried soul finds order and meaning in a simple world of work benches, old newspapers, plants, preserves, beer, pinochle cards, the furnace, and a secret collection of passbooks to neighborhood banks and savings & loans. A place for everything, everything in its place.

A time to set things straight, to put things in order. (Though part of the Bohemian's frustration is that everything is *always* in order.)

So I retreat to the basement, sit on the lowest step, nibble on a bag of dry mushrooms, and think houby, all the way . . . and am reminded mainly of that great big mushroom cloud in the sky. But that was a bad mushroom. Why didn't it come out shaped like a stalk of celery instead? or a head of cabbage? or a kohlrabi? Why something so comical, so comely, so comforting and folksy as a mushroom?

I am getting nowhere. I recall bits of houby lore from the past and conclude that one of the main problems is a simple one of being trustworthy. Even the Houby King admonished me for prying. "My houby hunting grounds are a secret," he fired at me point blank.

"They're not out of state are they?"

"No," was all he would say.

"Well, how do you know when the time is right?"

"I have houby watchers," he said. "Fellows who check every day for me and report."

"So then you'll call me, and I'll promise to not tell?"

No reply. "It's a bad year for houby," he confessed. "Too dry. You've got to have moisture for good houby hunting."

"When does the season end?"

"The first hard frost." Then he was gone.

Either it is still too dry, or more likely I failed to get the Official Houby Hunter Seal of Approval.

Rummaging through a stack of old Life newspapers, I come across a picture of James Drabek, posing with his bounty of baskets full of mushrooms, plus the greatest trophy of any Bohemian hunter, a kotrc (pronounced cut-torch) weighing 3½ pounds.

I call Drabek immediately. I promise him almost as much as a pint of pure Bohemian blood that I will not reveal his hunting grounds to anyone. He says he'll call me.

THE FALL OF '71

It was the best of times; it was the worst of times. It was an extraordinary season of balmy temperatures up in the 80s. But there was no rain, and mushrooms were hit hard in the hypha (something like a root . . . I had been reading into mycology) or vanquished at volva stage, unable to get it all together, to even peek past the earth and make the scene as a cute little button.

This lasted till into November when suddenly the frost hit. And in Bohemian basements everywhere, houby hunters could be heard reverently piling up their bushel baskets, putting away their knives, hanging their magic sticks in the dark till next fall.

The King is dead. Long live the King.

The rain never fell.

Nobody called.

A VOICE IN THE WILDERNESS

It was a young fellow of Bohemian extraction by the name of Kapoun who finally broke the spell. He was deep in the woods taking pictures one day, and who should appear from behind a tree but a houby hunter!

"Are you sure? In the middle of November?" I asked in amazement.

"Yes. He has a basket and everything. He's a nice old guy, well into his seventies. Only one thing wrong . . ."

"I know. I can't follow him on a hunt."

"No. He's not a Bohemian. He's Polish. His name's Ray Adamczyk, and he says he's been picking mushrooms for over 30 years. But I don't know what the hell he calls them . . . put-pink-ies and vesh-poof-ki or something. That's another thing. He's pretty hard to understand. Rough accent."

"No matter. I'll communicate somehow."

"Oh, yeah. He says this one mushroom, this veshpoofki whatever, you can get even in winter. Even under the snow."

"Houby hunting under the snow? Wait till the Bohemians find out. It'll spur a new winter sport. The Poles must have been keeping this a secret."

PUTPINKI, BOOZE ... BREAKFAST WITH THE OLD
POLISH HUNTER

He lives on the Southwest Side of Chicago in the first floor rear of a corner apartment building, with a basement where he keeps his cache of mushrooms preserved under lock and key. He's a neat little old man, a widower, who keeps his small living quarters spotless. He smiles frequently, seems almost serene, and does have a difficult time with the language.

"You like drink? Beer? Whisky?"

Although it isn't quite 10 in the morning. I don't want to hurt the old man's feelings, so I accept his hospitality.

He tries to explain the difference between putpinki and veshpoofki, where they're found, how he and his wife hunted them for years, and the way she used to prepare them.

"Do you remember exactly how she made them?" I ask.

"Sweet/sour," is all I can understand. "You taste?" he asks.

"Yes, I would like to taste."

He goes into the pantry and comes out with a dish, a spoon, a jar of mushrooms.

"Daughter make these," he explains. "Not so good like wife. This time too sour."

I can't tell the difference. They taste slimy, sour, and fine to me. But sweet/sour mushrooms washed down with whisky are a bit much for breakfast.

"This be putpinki," he explains. "Best, September, October. No more now. Only veshpoofki."

"We go? Go look for veshpoofki soon?"

"Sure," he smiles. "I give you call."

"No. I call you when it looks like veshpoofki time, okay?"

THE HUNT

We meet in the parking lot of an outlying forest preserve on Nov. 23, at 9 in the morning. It is a gray day with a temperature in the 20s. A fine snow filters periodically between the occasional sharp gusts of wind.

The old man is waiting ouside his car with basket in hand as I pull up. He is dressed in a pair of old blue-gray striped suit pants, a brown coat, rubbers, flannel shirt, and a blue-gray cap. He is making final adjustments to all of these. Then he shifts his bushel basket (with a rag handle) to his other arm, checks his knife, pulls on a pair of blue woolen gloves, starts walking toward the woods; stops, scrunches up a bit and says: "Cold. I put other coat on."

Finally we head down a well-worn path. He leads, I follow. About 50 feet into the path he stops before a stump which he seems to treat like an old friend.

"Veshpoofki sometime around stump," he says. "Sometime pick bushel around stump. Too late."

"You mean veshpoofki or putpinki?" I ask.

"Putpinki," he answers. I scratch my head in confusion and follow him deeper into the woods.

The woods are lovely, dark, and deep, but we have miles to go before lining up a veshpoofki in our sights. Occasionally the old man throws his arms up in mystery, "Don't know ... where's the veshpoofki?" which I think may be either the old man's sense of humor or a time-worn way of calling for help from the great mushroom spirit. So I try it, too ... "Don't know ... where the hell's the veshpoofki?"

We move then, stealthily through a noisy covering of dead leaves and cold twigs, down toward a riverbank. The old man is a tough mushroom to follow.

It is getting colder. There are some sparse patches of green for ground cover, some frost, but mostly leaves, fallen branches, and dead tree trunks.

The old man begins to slow his step, begins to hunch. I do the same.

He is sneaking up now behind an old willow tree along the riverbank.

He sets the bushel basket down carefully so as not to disturb all the silent forces of nature.

We crouch. He moves in, pouncing on the base of the willow with a knife gleaming for satisfaction.

"Veshpoofki!"

An innocent herd of russet little buttons clinging to the willow for dear, dead life. A small herd at that. He decapitates a few, fingers their less than meaty caps, and throws them into the basket with an "Auch!" Which either means "great" or "bad news" to an old Polish mushroom hunter. Considering the head count — 1, 2, 3, 4 veshpoofki in a row — probably bad news.

We keep moving. The riverbank is a well known stronghold of the valiant veshpoofki, and a treacherous terrain as well. Whole willow trees frequently blockade our path, and the path itself is a plot of holes and slick mud.

A few more sorties toward another old willow stump is unsuccessful. Not even a hint of an old veshpoofki village. Suddenly the old man takes a sharp turn and I lose sight of him.

From the other side of a huge stump I hear him exclaiming: "This is willow, was something once. Now nothing. I think is too dry." I nod in agreement.

Now the old man unexpectedly abandons the riverbank and heads for the interior through a wall of tall, dry weeds, wielding his knife like a machete, making them fall at his feet.

He stops momentarily, surveys the scene, edges toward the river once agains and explains: "With my wife, I come hunt all the time. Sometimes two, three times a week. Not just this place. I go Indiana. This veshpoofki grow 'round willow. But putpinki, I show you, grow all around ... don't have to move."

We head then to the old putpinki patch armed with his remembrance of putpinkis past. We come to a clearing and the old man stands tall in a familiar battle ground where putpinki by the hundreds once occupied the field.

Under a small pile of oak leaves, a few putpinki still peek. But they are black and shriveled—fallen soldiers, victims cut down by the sure death of hard frost. And here and there are a few more, their caps tipped over in silence . . . a veritable graveyard of brave putpinki.

"Look this stump," says the old man, "all around you . . . you don't have to move . . . just cut and cut, fill bushel and bushel!"

We are on the move again, this time toward a thicket of young trees. The old man is beginning to get angry, beginning to make excuses.

"Too dry now. Mostly I go to Indiana. No veshpoofki now." I am afraid we are on our way to Indiana when suddenly he turns and heads through an open woods.

He circles another stump, makes a dive, and comes up with only a dead putpinki.

"My daughter call yesterday," he says. "I tell her I go out hunt mushroom." He smiles. "Lotta people don't pick veshpoofki 'cause lotta people don't know you can eat. I go sometime even March. Under snow. March I find them. Not frozen, no. Not veshpoofki."

We have circled back to the parking lot. "No veshpoofki here. We go other place. Find Veshpoofki."

THE HUNT—PART II

Along another riverbank in another forest preserve a little farther west, we bag a wild herd of veshpoofki at the first stump.

"See! See!" exclaims the old man, "veshpoofki!"

"Great find!" I shout.

The old man executes the kill skillfully and drops a heavy handful in the basket. We move downriver some more, a little excited, and even stir up a flock of wild ducks.

"We should be hunting ducks," I say to him.

"Veshpoofki," he smiles.

We find no veshpoofki, nowhere. The old man's getting angry again. "I think if there be no veshpoofki, there be no veshpoofki," he concludes. I admire and accept that.

But we still stalk another few miles in the cold to search for an old landmark. "I show you one stump. Like I go after before. I pick bushel basket of putpinki." So we're back to putpinki again. . . .

But the stump has disappeared. "I don't know, maybe burn up or something. Was here once. I don't know what happen . . . someone put poison or something. They put something maybe on mushroom not supposed to grow. I used to come place before, fill two bushel and go home. Come to this place now and so little ... nothing."

We surrender an hour later and return to our cars. We sort through the 17 captives, and I go home with a small paper bag full.

"Only thing," the old man advises, "these not stay too long. Cook right away. Only stay two month maybe."

We shake hands on the hunt. "We go maybe March. You call," he says.

Later I check with a Polish newspaper to find out what the hell kind of mushrooms we were hunting, and come up with podbienki for putpinki and nothing even close to veshpoofki except maybe weslefki. I decide I like veshpoofki better anyway, for its magical sound, and so it will always remain to me ... veshpoofki, like a secret hidden under the snow.

GOIN' TO MEET THE MUSHROOM MAN

The houby hunting season is over. I have bagged my limit of eight veshpoofki. I cook two of them up and pass the famous mushroom test (they're not poisonous), but still I'm not satisfied. I'm left with a feeling that my own people have let me down.

That's when my man-about-the-woods, Kapoun, comes through again. He has found a genuine houby hunter, a Bohemian named Tony Blazek.

A clandestine meeting is arranged in Brookfield on a late night in December.

I case the block carefully for a house my informer said I couldn't miss because it was all made of stone. And sure enough, even there in the dark it looms unique, kind of a small castle, a fairy-tale-in-the-woods house ... a kind of mushroom house that popped up from the damp earth one night.

It is not Tony Blazek's house. It is owned by Louie and Marie Pekar. Louie has a black patch over his eye. Tony, I am told, will be here later.

Louie Pekar whisks me into the kitchen where Marie is seated at a table. I am not introduced to a heavyset man leaning against the sink.

Af first we make a little small talk, and again I have this sinking feeling that I am not trusted. Slowly, though, Louie and Marie become hospitable.

But still at the sink the heavyset man is eyeing me carefully and saying nothing ... the mushroom man.

"This is Tony," says Marie. "You want a beer?"

"Thank you," I say, and Tony gestures for me to sit across from him at a small counter. I ask him, "Ever hear of a mushroom the Poles call veshpoofki?" I explain what I think it looks like.

A magic word, Tony opens up immediately. He brings out books, he brings out mushrooms, trying to solve the mystery of the veshpoofki. He makes a tentative identification.

"I think it's a velvet stem collybia ... collybia velutipes ... a winter mushroom. It's not very good. The Bohemians don't go for it. You have to cook it at least two hours in salt."

What a find! Not a collybia velutipes but Tony Blazek ... a Bohemian, a houby hunter with the makings of a mycologist!

Marie brings out a jar of pickled mushrooms. We eat, we drink beer, I listen to Tony unfold a kind of folk history of houby entitled "Me & the Mushroom":

"I once found a kotrc (that prize trophy among Bohemian hunters, that superspreading houby) that weighed 35 pounds. I'll show you a picture of it later. You can bread them, fry them, chop them up in gravy. They're found mostly around oak stumps, even walnut. Indiana mushrooms? No good. Too much sand. A bad year for mushrooms? Well, too much moisture is, not enough is bad. It's always one or the other with mushrooms. But they're there!"

I ask him about what the old Polish hunter called putpinki, and Tony decides it must be what the Bohemians call vaclavka: "The honey mushroom. The true Bohemian favorite."

"Vaclav means Jim," adds Louie. "We call them little Jimmies."

"I think it has something to do with St. James' Day," says Tony.

I knew the Bohemians had some connection between religion and mushrooms, I say to myself.

"How's the pickled mushrooms?" asks Marie.

"Delicious, delicious. Could I have the recipe?"

"I'll find it," she promises.

Everything's coming up mushrooms. Even the house seems to be spreading out in the dark. I notice there is a mushroom mobile hanging in one corner of the kitchen. And there are mushroom platters, mushroom hot plates, and a mushroom wall hanging.

Tony is showing me a book. "Now here's a beautiful mushroom. When it's on a log, the top of it just glows." (He is pointing to a volvariella bombycina ... Silky Agaric). "The Constitution of the United States was written out of the ink of this one, coprinus atramentarius, Inky Cap. Now this one here, this Brick Cap, people sometimes pick by mistake for a vaclovka. I wouldn't pick one. You could get very sick. And here, the Fairy-Ring mushroom is one of my favorites. I went so far as to dig up the ground once, the whole ring in the woods, and set it in the back yard. Nothing. Wild mushrooms you just can't grow at home. They're in a habit all of their own."

He disappears momentarily into the basement and comes up with a jar of dried mushrooms. "Boletus Granultatus ... no gills. You find them mostly under pine trees. Good eating."

"But how do you know?" I ask. "How can you be sure it's not that fatal mushroom waiting there with your number on it?"

"You pick these so long, and your eyes tell you." Then he disappears into the basement again.

Louie retires for the night. Marie follows, leaving me her recipe for pickled mushrooms.

Pickled Mushrooms
5 quarts of mushrooms
2 or 2 1/2 cups of white vinegar
2 cups of water
20 whole allspice
1 teaspoon of whole black peppercorn
1 large pinch of salt
1 cup of sugar [more or less to suit]
2 medium onions [cut into 1/2-inch pieces]
Bring to a boil, add mushrooms, and boil for five minutes.
Then fill pint sterilized jars.

Come on down here," calls Tony. I go down to the basement and find the mushroom man at a small bar looking for a picture of his famous kotrc.

He says: "Best time for hunting mushroom is the middle of August till the killing frost. I never ate a really bad mushroom. But once, my partner George Firak and me found some of those mushrooms that will put you into orbit."

"The ledendary Sacred Mushroom?" I ask.

"It got me sort of weak, that's all. Sort of relaxed."

I look around and conclude that this is an authentic Bohemian basement. Once I spot the pinochle decks behind the bar, I am certain. In the corner, I see a collection of hunting sticks the Houby King told me about. "Are those magic or something?' I ask Tony.

He smiles. "They're mainly to brush the leaves aside to find the houby hiding underneath," he says, and hands me a picture of himself and his friend George holding the giant kotrc outside the houby house.

"How do you find something like this?" I ask.

"You won't believe this," he says. "But we were coming home from mushroom hunting one day and I was driving about 70 miles an hour. 'George,' I said, 'I think I saw a mushroom back there.' 'You're crazy,' he said. And I went back, and there it was."

It's around midnight now, and I'm in the kitchen still mulling over mushrooms with the mushroom man, trying to pin him down but getting nowhere.

"But then you don't really live in this house?"

"I'm here. I'm always around, you know."

"Well, maybe next fall, if you're here, I'll call and maybe I can go with you?" No answer.

"Listen, then. Why mushrooms? And the Bohemians in particular? Was it merely a way of life they brought over from the Old Country?"

"It's the object of finding them."

"You mean for nothing," I add. "Something free . . . the Bohemians like those odds."

"No, it's finding them . . . seeing the way they grow . . . you're walking and all of a sudden they're infront of you, and your heart starts pounding because you found such a lovely cache!"

"Then it's the buried treasure game, huh?"

"There was one time we came across a patch so big it took us over a day to pick them. You can't imagine finding something like that."

As I leave the mushroom man in the dark, to his reveries of fields and woods and the age-old mysteries of mushroom and man, he says:

"You can dry them, and pickle them, and freeze them. Mushrooms are incredible. I like to saute them with onions and a little caraway. . . ."

The door of the mushroom house opens and sets me adrift in the night like a spore. The voice of the mushroom man continues like an unfinished hymn:

"Napoleon, you know, lived on mushrooms when he made the big push into Russia . . ."

I ponder the possibilities of Napolean, a houby hunter, scrounging for veshpoofki under the snow.

The Neighborhood Pub

It's the wrong neighborhood for one thing. Places like The Princess Pub glow beautifully and naturally in the daily night of Old Town Chicago or the Near Northside.

Pure neighborhoods breed beery corner taverns: red vinyl bar stools with the stuffing out, cheap electric beer plaques on the hustle (bouncing, humming, flashing all kinds of colored liquid comfort) ... "Hey, gimme a Bud" ... sticky formica bars with a wet mosaic of wet rings, dumb gray ballgames on a propped-up TV, front doors slightly opened, and the owners, Fred & Elsie, of course, dressed in traditional flannel shirt and mickey mouse apron.

But the soft pubs and lounges continue to move in. And with them comes the cocktail waitress. What was once Fred & Elsie's is suddenly The Princess Pub. The front door is heavy, windowless, wooden, and shut. It takes a lot of man to step out of the broken sidewalk sunlight and push against that door for the first time to see what the hell's going on in his own neighborhood.

"What's going on" is that he's the only guy in there without a tie to begin with. And the TV's been taken out. It's dark, air-conditioned, jukebox-quiet, and full of strangers. The innkeeper is dressed like Old King Cole. The bar stools have backs to keep a man from falling, and there are no signs telling anyone what to drink. He wants to crawl out and go home, but he can't find the door. Walking into a chair, he decides to sit down.

"Hello," a whispery voice nudges him from behind and drops a lacy napkin.

"Yeah, hi." He answers a voice he hasn't heard the likes of since his first girl was 17 and anxious in the gangway of her father's bungalow.

"We're serving dragon tails today," her breath aflame.

"Dragon tails, huh? Sure, gimme a dragon tail."

And as she leaves the table, his eyes slowly focus on the voice miraculously transformed into a tight little mini-skirted, booted, bashful body who is off to get HIM a dragon tail.

"1.25," hush, hush, hush. (Enough boilermakers to turn his old black and white TV into living color, he thinks.)

"Not bad."

"I'll be back," flame, flame, flame.

"So will I," he replies, looking around to see who said that.

And so he returns time and time again, gradually absorbed in the English mystery of pubs and ale, darts and dragon-tail waitresses. And he brings friends, pulling them off local bar stools like suction cups, "Look, look! (like a kid) Come see what I found! Follow me. Here, push the door hard."

"I can't see anything. Where the hell's the TV?"

"Wait, wait. Things will clear up in a second."

"We're serving dragon tails today," flame, flame, flame.

"What the hell was that?"

"See! See!"

"Oh my God. Call my old lady and tell her I was hit by a Douglas Park El and won't be home till after Johnny Carson."

Her name? What's in a name? Call her Lady. She's all that.

With time, Lady learns his name. And it becomes increasingly clear that more and more strangers are regulars, everybody has a name, and Lady knows them all. But for a MOMENT, a WHILE, a SECOND, sometimes MINUTES UPON MINUTES, she is his. And his, and his, and his.

Her story is not a happy-ever-after story after all. Her story is a broken marriage story, kids, responsibilities, three jobs, religion and deep motherly instincts; everything any man does not want to hear from a mini-skirted young fantasy that often dances alone while waiting for orders.

And when Lady talks, Lady jousts ...

"Of all the men who come here to see you, Lady, which do you prefer?"

"The men who come in to watch the animals with me."

In time, the innkeeper calls, "Time!" The lights are turned on. Lady looks even better. Everyone blinks and feels guilty about something. Farewells are mumbled as the regulars, their armor a trifle rusty, meet the door, the night, and everything they left waiting on the outside. Some one has stolen their horses.

He joins them with a gallant, "Good night," to Lady as he moves backwards down the fairy tale alleys, feeling a little like Jake Barnes.

Thanksgiving

If I am home for Thanksgiving (home is the Cicero/Berwyn area), I know just how the day will go. Thanksgivings there have been the same for me forever, it seems.

It's a day difficult to define. As a boy, as a student, as a teacher, it had that air of "holiday" to it. As a writer, days have become almost indistinguishable. All holidays, I suspect, have been homogenized.

Thanksgiving was always a gray day, regardless if the sun made the scene or if there was a touch of early snow to the neighborhood. Thanksgiving was as gray as the clothes the Pilgrims wore. And almost as dull.

It is a day of great expectation where nothing finally happens. We eat, we talk, we mouth our thank yous, we eat some more, we go to bed.

Ironically (perhaps not so ironically in America today), there is very little *thanks* or *giving* involved. It's an uncomfortable holiday at best for most Americans. It's the one holiday we've never been able to put a handle on. Oh, the advertising mind tries to make it annually with Macy's parade on national TV. But what they're really asking us to celebrate is the number of shopping days till Christmas.

So if I am home on Thanksgiving, and if I act true to form, I will be up early, leave the kids to their mom, Grandma and Grandpa, Macy's parade, all the preparations for Thanksgiving dinner, and go for the morning newspaper, walking the neighborhood streets and alleys toward Cermak Road.

I hope it is cold. I know it will be gray. I might even welcome a little snow in the backyards and front lawns. I will feel warm within my jacket, comfortably romantic in the deep, long pulls of smoking tobacco, cocooning myself in my own shade of gray to thank the day.

There's a selfishness to my walks, especially these morning walks through the neighborhood, checking the quietness of backyards, flowers and gardens past their prime, blackbirds waiting it out on garage roofs. I think of the warmth and smell of a fresh newspaper at the corner stand just ahead, the taste and the satisfaction of a cup of hot, black coffee.

I won't think much of "giving thanks." Not consciously, anyway. That's something to think about, I don't imagine many of us do. And whether or not we go through the thanksgiving motions in the churchly act of reverence, whatever the chapter or verse, whatever the gospel, whatever the memorable message in the sermon, it's a momentary feeling at best.

So let's get on with it; let's get home and eat. There's a turkey roasting in the oven, and all this company coming.

It seems that whenever we make a big thing about a very human gesture, we lose it. I've been thinking about that lately. I've been thinking about that for a long time.

If I'm home for Thanksgiving, I'll be thinking about it again as I buy my morning paper on the corner of Cermak and Oak Park and slip into the Seneca restaurant. The waitress will lay down a steaming cup of coffee in front of me without asking, and I'll say: "Thank you."

Thank you. It's the first common courtesy we teach the child (couched in a threat . . . "Say thank you, or you can't have it") and the last one we ever learn ourselves — those of us who survive the fate of thankless creatures.

Something's wrong with our thanking capacity. It's such a frivolous gesture. Frankly, thank-yous come too damned easy these days . . . "Thank Thee God for everything."

A Day of Thanksgiving! I can hear the homilies all over America today. The classic calls from the pulpits to count our blessings, as if we had to keep them numbered on the shelf and bring them down each year to dust them off. I know what all the newspaper editorials are going to say, and I won't even bother to read them. And if I see another classroom window display of perfect orange pumpkins, black Pilgrim hats, and brown turkey silhouettes, I just might take the ax to them myself.

"Yes, more coffee, please. Thank you. I'll take a chocolate donut, too. Thank you."

Losing them . . . losing these very human gestures. How we speak them without feeling. How we wear them out under the burden of "holiday." We have this tendency in America to diminish the significance of all our celebrations until we lose them completely. The more we have, the more thankless we are, now, in our time. The quality of celebration lessens with the material advancement of the people to the point where the celebration parodies itself. I just thought of that. Call it: Blei's Goodtime Law.

To get back somehow to the primitive. Who can really envision the first Thanksgiving today? The Pilgrims who survived, plus 90 Indians? That first and truest thanks giving to God? How the Pilgrims must have felt deeply, thanking their God while the Indians looked on, no doubt in wonder, watching this strange religious rite of the whites ... no stranger, perhaps, than the Indians' reverence toward the Great Spirit. Offering thanks to whatever the name of the Unknown; thanks for survival, for the plentiful earth. That's all. That's it, very simply.

But the Indians lived the prayer, from morning sun to nights of stars and moon ... from season to season. While the whites quickly went about their business of civilizing things, including the Indian, until a time would come when a special day would be set aside each year to give thanks. A *special* day!

That's the folk history. And much of the problem, thank you.

We pass it down, of course. We make it history. We distill the initial act. Children and the indoctrination of myth; stuffing them with First Thanksgivings. Nothing wrong with that — we've got to know where we came from, to know which way we're going. So we celebrate the history and sacrifice the act of kindness, the real thing.

Man, those were fine people, those Pilgrims. Did you know there was a woman aboard the Mayflower named Desire? Three boys named Love and Wrestling and Resolved? And a boy, too, called Remember. There was a child born at sea and they named him Oceanus. I give a kind of silent thanks to those Pilgrims and all that beautiful naming.

They suffered, they sacrificed, and their thank-yous were genuine because they had so little and were given so much almost miraculously. You planted a certain seed, and in time you harvested corn, which contained even more miracles in itself. Not the least of which was planting the seed once again for more, full circle. Thanks, to the infinite wonder of it all.

And those Indians ... those were some Indians: Chief Massasoit, Samoset, and Squanto. Squanto, who stayed on to live in Plymouth Colony, who taught the Pilgrims how to live with the earth, planting herrings in each corn hill to help the corn grow tall, hunting with bow and arrow, digging clams, refining maple sugar, healing with medicinal herbs. Organic living ... harmony. Squanto was where we're at, where many of us are trying to get back to, to be, today.

So the Pilgrims threw a feast and thanked the Indians. That was good, but not enough for the Indians. The Indians were forever givers. (Not the "Indian givers" connotation we gave them in time.) The feast was turkey, deer, geese, fish, corn, beans, pumpkins, squash, grapes, cranberries, nuts — so overwhelming that the Indians stayed three days. Chief Massasoit, responding in gesture, in mutual feeling, in something unspoken but thanks giving, sent Indian hunters to the woods who returned with five deer for the Pilgrims.

After the feast came the fun. The Indians danced! Then, Captain Myles Standish marched his men and boys around in parade. I like that best. It reveals so damn much. Old America broke out into a dance, and New America marched. Maybe we blew it all right then. Where did I read the words, just lately? *Primitive religion is not believed. It is danced.*

Today, children still cut and draw and paint pumpkins and turkeys until they're sick of them. We study the First Thanksgiving over and over as if somehow it's supposed to make us thankful.

By the time kids reach the age of Give and Receive, all they really know or care about Thanksgiving is that it comes after Halloween (tricks or treats, receiving, receiving), and just before the celebration we've managed to raise to the level of grotesque: Christmas, when we adults sit hungrily around awaiting our fat but hollow thank-yous.

"Fill it up?" says the waitress, holding the bottomless coffee urn. "Thank you ... my cup runneth over ..."

Does anybody truly feel anything *good* anymore? What does a *thank you* really feel like, where does it come from? The mind? The mouth? The hand? The heart? Or just the pocketbook?

How is a kid, an adult, to get an authentic measure of it these days in a time and a land of Everything-Taken-For-Granted?

So you thank me for my offering, and I'll thank you for yours, and in times of stress or danger (overcome or at least diminished by the help of God), we'll both "thank our lucky stars." Or, if we're really feeling our faith, "Thank the Lord above." Now, then, let's get on with the getting, and oh, by the way, thanks a million.

If I am home on Thanksgiving, I will finish my fourth or fifth cup of coffee at the Seneca, fold the morning newspaper under my arm, light up again, and leave a tip under the saucer for the waitress ... my way of showing gratitude. A good waitress, of course, knows how to work the gratitude out of any customer. But I do appreciate the extra service, the small talk, and she knows it; it's part of our contemporary, unquestionable ritual of thanks giving.

From the restaurant, it's over the river and through the woods; but more likely, in Berwyn, down the block and through the alley to Grandmother's house. I know the turkey will be roasting in the oven, the kitchen will smell delicious, the dining room table will be set for a dozen people or more.

There will be bowls of dressing, gravy, cranberries and a slice of pumpkin pie with whip cream.

And that will be good. All the family together will be fine, very nice. I will probably imagine and see again, as I often do at Thanksgiving and Christmas, a hokey but true Norman Rockwell painting, "Freedom from Want": the beautiful table, the smiling faces, young and old, the huge turkey on a gleaming white platter. I might even think about how half the world is starving. But

I won't dwell on it too long because, after all, I'm only human.

Most likely, no one will say grace; no one will offer any thanks aloud. It's not that we won't feel it inside of us; it's just not customary in our family. In fact, group grace is downright embarrassing. So, unless one of the children has recently undergone a brief Sunday school conversion and can be coaxed and bribed and teased into saying some kind of "Thank Thee," we will fix our napkins, pass the food, fill up our plates, take up our knives and forks, and eat. And someone will say, "It's good," and the rest of us will nod our heads in agreement. Grandma will smile.

If I am not in Chicago for Thanksgiving, if instead I find myself at my half-way home in the country, then it will be a little different:

I have no corner, no Cermak Road, no newspaper to go for in the morning. Instead, I will take my usual walk down the road, through the woods and fields, maybe as far as the lake. It will be cold. The day will be gray. The fog horn will probably be blowing. Separated from family and friends, Thanksgiving will be celebrated in one of the local restaurants. The food will be good; it usually is. And there will be just enough of everything. But it will be a good deal less than Thanksgiving at Grandma's.

Nostalgia, perhaps, for Thanksgiving past. Maybe the whole celebration is just a state of mind.

But there was a Thanksgiving morning some years ago on Cermak Road in Cicero when I walked through another gray day to a small Bohemian restaurant called Frank's, which I often frequented.

Frank's had a long counter, a few tables, bright lights, delicious food, and Frank himself, who seldom smiled. But I liked him; he cared about the food and there was a peacefulness about the place.

Oldtimers made a home for themselves there, each day. Widowers, pensioners, just plain loners. They'd gather there for coffee and homemade bakery each morning. They stayed for a half hour or so, talked the usual talk of taxes, weather, sickness, death, and then disappeared, one their separate ways until the next morning when they would return and take up yesterday's conversation. They would speak in English and Czech. They would talk to Frank, but he would seldom answer them; he was usually too busy.

And on Thanksgiving Day, I remember, they would come into Frank's one at a time, a little dressed up, feeling good about the holiday, talking it up like it really meant something and were thankful they had somewhere to go. Then they would order turkey dinner for breakfast. He would tell them it wasn't ready yet, and they would wait. After eating, they would quietly disappear and go back to where they came from.

That, very simply, was an acting out of thanks.

Even more simply . . . here in the country one gray and white Thanksgiving Day . . . the silent blessing, gratuity unexpressed . . . I remember crossing through an old orchard landscaped the night before in snow. The apple trees were dead and twisted and broken, and sang so eloquently of all the sadness in life, the loneliness, the hopelessness, the despair ...

But for the sudden madness and richness of one tree, still desperately clinging to red ripe fruits. Bluejays were laughing it up in the branches in the midst of all the unexpected wonder ... cold and snow, and soon darkness and the long winter were inevitable.

Yet that apple tree danced and whirled in birds and snow. . . . Say "thanks," I said to myself, snapping a cold apple from a branch, feeling fully the naturalness of the celebration, whatever the season ... tasting it.

The Polka King: Frankie Yankovic

The Polka King is in the kitchen. In late afternoon, the King — Frankie Yankovic — sits at the head of the table at Carl and Ann Birsa's home in southwest-suburban Summit, drinking a small bottle of cold duck, laughing and joking, waiting for a bowl of Ann's mushroom soup (made in his honor).

He wears a rust-colored shirt outside his belt in a sporty fashion, a diamond ring on his pinkie (a sign of royalty, certainly). His hair, now graying, is neatly slicked back in 1940s fashion. Nothing out of place about the King, especially his sure smile.

He arrived a few hours ago from his hometown, Cleveland, to play a one-nighter at the Red Anchor Inn in Lyons. "I love one-nighters. To me it's more excitement. I look forward to meeting friends wherever I go. I rarely stay in a hotel; friends would get mad at us. Like my daughter here (Ann Birsa, whom he nicknamed Daughter years ago) ... it's like home."

"Yeah," says Ann. "He's got mothers and daughters all over the country who cook and take care of him. He's got it made."

"Daughter," laughs the Polka King, "where's some of that soup? Jesus, it smells so good."

Although I was brought up with heavy doses of polka music at weddings and family celebrations, I think I first heard Frankie Yankovic on a crank record player in the Cicero basement of my boyhood friend Ed Tomse (Ann Birsa's brother). I remember the effect: an instinctive jumping up and down as soon as one heard the music. Instant joy — that's one of the secrets of the polka. That's the way it must have hit Yankovic as a child in Cleveland.

"My mother used to take in boarders," he says, "and one of them played the button box concertina. I was eight or nine at the time. After work, these fellas would drink and play cards, and Max Zolodic would play the button box, and all of them would sing. When they were at work, I would try to play it.

"I was sixteen when I got my first piano accordian. My mother bought it for me without the old man knowing. It cost $500. My dad was old-fashioned; he believed in the button box. I had only about eight lessons in my life. It seemed like overnight I learned how to play. My friend Joe Trolli taught me the most."

"You want more soup?" asks Ann.

"Oooh, this is great soup, Daughter. I'll have some more."

"More wine?"

"I'll have a little more of that too. I have to watch, though. Christ, I have to play tonight.

"Tomorrow night it's South Bend. I was in Milwaukee last week. Going on tour to Hawaii . . . in May I go to Spain. And Dubrovnik in October. They got hotels in Dubrovnik that would put Miami to shame. In June we're goin' on a cruise, the Rotterdam out of New York.

"What am I gonna do? The people keep asking for me. I got more work than I can handle. But I don't like to turn anybody down. I average three, four, five engagements a week. I'll never retire."

It may be hard to imagine that in the days of country, folk, jazz, and rock, there still reigns an American Polka King, Frankie Yankovic, still in constant demand.

"It's not like before, admits Yankovic. "Every town has its own polka band now. Joliet, St. Louis, Chicago . . . it's almost impossible to establish ground as a polka player today on a national level. The expense is too high . . . traveling from place to place. And then, the ballroom business is gone. They're not open on Tuesdays, Wednesdays, and Thursdays anymore.

"The polka audience is still there, but it's different too. Take Chicago. I hardly play here anymore. I used to play the Trianon, all the ballrooms. But that's gone. TV killed the weeknight audience. People stay home now, buy a case of beer, maybe watch polka shows on TV. And those are so damn bad, most of them. Poor direction, poor bands . . . All you see is two women dancing. What the hell kind of polka dance is that? I get up and turn it off.

"The audience is there, though. I played in Bismarck, North Dakota. There people were no special nationality. And it went terrific! They had 1,200 the first night and a thousand the next. And on a Thursday, mind you.

"Canada, now there's something. The crowds are 2-to-1 compared with the States. It seems the people there are happier. Here you see all these worried faces even when they're dancing. And they break up earlier here; 11 o'clock and they're tired, they want to go home. At 1 in the morning in Canada the people are still dancing, and they have to get to work in a few hours! Most of them are farmers, French, German, Belgian ... they're great!"

Yankovic savors the aroma of his third bowl of soup, takes a swig of wine, and reaches for the pepper mill, grinding hills of pepper into his soup, onto the table, into his lap.

"We gonna eat later, or what?" he asks.

His reign on the national scene goes way back. "From 1948 to 1960 was my biggest time," he acknowleges. "I started to write music with Joe Trolli about 1932. In the late '30s the lyrics became important; the people could remember the songs better. In those years I made four sides on the Yankee label. The records went like hotcakes. Then I opened my first nightclub, Dec. 6, 1941 ... the day before Pearl Harbor.

"I went to work at Fisher Body in Cleveland and played the bar at night. I was drafted in 1942, in the infantry, and left the club to my dad and the bartender to run. I cut 32 sides before going overseas, and they sold so fast they couldn't keep up. When I came back to the club after the war, Columbia records was waiting for me. I was with them 20-some years.

"My first big hit was in 1948 with 'Just Because.' The first week it sold 10,000 copies in *Boston*, where they never heard a polka before. I followed that up with 'Blue Skirt Waltz.' Both of them were million-sellers."

Yankovic was crowned Polka King in Milwaukee, where a "Battle of the Polka Bands" was held before 8,000 people in 1950. It lasted three hours, and Yankovic won by secret ballot of the audience over five other bands. He also recalls another Milwaukee contest, "Jazz Versus Old-Time Music," in which he took on Duke Ellington and three other bands. Ellington should have asked for a change of venue; only in Milwaukee, probably, could a King of Polka beat a Duke of Jazz.

Since then? Well ... there've been "Tick-Tock Polka," "Bye Bye Baby," and, most recently, the "Barking Dog Polka." But nothing like "Just Because" or "Blue Skirt Waltz"; perhaps nothing like that for him again.

His group these days is a "pickup" band, the best of whatever polka men he can find in each town. "When I play in Vegas, for example, or Reno, those audiences expect a real show, entertainment, so I try to find polka players who can sing real good too."

His band at the Red Anchor Inn tonight ("I don't know anything about the joint," he confesses; "My drummer lined it up") will consist of guys he frequently uses in this area: Bob Lorenz, accordian, from Oshkosh; Denny, on bass, from Milwaukee; Bobby the drummer, from Riverside; and Adolph, banjo and guitar, from Chicago.

"You see," he says earnestly, "I was trying to give the polka a certain beat where it wouldn't be tied to no ethnic group in particular. I never liked wind instruments. I found I had enough lead in the accordion...."

"What time we got, Daughter? Are the shirts ready?"

"They're in the basement, all ironed, don't worry about it. How do you like that?" says Ann. "I'm even his maid." The King is honored wherever he goes. Polka groupies, in a sense, these women, making shirts for him and his band, laundering them, cooking for him and the boys, putting them up for the night or two, creating a sense of home all over America.

"The thing that keeps me going is that every town I go to, I know who I'm going to see," Yankovic says. "All these friendships are more important to me than anything."

The Red Anchor Inn on Ogden Avenue in Lyons is a combination bar and lounge, hardly the classic polka setting. The tiny marquee and a sign on the door announce, "Frankie Yankovic, One Night Only." A Thursday night at that. But the King has a strong polka faith. And a strong following.

It is 7:30. Yankovic is to play from 9 'til 1 a.m., and nobody else is here yet. I have visions of a quiet night with just the King and a few of his cronies. After Frankie's Red Anchor dinner of steak, dumplings, and gravy, it's 8:30, and he's on the bandstand testing the mikes. Now all the front and middle tables are full, and by the time Yankovic plays his first polka, the place is packed.

He's ready now. The men are up there in their fancy old-world shirts with the puffed cuffs. Silence. The King speaks:

"Good evening everybody. We're gonna have a hell of a good time tonight. But first I want you to stand up ... come on, let's all stand up ... now shake hands with the person behind you ... that's good ... good."

The Polka King is warming them up in classic fashion. He talls an anecdote about Don Ho, the Hawaiian singer, and follows with a couple of quick jokes. Laughter, a little applause, and then, "All right, we're gonna start right in with the 'Tick-Tock Polka'!" The bouncing sound of polka music hits the Red Anchor Inn like an explosion, constant crescendo, flat out. Polka music. And the more you drink and dance, the better it sounds. But for now, the dance floor is empty.

"Wait a minute! Wait a minute!" yells Yankovic, and the music stops. "What the hell is this? What do you think this is, a concert? I'll buy a drink for the first couple dancing." Then the first couple steps out, then another, and another, and the evening has begun.

The songs keep coming — polkas, waltzes, just plain popular tunes. Polka people carry them in their heads, their hearts, their dancing feet. All it takes is a man like Yankovic to bring them out again.

Polka people come up to him at the bandstand all night long it; it becomes almost a royal receiving line. Even in the middle of a number they dance or walk up, shake a hand, say hello, request a song, tell him how they love his music, exchange stories about mutual friends, and inquire when they'll be able to see him again. Then he's explaining the universal ethnic polka quality to his people: "I'm gonna play a little medley, German, Bohemian, Croatian, Italian, Slovenian, Polish...."

Halfway through the night, you can barely find room to polka. For a Thursday night at the Red Anchor in Lyons, Illinois, the crowd is a minor miracle. Most will probably never come here again, unless the Polka King returns.

There are certain types of couples who will forever be found on polka dancing floors, starting with the kids, especially at weddings, jumping and hopping and crashing into people. They feel this call to the blood at an early age.

Then there are always the two women who dance with each other. They dance and enjoy . . . but it's less than pure polka. A man and wife polkaing are easy to spot. Though their feet may slide and jump, their eyes stare off in the distance, as if they are not enjoying it one damn bit.

And young lovers, perhaps engaged, with eyes and polka steps only for each other. There's a seriousness and hopefulness to their dance.

The real zestiness of the dance is left to the slightly drunk, middle-aged dancers, the old-timers — with the perfectly, delicately drunken polka man holding the edge. To whirl, to jump, to stomp, to holler, to laugh, to squeeze the woman (never your wife), to become one with her and the music and the whole big dance called life without falling on your face . . . *that's* the ultimate polka dance. And it's contagious.

The King and I get into this later. "Polka music is the happiest kind this side of heaven," Yankovic tells me. "Old people come up and say, 'Frank, your music is better than any doctor. I can polka, I can dance! I can do anything!' No, it's not sophisticated. So what? It appeals to the working class. The sophisticated people never could express themselves."

He launches into his million-seller "Just Because." And I discover that all the words are still where I must have left them twenty years ago:

Just because you think you're so pretty.
Just because you think you're so hot.
Just because you think you've got something
That nobody else has got . . .
You made me spend all my money.
You laughed and called me Old Santa Claus,
Well I'm telling you, baby, I'm through with you,
Just because . . .

At 1 o'clock, the polka people in Lyons are proving themselves the equals of any group of Canadians you care to mention; they will carry the sound of polka long into the night. But the King is tired.

"I wouldn't recommend this life to anyone," Yankovic says, suddenly serious. "I never had the time to get to know my kids [eight by his first marriage, one more by his second], if you want to be a family man, this is not the life.

"But it's been the happiest life for me."

The Ice Cream Man

I

It was a candy store. A Chicago corner. A neighborhood. Kids, churches, schools, alleys, dogs, curbs, gangways, and backyards. And ice cream. An ice cream cone every Sunday afternoon. There was a little piece of paper stuffed into the bottom tip of some of the cones. Only some of the cones. The message read FREE ICE CREAM CONE. Whenever there was a message.

I paid for an interminable run of Sundays a nickel-at-a-time. Strawberry cone Sunday afternoons. Sometimes chocolate. I ate the cones upside down looking for a reason. Looking for a FREE cone of Sunday vanilla ice cream or butter pecan. Even a hint of an unpronounceable pistachio. One day Sunday I won. Once. My birthday. And I have reason now to suspect that the cone was hand packed by the candy man. A Bohemian named Zeka. But a FREE strawberry cone Sunday nonetheless. Once more once, please. Zeka played the horses.

He also played the violin when he was sad. And made Mrs. Zeka cry. And as time touched his hands old Zeka played the women as well. A lady teller at the bank kept giving him more money without telling. For being just good old Frank Zeka the candy man and packer of neighborhood ice cream cones. Chocolate Vanilla Strawberry. In time she was fired for giving him treats to the cone crunching bite of a couple grand. He went to jail: The candy store closed. I lost forever the Sunday combination of FREE ICE CREAM hand packed.

II

I lived on a farm in Michigan each summer when I was a child. I childhood-hiked down the path past the white chickens to the mailbox and sat against an oak tree belonging to a farmer who was dying but who still fed the pigs and waited and watched the highway for the rural delivery carrier who would chug down the road in an old Ford and play games with the little red flag on the mailbox. The flag is up! The flag is down! SURPRISE! Guess what? Mail. Money from home.

I hiked three miles along the road into town and found my place at the counter of the Rexall drugstore and immediately converted the magic message from home into ice cram. A morning ritual, mail or not. A pineapple sundae six days a week, no delivery on Sunday. God don't need no ice cream. I watched the white-aproned ice cream man bury his right arm to the shoulder in the freezer each day as he scooped and scooped vanilla from the frosty dark depths, ladled on the mushy miracle of pineapple, and stood back against the mirror waiting for my applause. Later I walked back to the farm on the railroad tracks, balancing the rail, an ice cream cone in each hand, waving, dripping, an equilibrium in the universe, a brave boy on a high wire, ice cream and the center of things.

III

The ice cream man cometh. A man of goodness and humor. Pushing a white cart shaped like a great ship cut in half. There was a front wheel that twirled around under the bow in absolute freedom which gave the white uniformed captain the power of starboard and port with his heavy cargo of ice cream under the hatch. And there were also bells. One bell. Three bells. Six

bells. The time was always now. He pushed-sailed this white vessel of ice cream, rang the bells and sang, ICE CREAMMMMM! ICE CREAMMMMM! down the asphalt rivers of my neighborhood and came to port at the front curb and opened the hatch in a cloud of freezing smoke and handed me a fudgicle (Fudgsicle) as hard as a bone. And a piece of hot ice, FREE! The fudgicle could wait for the sun. It was the metaphysics of hot ice that held the mystery of the universe. I held it, pressed coins into it, listend for the zinging sounds of CRAAAAAKKKKK!, dipped it into water for a bubbling broth, and handpacked it in a handkerchief to conjure at home. Long live the hot little hands of the ice cream man and his mystery ship.

IV

I grew up, a boy at the age of 13, to become an ice cream man. I was captain of the slickest white ship in the neighborhood. There were orange Popsicles painted on the broadsides, strawberry, lemon, lime, real-looking chocolate-covered ice cream bars, and hints of things to come in a pink fantasy some poet dubbed a Dreamsicle. And such a munificence of hot ice smoldering in the secret hatch with the bright chrome handle. I gave away the ice cream to a hundred small hands and put on street shows for unbelievers with hot ice puddles along the curb. I was not too hot as an ice cream man. My head and hands were just not into it. It was basically a religious problem. Here I was all dressed up in Holy Communion white with wheels and bells and answered prayers and supposed to be Christian when I was really invisibly wrapped in Tao and the zinging Zen of hot ice . . . the sound of one frozen hand packing . . . smoke.

V

> Sitting in the back booth of an ice
>   cream parlor on Cermak Road
> 'How about a strawberry malt?'
>   I asked her
> 'Yes' she said. 'Yes, mmmmmmmm'
> And how about this,' I looked
>   into her eyes
> And yes, they said, mmmmmmm,
>   yes
> 'And what about us?' I whispered
> 'Oh yes,' she said, 'Ooooooo yessssss'
> 'And here is your strawberry malt,'
>   I said

'Thanks' she murmured through a
strawberry thick straw
'And how about this?' I sipped
through her lips
'Mmmmmmmmm,' came the
strawberry taste
And later much later we held
strawberry hands and packed
away the flavor real good,
real good

VI

Chocolate frozen custard became a mania. I ate them six times a day. There was a store next to the alley on 16th Street. that had this amazing machine with a bright chrome handle which a fat lady turned open and then guided a gush of frozen custard into a mountainous whirl of a delicate crunchy cup. At night, under the streetlights, the custard flowed even faster.

We walked then, Sada and I, in the dark, hand in hand down all the frozen custard alleys to her home. I bit into mine, she teased hers to a thready tip of a Turkish temple, till the tip toppled and she sculpted the softness in chocolate all over again. It was plain she sought a certain permanence of passion that frozen custard would not allow.

'No' was all she smiled as my right hand stole past her frozen custard hand seeking solace in some fullness, some permanence of form.

'But no is never never,' I smiled as she dropped her frozen custard in the dark.

VII

banana split . . . i want a banana split . . . you can't have a banana split, you're too fat, and stop acting like a kid . . . i want a banana split . . . you can't have one . . . why ?. . you're too fat . . . so what . . . you want to die from a heart attack ?. . i have a good heart, a heart beating for banana splits . . . you'll die from a heart attack . . . a sweet banana split attack of love . . . no, a fat heart . . . maybe forget the bananas, just three dips of ice cream, chocolate, vanilla, and strawberry, maybe marshmellow, butterscotch and chocolate topping with whipped cream and sprinkled nuts and three bright cherries . . . that's still a banana split . . . no, not a banana split yes there are no bananas . . . that's a banana split and it's no bananas for you . . . i still crave a banana split . . . eat some pudding instead, pudding's good for you . . . pudding's no good for me when my stomach feels it needs a banana split . . . i made the pudding myself, with my own little hands . . . i don't care, it's not a banana split, nothing, never in the whole world can compare to a banana split . . . you don't love me . . . our love has nothing to do with banana splits . . . yes it does, i made this lovely pudding just for you with my own two hands, and anybody in the whole damn world can make a banana split without love . . . that's not true, only one who loves can make the majesty of banana splits, still i will love you just the same only now i'm going, i'm splitting . . . where? . . you know where, where all men must go just because it's there . . . you're going to die mounting the calorific cliffs of some distant split in the lost horizon just because it's there? . . . i hope so, i hope so . . . then here, my love, take a spoonful of my banana pudding before you leave

The Latin Mass

Laramie Avenue in Cicero is not one of the more scenic routes in the community or necessarily the way to salvation. Taking it south from 12th Street, it's a ragged street, at best, of factories, restaurants, marginal shops, bars, old book joints, all leading to the true spirit at the end of the line: Sportsman's and Hawthorne racetracks.

It's the kind of street that seems to be struggling to maintain some kind of propriety, but losing ground in a historically ethnic neighborhood trying to hold its own but nevertheless undergoing changes.

It's a ripe place to start a revolution or build a new church.

The old Raleigh Funeral Parlor at 2307 S. Laramie (where, legend has it, some of Cicero's finest hoods were laid to rest) now sets out a rather heretical sign of the times:

THE LATIN RITE
CHURCH OF ST. JOSEPH
ALL MASSES IN TRADITIONAL LATIN
Sunday Masses 7:45 a.m., 10:45 a.m.

I have been thinking about the old Latin mass for some time now. Last year, after almost 20 years of wandering from the Catholic flock, I sat in on a guitar mass in my old Cicero parish, St. Francis of Rome. I came away pleasantly surprised, mildly entertained, and somewhat at a loss for words, though the new mass was trying hard to speak my language.

But it came on the scene a little too late and a little too folksy for me. I was looking for this before the time of Pope John. I was moving on to other things now. If anything, I was probably moving backwards.

The aluminum door to the Church of St. Joseph has an aura of secrecy about it. Five minutes before mass is to begin, and no one is in sight rushing ahead or behind me to get a seat. A Xeroxed message posted on the door holds me back momentarily: "Woman's Dress Regulations in This Church. SLACKS NEVER 1. No low neck. 2. Sleeves to elbow. 3. Knees must be covered. 4. Head covered always."

I had come not as a penitent, a convert, or even a journalist or rabble-rouser. I was born and raised in the mood and mystery of the Catholic Church. My old parish is still the parish of my parents.

I went ot school there, was confirmed there, sang in the choir, served as an altar boy. I even entertained strange aspirations for the priesthood, as most of us did who were educated by nuns and fed an overdose of religious guidance.

I grew out of it, though, after graduation from grammar school and the taste of fresh and free air found only in a public high school. Secularization began to take hold of me. Classifications of sin no longer mortified me. Confession was of no one's concern. Faith in the "One, Holy, Catholic and Apostolic Church" began to fade.

There was more to life than guilt. Catholics all around me were leading lives of mass contradictions. And, as I seriously began to read for the first time, I learned, for example, about Buddha, and he sounded damn good to me then. To date, all organized religion seems insufferable to me.

I left the church soon after. Eventually married outside the church. And have not been back in almost 20 years. The marks remain, though, like indelible etchings on a man's psyche. It's been said that all one had to hear was the tinkling of a bell, and you would find a Catholic genuflecting.

Last Christmas I though I'd give the old church, on 15th and Austin, one last try. I brought the kids along too, neither of whom have ever been baptized, attend Sunday school or had any specific church affiliation whatsoever. When it comes time for them, I hope they'll find their own way. But I guess I was kind of nostalgically wrapped up in the pomp and circumstance of Midnight Masses I remembered as a choir boy, and all the obligatory Sunday masses of my childhood.

It was like a hunger upon me to hear the Latin hymns, the priest chanting: *Pax Domini sit semper vobiscum* (May the peace of the Lord be with you always) and voices replying, *Et cum spiritu tuo* (And with thy spirit).

There was a rememberance, too, of sun pouring through stained glass windows, priests lording in their colorful robes, altar boys in black cassocks and blinding white surplices ... bells, incense, the flashing gold tabernacle and chalice ... the preponderance of statues ... the Virgin Mary in blue and white, stepping on a serpent; Christ in red and white robes, the Sacred Heart exposed, his arms outstretched; St. Joseph, the Infant of Prague, the large crucifix above the altar.

And candles. From the smallest red vigil candle, burned in memory of the departed or someone ill, to the tallest candles on the altar which forever held your eyes.

I wanted my children to experience this, at least once. I wanted them to have some memory of what ritual might mean in a person's life. I wanted to tell them how, as a kid, I sometimes hypnotized myself through an entire mass by merely concentrating my eyes on the candlelight. (An old yoga and meditation technique, I later discovered.)

If just some of this could be left for them ... But the church was bare. There was a monotony to the bland painted walls. Statues had disappeared. A modern, meaningless cross, replaced the crucifix. The priests could have been anyone. The Latin liturgy of the mass had been diluted to a pure Protestant ceremony.

Only some of the candles remained, and the stained glass windows. Vatican II had done its stuff. Ritual was passe. I had nothing to show my kids. No gift of a miraculous old rite to pass down to them, to do with it what they would in their own time. The church looked like a bingo hall.

So it is with some confusion and even trepidation that I step into the Church of Saint Joseph on Laramie Avenue in Cicero this Sunday morning, wondering just what the hell I am getting myself into. The Tridentine mass, some 400 years old, has been outlawed by Rome since 1969, when change swept away most of the traditions Catholics understood in their blood.

I could be excommunicated for this ... but then again, I probably am anyway since I married outside the church and gave up all the sacraments years ago. Still, there was something ingrained upon my old Catholic conscience ... this is wrong ... this is a rebel church ... this is trouble.

There are 15 people present when I enter. I take a pew in the back, next to the last, as I customarily did in my growing up years at St. Francis.

Unconsciously I find myself kneeling down and staring at the altar. "It's been a long time" keeps echoing through my head. Am I here to participate or observe? I don't know. I always found myself doing both, even inside the trappings of the faith.

Gradually, more people begin filtering in till the congregation reaches a total of approximately 35 people for the first mass. Who are they? Where are they from? Why do they come?

These are mostly middle-aged people ... families. Even young people and newly marrieds with babies in their arms. The young must have experienced at least a traditional Catholic grammar school or high school before the changes came. And then they couldn't adapt. Or wouldn't. Joining hands with strangers on each side of you in a contemporary display of unity friendship, and love (which the new Catholic Church now practices) was perhaps just one of the things they couldn't handle. Singing folk songs was probably another. And abandoning the mystery, the mysticism, of the Latin ritual was worse than death.

So it had come to this ... a counter-revolution. A Catholic Traditional Movement, which in itself has already begun to break into factions — those who accept Pope Paul VI as the true Pope, and those who do not. For now, however, all that matters is the celebration of the old Latin mass. I wish my kids could see this.

It's all here, carefully preserved. And a High Mass, no less. Doors swing open at the back and side of the church, and a procession of six altar boys, two sub-deacons, and an old priest move miraculously down the center aisle of the church. We are blessed ... incense is floated through the air ... that scent alone triggers so many sweet smelling memories of an old faith I have just barely begun to feel again.

The mass proceeds, the mass continues in true form. From *Introibo ad altare Dei* (I will go to the altar of God), to the Confiteor ... I confess to almighty God ... to the Kyrie, *Kyrie eleison* (Lord, have mercy on us), *Christe eleison* (Christ, have mercy on us) ... to the Gloria, the Gospel, the Sermon, th Creed, the Offertory, the Washing of Fingers, the Preface, the Consecration of Bread and Wine, the Communion.

The old priest is in fine form, even in preaching a short sermon on the Good Shepherd, reminding his parishoners frequently of their unique position within or without the framework of the Vatican Church. "We are not another parish. We are another church!" Then adding, "How strange, that of all places, God, in his infinite wisdom, should choose Cicero, Illinois, for the rebirth of the church."

The parishioners clutch old Sunday Missals, rosaries ... They are partially with the priest's celebration of the mass, partially out of it, as Catholics have always been.

The Latin mass is a difficult ritual to concentrate on. (One of the reasons why the English changes came about.) So the mind often drifts, as mine did when I was a child. You say some silent prayers ... you feast your eyes on the colorful chasuble the priest is wearing ... you hear the bells, watch the chalice and the host being upraised ... or lose yourself in the flickering flames of the candles. One way or another, though, you experience God. You are often transcended by the ritual of the old Latin mass.

And at communion, everyone — virtually everyone but me — goes up to the altar railing to receive Holy Communion this morning at St. Joseph's in Cicero.

The faces: I read some of the faces coming back to the pews, ethnic faces, most of them ... Slavic ... Irish ... Swede ... German ... no Italians, that I can perceive; not yet, anyway. As for the very young, I cannot read their faces at all.

The priest, however, the Rev. John Higgins, gray-haired, erect, is all Irish. I have no doubt about that. The brogue comes through. Serious in the pulpit, in reading the Gospel, in singing the Latin. A power in his voice ... sonorous. And as humorless and high-and-mighty sounding as all the old priests often were in my youth, whenever they donned the vestments, perormed the sacred mass, spoke the Gospel, heard confession and gave penance.

Priests intimidated you by their very presence. How am I going to approach this man, this tough old priest, I wonder? I'm no longer a Catholic school kid, waiting to be reprimanded for throwing snowballs, missing mass, or confessing a string of venal sins. Do I call him "Father"? How can he run a church like this in defiance of the Vatican? How does he get away with it?

I wait until the mass is over, until most of the congregation disperses. But I am easily spotted by an usher as an outsider. Perhap's it's the long hair.

"Would you like to see one of the priests?" he asks.

Yes, I'd like to speak to the old priest. I am led outside, around, and to the rear into a small, dark, chapel-like room adjoining the church, where I am taken in hand by Brother William Rochelle, 33, a sub-deacon, who arranges for me to meet the old priest.

Two women are also waiting to see him about a mass they want said. One of the women says to me, "It's just like old times, isn't it? Isn't it good to hear the old mass again?" I smile and nod in agreement.

Soon, I'm called into an even smaller room between the chapel and the church, used, it seems, as some sort of dressing room where the priestly vestments are kept. The old priest, stripped down to his black, unbuttoned cassock, stands next to a table, casts a stony eye upon me, then extends his hand and breaks into a warm smile.

"Now then, tell me. Who are you? And what can I do for you? You're not from the Benedictines, are you? We're expecting someone from the Benedictines today, and someone spotted you in the back of the church, you know, with your long hair and everything, and thought you might be one."

I explain my presence to him briefly, and he invites me back a few days later for a longer talk. "I suppose this is a renegade church," he says, "but we know that what we are doing is right. Sure, you can take photographs. Not during mass. But I'll put on the robes, if you like. Re-enact the mass. We have nothing to hide."

I return a few days later on a rainy, gray morning and am met once again by the young Brother William Rochelle. Not yet a priest, I discover, but expecting to be ordained soon by the old priest. Brother Rochelle, only one year away from ordination in the new church at a Catholic seminary in Ohio, finally dropped out when he could no longer accept the changes going on within the church.

He leaves to inform the old priest of my arrival, and I stand alone in the dark chapel. I remember the funereal overtones to the room . . . I look around and see a bleeding statue of Christ. There is a heavy and ominous feeling about the scene. Something like being in church on an inevitably rainy and gray Good Friday afternoon for the Stations of the Cross.

The entrance of the old priest, though, lifts the darkness considerably. The three of us sit down at a card table and attempt to put the story together. He carries with him a framed, Xeroxed copy of an official document, which, he claims, proves his appointment as Bishop. He has been called a self-proclaimed Bishop, much to his and his congregation's displeasure. He wants it understood that this is not so.

"I am a Bishop," he says. "And here's the proof."

It's an erratic history; even the Bishop is not precisely sure of the dates. And no one, it seems, has bothered to record anything yet as to the history of this movement away form the Vatican Church. It's a question, though, of authority. And the intrigue at times seems almost medieval.

There is the Catholic Traditionalist Movement, some 10 years old, centered in New York, under the leadership of the Rev. Gommar DePauw. A Rev. Henry Lovett, from New Jersey, was part of that movement at first. Lovett was sent to Wheaton to establish a church, but disagreements arose and Lovett started the Church of St. Joseph in Cicero, in 1968.

"I came here officially, at the request of Father Lovett, on December 1, 1970," says Bishop Higgins. "Something happened there [Wheaton] and there was a break between him and Father DePauw. Lovett wanted authority. He didn't have it from Father DePauw. Where was he to get it?

"There was a Chicago Chapter of the Knights of Malta which Father Lovett signed up. The Knights of Malta were an historic Middle Age order organized to arrest the holy areas from the Turks. They had authority and rights, operative only insofar as they were associated with the true Pope.

"These people [the Chicago Chapter] claimed they had the authority which Father Lovett needed to run his church. But then this group, too, became filled with division and quarreling, and again Father Lovett felt he did not have a leader. Father Lovett, by the way, was here until a year ago, when he had the opportunity to start a new parish in New Jersey.

"So they opened this place [in Cicero] under the Knights of Malta, but not to Lovett's satisfaction. He knew he needed a Bishop. They knew that God would send them someone."

Authority is still a central issue; that and whatever personal history this man, Rev. John Higgins, is willing to reveal.

"I've been traveling now for 20 years. I came to Chicago because it was the central headquarters. When Pope John died, I broke with the Church. Father Lovett wanted to see me. . . . They were praying for a leader. I gave them my story. 'I am satisfied that you are the man we are looking for,' said Father Lovett.

"He watched me from February to August, 1969. And in August he came in and asked me to be presented to the people. And he proposed that we move over, lock, stock, and barrel and form the true church. Then the storm broke. The Knights of Malta went their way, and we went ours."

Without the Knights of Malta, though, they once again lacked the authority to build their church. Father Lovett had found the leader he was seeking in Father Higgins. They were both certain that the Vatican Church, under Pope Paul VI, was wrong. They knew many Catholics felt this way too. But where was the authority to come from?

"I'm an Irishman," smiles the old priest, "born in England, a parish in California ... I'm a real gypsy. And I was in Rome, you see, and I had come into possession of the Secret of Fatima which informed me that Clement XV was the True Pope, not Paul VI. But that I had to prove to myself."

The church then, as Father Higgins sees it, and intends to rebuild it, rests upon a strange and little understood premise: That the succession of Popes was broken after Pope John.

This is, allegedly, the Secret Message of Fatima (the Virgin Mary appeared to three children in Fatima, Portugal, in 1917, leaving a message. The secret was to be left with the Pope and not made public until 1960. "There shall be no more conclaves for the election of the Pope" and in the future each Pope would select his successor, which had been Church practice for centuries before).

Pope John, who reportedly knew the Secret of Fatima, had chosen Clement XV as his successor. Nevertheless, a conclave was held after the death of Pope John, and they elected Paul VI as Pope.

Clement XV, however, was "ordered from above" in 1961 to begin functioning as the True Pope. He did just that from Clemery, France, in a community involving bishops, priests, sisters and laymen from other countries.

Father Higgins, who met and prayed with Pope Clement XV on a visit to this country in 1963, now found the authority he needed to return the Church to its Latin rites and true history. Or, as he states, "We are a continuation of the old church ... the one, holy, and apostolic church ..."

And, as Brother Rochelle interjects, "this time we are the Lutherans. Luther thought that he was right. We think we are right. Now the small group differs from the institution."

Bishop Higgins continues with his personal story: "I saw the disintegration of the Church. The state of nuns, dressing like lay people. Priests getting married ... the extraordinary number of priests who are quitting altogether ..."

He recalls a modern mass he witnessed in Rome, and stands up now to illustrate how the Italian priest said, "Confesso, Confesso" as if it meant nothing. "Blasphemy," says the Bishop.

"I was living in Necedah, then Germantown, Wisconsin," continues the Bishop. "I was living in seclusion, on my own money. I was there until Pope Clement XV came in 1963, and he convinced me. I had all the proof I needed that he was the True Pope. Then he went back to France. I visited him over there and grew move convinced.

"He was a monk, where I would be considered a secular priest. He was running a monastery and convent there, and pilgrims came from all over Europe."

Back to Laramie Avenue in Cicero ... why Cicero? The old priest busts out laughing: "God working through human events ... Father Lovett used to say, "The early Christians had the catacombs, and we have a mortuary!"

And who are these people? How large is the flock? "Actually, most of the people don't live in Cicero," he reveals. "They come from all over. Mainly suburban people, people from as far as Crystal Lake, Morton Grove, LaGrange, Joliet. There's a happiness here. That's the thing that gets them in this church. Nearly everyone goes to confession and communion. And there's no social organization whatsoever."

But he is dead serious about membership in his church. He tells the congregation at mass: "Please, if you are here for the first time, please do not take Holy Communion until you have met with us and know who we are. You must be registered with us to receive the sacraments. You must investigate who we are, and you must be convinced that we are the true church."

"They must observe the laws, decorum and dignity," he explains. "The way to kill the faith is to socialize it. If they [the new church] are going to take the priest down to the level of being a football coach and ticket salesman ... it's wrong."

You mean, Father, no Bingo? I smile.

"No Bingo. Ours is strictly a spiritual program."

Dignity is unquestionably the keynote to his church and the old Latin mass. The Bishop is well aware of this and understands that the people respect him for it. "Why the Latin mass? Because that is the law, laid down for safety's sake," he explains. "A contributor for a mass once demanded this of me, 'Do not surrender the Latin!' When you start using living language, then it becomes a threat to substance. Meanings change.'

"You observed the mass here. Don't you agree it was conducted with dignity, propriety, a definite order and form?" I agree.

Nevertheless, he and his whole church seem so vulnerable. What chance does he have against the organization of the Vatican, especially since the recent death of Clement XV?

The Bishop remarks, quite honestly, "Counting adults, children, babies, even the statues, some say, we cannot get over 50 people here ... altogether, about 89 people signed. Maybe 20 families ... You have to go by number of families. In the main, though, what is important is that they are staying, and

their roots are deepening. They are growing. The biggest proof is that we are keeping the place open."

And what of his congregation? It must take courage to reject the new church completely. "They're terribly afraid of the clergy," admits the Bishop. "They've been intimidated with excommunication."

I look at the old priest and can't help but be moved by his sense of history, dedication, faith. Whether Pope Clement was the true Pope or not, whether his successor is eventually announced, whether Brother Rochelle is ever ordained a priest, I can only honor the dignity of this troubled old priest, and the history of a rite he is trying to preserve.

"In June, I'll be 68," he confesses. "I was born in 1907 . . . that should make me 68, shouldn't it?"

And how do you survive in this old funeral parlor? I try to ask him as I prepare to leave.

"Oh, everything is here," he says. "Everything in miniature. We live upstairs, take care of our own laundry . . . We get just enough to pay our bills. It takes $450 a month just to pay the mortgage."

Who does the cooking? I ask. Brother Rochelle meekly raises his hand.

"Don't say cooking," laughs the old priest. "Here, now, before you leave I want you to look at this statement of Clement XV appointing me to found churches in the English speaking world."

And he shows me again the framed, Xeroxed copy of his appointment as Bishop. This is the proof. He wants it known that he has the authority.

So I acknowledge the Bill of Appointment with respect, signed August 8, 1969 by Pope Clement XV with a Papal seal. I assure him that I will do my best to clarify the matter. I shake his hand and leave the dark church on Laramie Avenue in Cicero, mumbling whatever parts of the Latin mass and prayers I can recall from the liturgy of my youth, as some kind of absolution and hope for him, and all of us.

Tennis

Tennis without the net ...

It was not a neighborhood game. Or a street game, an alley game, a vacant lot game, a school game, or a playground game. To play tennis you needed the confines of a "court" (not to mention the possibility of a "racket") and we were not to be confined. Playing tennis was something people with money did, somewhere on the North Side of Chicago. It had that Cadillac, bridge, golf air about it ... short white pants, white tee shirt, white socks and tennis shoes. We wouldn't walk down an alley and be caught in an outfit like that. Tennis, Jesus, that's a sport for those guys who have wings! ... A neighbor gave me my first and only tennis racket, a warped and almost gutless piece of equipment, when I was only about 10 years old. So I stood there in the alley holding this goddam thing like a baseball bat with holes, wondering just what I was supposed to hit.   I think my neighborhood friend John Cibulka came out then, and so I tried it on him. Only he hit back. After another attempt at John's head, there was a succession of objects to be swung at — rocks, cans, bugs and even butterflies.

That's the way it is with neighborhood sports heroes. You give them a strange piece of equipment, and they discover their own games. Soon every kid on the block wanted a racket to ping stones with. And "ping" was exactly the new sound we heard with a racket. It was much more refined, more musical than the "whop" of a bat ... When, weeks later, another broken racket appeared on the scene, we had this brand-new alley game of pinging stones at one another till someone got hit real good ... One thing we all had were gym shoes — later dubbed "tennis shoes" and popularized to the point of Now with the American flag, red, white and blue, and Peter Max. And stars.

But back then they were just ugly old gym shoes, black canvas with a heavy rubber sole and toe, and a little circular patch on the ankle bones. The shoe laces were either broken or else came up to about the top of your head and had to be wound around and around your ankle till the circulation stopped. But no matter what the sport was, pinging stones with a racket or running for your life, with gym shoes you had Power! Power to take flight or stop on a dime. They improved with age. And their peculiar smell ripened through the summer season. Tennis shoes are just for playing tennis in. Or for showing off your colors. Gym shoes were for living in the whole day and a good part of the night and then sitting down on the bed to take them off before going to sleep and dropping them softly to the floor in the sweet sweat of hard play only to be rudely awaked by Mother's gentle reminder, "Put those damn shoes on the back porch before the bedroom smells like a barn!" Christ, all I want is a pair of smelly old gym shoes, a broken racket, and an alley to play in. We had tennis balls, old ones, before we knew just what they were used for or how the game was played. Soft, old tennis balls somehow appeared and multiplied overnight in a bushel basket in the garage, along with torn softballs and league hard balls. But the very airy nature of the tennis ball made it something to suspect or disdain. Tennis balls were for girls and old people to play catch with. Their very bounce was feminine. You throw a tennis ball in the air, and it might float away. And you hit a kid with a tennis ball and it never hurt. No tears or anything. My favorite tennis ball had a soft dent in it where the air used to be. This was the one I used with my broken racket. This is the one that took to the air with such a crazy flight pattern as I continually bounced it up and down in a newly discovered Hi-Li game, without the rubber string. This was the ball that didn't bounce or roll along the ground, but met the pavement in dead earnestness like a ball of mud. Such were the days of tennis in my youth on the West Side of Chicago. Love? You bet we did . . . though we didn't know the score . . . In less than record time I left the alleys of my youth and one sunny Saturday morning I found myself on the red clay tennis courts of Illinois State University, Normal, on the make and matched with Yvonne, a sweet young farm girl from southern Illinois who thought Chicago was Evil and whose real calling in life was making hay. And teaching. Which was why we were both there. And I was learning . . . "Love 15," she called, that prancing angel in white trying to escape the net . . . "I gotch ya," I answered as all the tennis balls in the world seemed to escape my borrowed "professional" racket. "Love 30, love 40 . . . " she trilled as the score seemed to be getting better all the time. Who knew how it would end? . . . "You're supposed to hit the ball over the net, not under it," she sparkled. "Shut up or I'll remove the seat from your Massey Ferguson," I threatened.

    I wore a white tee shirt, Levi's, and white buck shoes with red soles, but that didn't help. It wasn't my kind of game. Besides, I was perspiring. Those farm girls sure know how to make you work . . . Finally, I pinged a stone at her and she took a leap that defied all laws of tennis. White blouse sailing, tight white shorts in tow, sneakers snuggled ... she was game and returned the stone with a haymaker of a ping that saw my feet leave the ground for the first time ... Talk about "Claire's Knee!" You should have seen Yvonne's derriere in those little tennis shorts ... The sun never sets on Victor Gut Strings. ... Wilson T2000. The little wires are a big help to your game ... The Guys Who Took The Davis Cup Doubles Wear Pro-Keds ... How to play tennis and make friends in 14 languages. Pan Am ... Ask for Wick-Dry tennis socks ... The fun to make Pre-Cut Tennis Dress ... Tenni-Pro Automatic tennis machines ... For the only true tennis ... "WRITING FREE VERSE IS LIKE PLAYING TENNIS WITHOUT A NET," Robert Frost was supposed to have said about the free swinging style of that old neighborhood ballplayer, Carl Sandburg. And that's all I ever learned about the game in college, in my young manhood ... Yvonne on the ascent notwithstanding ... Whether one is into it or not, the game nevertheless is still being played out there ... all over Chicago, including the old neighborhood, all over the country, all over the world. It has reached down to the very young and touched the very old as well. There must be something to it. And as the years keep bouncing by, I keep promising myself that one day I will return to the nets. But I still don't have a tennis outfit. Not even a pair of sneakers. And my gutless racket still hangs from a bent nail in my father's garage on the West Side of Chicago. God only knows how promiscuous those old tennis balls have been in that bushel basket through all these years. And no one, in the recorded history of my life has ever said to me, "Hey, Blei, how about a game of tennis?" I'm not sure how I would answer that. Looking upon The Game from a distance, I have only images to behold ... Somehow I always see tennis players in flight, a whirl in white, a ballet of attempts off the ground above the net, arms clutching at space looking for the handle to stay up there to ramain aloft and aloof from all those strictures of courts and nets down below. I remember the tennis game in "Carnal Knowledge." A very real game indeed. And I remember the tennis game at the end of "Blow Up." A very unreal game indeed, but more real in my imagination of what, perhaps, the game is all about ... a kind of pantomime of the human condition, etched in space ... There stands Robert Frost, eyeing the net, clutching his Official Racquet with his traditional New Englander's grip, reading a measured serve. The tips of his toes touch the ground ... Carl Sandburg, about so high above the net and climbing steadily, wafts his guitar at the wind and makes music for the oncoming moon ... Somewhere in the alleys of the old neighborhood, kids are pinging stones with broken rackets ... Somewhere in the prairies of Downstate Illinois Yvonne is still teaching the game ... Somewhere in northern Wisconsin I keep trying to do away with all the nets.

Requiem for a Neighborhood Winemaker

And so in fall when men think mostly about leaves turning gold and the approaching white of winter, he remembers again the warmth of wine and that time of the year that was red.

The winemakers are gone. The presses that have not been chopped up or bound for the inevitable journey to antique shops, remain dry yet solid artifacts in the corners of the basements of his youth. And there is still the scent of red wine about them.

His own heritage was not wine, but beer. And this, to his knowledge, was never brewed in the basements of his neighborhood. But across the street, down the block, near the corner where the Slovenians lived, there in those basements, every fall came the time of the year that was wine.

Ed Tomse was the friend's name. A short, heavy, tough little kid who taught the rest of the neighborhood boys the power of tavern language, something he learned first-hand in the old neighborhood around St. Stephen's church, Wolcott and 22nd place. But this was the new neighborhood. And along with the new language, Ed Tomse brought with him a still stranger language, Slovenian, he called it, which he, his family, and relatives found more comfortable than English and would always hold onto, while Ed would gradually yield to the times. Like the making of wine.

Matt Tomse was the father. The first winemaker he ever met. And Mary Tomse the mother, who, in the European tradition, was everything the husband expected of her yet still mother and woman of the house. So she, too, in a way, was a winemaker.

And that time always began in fall, the middle of October, when the grapes were ready, when they stood in 42- and 36-pound boxes in the market of the

Santa Fe yards on Ashland, and the Slovenians in the neighborhood went down to look them over and buy. Both red (zinfandel) and white (muscatel), he remembers coffee break before sliding the note under his door on which he had scrawled the words, "I don't want to play any more. I quit. Andy."

But the difficulty now about remembering that time of wine is that most of the particulars are so hard to recall now that the winemakers are gone. Yet even then, the particulars meant nothing. What mattered only was that the time of wine was coming. And one Saturday morning in October a truck, which the men had hired at the market, would deliver the grapes. And more than 100 boxes of them would be piled on the sidewalk while the winemakers counted, looked them over, divided them, and began carrying the boxes to their basements.

And there would be no homework now for nights as he ran across the street to the Tomses after supper and watched Matt Tomse in the basement as he began grinding the grapes, for the first wine, into two open barrels of 50 gallons each. Watched, three or four nights later, this white-haired giant of a man turn and turn the press of the second wine while Ed and his mother stood by listening to the winemaker's orders. Matt Tomse scared the hell out of him.

Why, he often wondered, when the old-timers settled in the neighborhoods, why did they always gravitate to the basement to carry on the work of their hands? He still wonders about this now. And he is sure it is more than mere practicality For others on the block it was the place to make sausage, to do tailoring, to cook, to put up preserves, to grow plants, to drink beer and play pinochle. They could never adapt themselves to the upstairs, these old-timers. The upstairs was for eating, sleeping, keeping clean. But it was down below, close to the earth, where they were most alive. And this was what he loved about winemaking in the basement at night.

Lights were on in all the basements of the winemakers at that time of year. And the scent of wine came through the windows and hung in the gangways and along the front walks. A single light bulb burned above the cement washtubs of Tomse's basement. And there was an old clock with a brass pendulum that ticktocked the time in a rather loud but hollow sound.

The winepress stood like some ancient altar in a nearby corner. Close to the back entrance of the basement was still another door, a gray door. (All the basements were painted gray, it seemed.) A magic door of sorts, for when this door was opened one was overpowered by the winey depths of the dark cellar. A light bulb quickly revealed three or four 50-gallon wooden barrels about a foot off the floor. Wooden spigots worn and red from turning. Empty bottles and jugs of all sizes. A treasure house of wine.

He tries again to remember just how it was made. The formulas, the recipes. How many boxes of red zinfandel? How many boxes of white muscatel for 50 gallons of wine? Was it 17 boxes of white and 4 red? Didn't John Kozar say that was the way of winemaking? One of the ways. And how many pounds of sugar for the second wine? Wasn't it 5 or 10 pounds? But the first wine was the best, pure juice. No sugar at all. No chemicals whatsoever like the bigtime winemakers. Just grapes and hands and time. How long did it all take? A week and a half? And when was the wine ready? Thanksgiving. Yes. it was on the table for Thanksgiving. But it wasn't clear, really clear, until Christmas.

So much of this is lost. But most of it no longer matters. Part of what remains of those winemaking nights in the basement is the remembrance of dried cakes of crushed grapes from the second wine. Of upright barrels and the feverish sound and sight and smell of wine fermenting. Of mixing the stuff that rose to the top those first few days. Of waiting. Of seeing Uncle John stop by from next door to joke with the Tomses and compare the wine. Of finally attempting a first taste of the wine, only a taste at this time for it was still very cloudy—and very dangerous for the insides of any man.

Mogen David was all he had ever tasted before. There was beer on his table every Sunday with the traditional Bohemian dish of roast pork, dumplings, and sauerkraut. But on holidays, sometimes, a bottle of Mogen David sat on the table, and what he tasted then was sweeter and warmer than any grape soda—and maybe better than beer. He always wanted more.

And so he was not quite prepared for that first taste of Tomse's homemade wine. It turned his mouth inside out, bent his ears, and burned his eyes.

"Drink, Norbul. You like?" said Matt Tomse with a grin. (And they would always call him that name, all of the old Slovenians on the block. They would never learn to pronounce his first name.)

"Yes, it's good," he lied. "No, that's enough." And Matt Tomse would laugh out loud.

And after the wine was ready that first year, and then many years to follow, and always around Christmas, there would be a bottle for him to take home to his parents.

"Mr. Tomse gave us some wine." And it was gladly accepted but never seen or tasted by him again.

Many seasons of wine passed in that neighborhood. And he did not witness the winemaking in all of them. Things on the outside and away from the neighborhood gradually took precedence over the old-timers who had nothing better to do each fall than bury themselves in the basement with their winepresses.

But there were still times of red wine he could not forget. There was a time one Halloween when he and Ed Tomse and a few of the others on the block broke a window accidentally and were brought home, to Ed Tomse's home of all places, by the police. The other kids scattered. We were all free to go. But he and Ed Tomse stood on the sidewalk under the streetlight and waited for Matt Tomse. He was already at the door. He was the door. Ed walked up with careful steps and tearfully told what happened as the squad car turned around the corner and was gone.

All Matt Tomse hollered was, "Come in house! You too, Norbul." And we followed him into the kitchen and sat down at the table and watched Matt Tomse smile and pour the wine. "Is all right. Drink." And it was good.

And there was a time, years later, the very last time he can remember Matt Tomse. Ed was now in the army and gone from home a long, long time. And Matt, for as big and fearsome a man as he was (a meatpacker who would often tell of the bad times and how he would walk to the stockyards to save carfare), could often be seen alone outside the house watering the lawn and talking about Ed, his only son, who would be coming home soon. And talking always in beautifully broken language and watery eyes. Ed would never realize how much the old man missed him. And all the while Matt Tomse made the wine and waited.

"Norbul," Matt Tomse said to him one day across the backyard fence, "Eddie come home next week. You come see him."

And he did. But he no longer had to cross the street to see his friend. For he was married now and lived next door. Lived, in fact, in Ed's uncle's house— Uncle John Zbasnik, another winemaker. And the night came when he went next door to see Ed after so long a time.

Matt and Mary Tomse met him at the door. Ed was at the kitchen table eating. The same old Ed. They said the usual inane things that friends usually say. And then Matt brought out the wine. Two decanters of it, if decanter is the proper word. Two bottles that looked like decanters. Probably two old Mogen David bottles. And Matt poured the wine in clumsy drinking glasses that never matched. And the taste was the same and got better through the night as he learned now to live with their wine.

"Vell, Norbul, my Eddie's home now. No more army."

"Good wine, Pa," was all Ed said.

"Vy sure, good! Me make, no?" and a hearty, raw laugh.

Matt died sometime after that. And neither Ed nor his mother bothered to make wine again. The press was chopped up in the basement.

But Uncle John Zbasnik kept the faith. It was up to Uncle John now and his son-in-law across the street, John Kozar, cousin John, to put the barrels in the gangway to dry each summer, to go to the markets to buy the grapes, to make the wine in their basements, to distribute it to friends and relatives, to drink and keep what was left in the family.

He was not part of that family of Tomse, Zbasnik, and Kozar. There were so many times he wished he were. And although they were convinced at times that similarities did exist between their old language and his own, he would never be able to decipher a word of their laughter or sadness at weddings or funerals. There was the wine, though, that bound them. And living close to it now in the back of Uncle John's first-floor apartment.

Living with his wife over a small section of the basement where the empty wine barrels were stored. Their bedroom, in fact, right above that scent of wine. He recalls visitors for the first time always remarking as they came up the back stairs, "What's that smell? You live in a brewery or something?"

"No," he smiled, "a wine cellar. You find me a better place to live."

Each fall he thinks back to that time of wine, what better place in the world to live than that 2½-room apartment with hot and cold running wine? And what better landlord than Uncle John, who never raised the rent, but lowered it at least twice?

Uncle John, the winemaker, not as big as Matt Tomse. Not as outwardly tough. But a short, sometimes heavyset man, who kept his hair cut close to the scalp and found laughter and good times in almost every man as he ceaselessly walked around his house never really finding anything more important to do than joke with Ed about who was getting fatter or whose hair was thinner.

We could always hear him out there. He always gave himself away with a loud "Ya," instead of yes. For Uncle John Zbasnik never could say yes, only "Ya" followed by laughter, and this was so much better than yes.

"Ya Norbul, make vine next week. You come vatch."

But Norbul never did see Uncle John make wine. The time was wrong or something. The neighborhood, the apartment, none of this was quite home anymore. There were too many things going on in downtown Chicago or the near northside. There were too many books to read, movies to see, friends to visit. So he left the old man to do his own winemaking.

Yet Uncle John and his gentle wife, Rose, never forgot him — Norbul and his wife — in the back apartment. There was always a bottle of wine behind the door.

And there was always Uncle John outside on the sidewalk in his undershirt, maybe sprinkling the lawn, but really waiting to talk to someone.

And often it was Norbul coming home from work in the late afternoon.

"You vorm enough in apartment, Norbul? You vant more heat?"

"No, John, fine. It's nice and warm."

"Ya, is good apartment. You got minute, Norbul?"

"Sure."

"Come." And we would go down in the basement through the back entrance and walk all the way to the front to a small cellar under the steps where John kept the new wine.

"Is good vine this year, ya?"

"Is good, John. Is very good. The best I've ever tasted."

Nobody knows how often he and Uncle John went down in that basement to sample the wine. Nobody knows how often Uncle John said, "Is good vine this year, ya?" Nobody knows how often on Sunday afternoons old men with brown paper bags went down in the basement to see Uncle John. Nobody knows for certain whether or not Uncle John found the secret of a Slovenian brand of white lightning. Nobody knows just how often he was in the basement with Uncle John and came up late for supper, slightly flushed, searching for the back stairs to the small apartment. And even now he can remember nothing more than the taste of wine.

And the time came when he, no longer living in the neighborhood, went to the wake for Uncle John and said the usual meaningless things that could never express the regret over a man dying, a simple man who loved life and people and wine. And he looked around him at the Zbasniks and the Tomses and the Kozars who were still left, and he realized that except for John Kozar, the time of the winemakers was gone. And when the talk, even at a wake, turned to wine, he asked John, "Did you make wine this year?" And John Kozar, with the most infectious laugh of all the Slovenians, only smiled a little, his thin mustache the last vestige of the old country. "No," he said, "I don't think I'll make anymore. There's nobody left to drink it."

There are books now about the art of winemaking. And one can imagine, in our time, how fashionable this could all become. But there are no books about these neighborhood men who made and loved and drank the wine. And they have taken all the art, all the recipes, all the life of that time with them.

The Butcher Shop

The Polacek Brothers are right out of Chicago's past. They own a Bohemian butcher shop on Cermak road in Cicero. A butcher shop with real butchers in bloody aprons. A butcher shop with smells of fresh meat and sausage. A butcher shop of signs:

TRY OUR HOMEMADE
LIVER DUMPLINGS:
FRESH MADE EVERY TUESDAY
AND FRIDAY, PRAZSKY
FRESH MADE KLOBASY

and in the window:

FRESH DOMACI
(homemade) FRANKFORTS
THEY'RE REALLY GOOD
FREE SAMPLE EVERY MONDAY
10:30 A.M. to 1:30 P.M.

A butcher shop with sounds of real butchering—the singing of the long hand saw working away through meat and bone; the slippery slap of fresh liver hitting the scale; the cleaver whacking through bone; the cleaver flattening tenderloin on a block, worn with time into woody waves—slap! slap! slap!

There is a primitive poetry about butcher shops. Something in blood and bone, meat and butchering that speaks to an ancient nature in all men.

Bill and Otto Polacek (twin brothers) have been butchering some 32 years. They came to it because of the depression—"There was nothing else to be had," says Otto. Then, with a smile, "I use to go with a butcher's daughter."

They are at their work each morning hours before opening. They come through the back door, hang their coats and hats in a closet, put on their fresh white aprons and prepare for another day. Otto heading for the front door, walking outside in the 7 a.m. quiet of Cermak Road, and slowly cranking down the awning. "That's the first thing I do every day, put down the awning. Later in the afternoon when the sun's out of the way, I roll it up again. You got to keep the sun away from the pickles and sausage."

Inside, Bill hangs brown shopping bags in the front window, "so the people walking by won't think we're open," and then moves to the small room at the back of the store and prepares a huge pot of coffee. Otto returns with fresh rolls from the bakery next door. They sit together at an enamel table in the back room and talk about meat.

Today is Thursday—market day for the Polacek butchers. Together they prepare their order for the busy weekend. In a few hours, Otto will pull out the small van from the garage and head for Fulton street to do his own selecting and buying of meats. Bill, and three other butchers, will open the shop.

Twin brothers, these Polacek butchers, at times difficult to tell apart. The customers often confuse one for the other. Bill taking an order and disappearing into the cooler. Otto suddenly appearing. The customer continuing a conversation with Otto that Bill began a few minutes before.

Their old shop was on 31st near Crawford (a predominantly Czech area now called "the little village"). Eight years ago they moved to Cermak Road, "because of the opportunity to get on a main street and a little bigger market."

Years ago there were butcher shops, bakeries, and milk stores on all the blocks in all the neighborhoods. And then the neighborhood stores, family owned with an apartment in the rear, slowly gave way to the chain stores. In time the old stores themselves were "remodeled"—bricked up, new picture windows and glass blocks added, and the entire inside of the shop turned into modern living quarters.

"But the old-timers still go to the small stores . . . when they can find them. We have Bohemians, Italians, Croatians, Polish, Germans, even some Irish. We speak everything. All the butchers speak Bohemian. We try Polish, even a little Italian.

"We have people here from outside the neighborhood, from all over. From Lombard, Evanston, Milwaukee, Palatine, Deerfield. Even when our own people move away, they still come back. They keep in touch."

Distance does not separate men from a tradition, a heritage of meat remembered. Bill removes some "orders" from a spindle:

Tulsa, Okla.

Dear Otto and Bill,

Please send me four 2 lb. prazsky if you have them, if you have them now send them instead of waiting for the real fresh ones. I am late in asking and afraid to wait for those on Tuesday.

And an old man writing from Milwaukee:

"... please enter the following order viz
15 links of jaternice
15 jelata
We have been experiencing some trouble getting a fresh weiner."

And a letter from as far as Albuquerque, N.M.

Dear Mr. Polacek,

My good friend George Duda, informed me that you're good people and since I'm an old Bohak formerly from Chicago I'm hoping you would be so kind to do the same for my wife and me.
The sausage they pass on to unfortunates here is disgustingly poor. The sausage I appreciate if you would send me are:
2 lbs. of debrecinky
1 each prazsky
1 each hard summer sausage
Yes it will be a joy to feast on some of those longed for Bohemian delicacies. You would make a fortune out here if you could get an outlet to sell some of your specialties.

Sincerely,
Jerry F. Dusek

A neighborhood butcher knows the traditions of its people. With the Bohemians it is *jaternice* (Bohemian sausage—"jets" Otto calls them, or "Bohemian bananas"). The butchers begin making *jaternice* each fall on St. James' day and continue through the winter 'til St. Patricks's. Tripe soup (tripe, the inside of a cow's stomach) is also seasonal. A good winter soup (which they now freeze for summer consumption as well), prepared by Otto's wife and mother-in-law. Homemade. So many of the specialties, the food of time-past, marked with the Polacek (and Czech) taste: *prazsky* sausage, *buchta* (veal loaf), *debrecinky* (small, seasoned sausage), *cerbulaty* (fat, garlic sausage), *sulc* (pieces of tongue and snouts suspended in jelly with vinegar), cream sausage, liver sausage, hot dogs, paprika bacon, and liver dumplings.

Neighborhood butchers do not forget the young. Traditions must be passed down to them. "We always give the kids something to eat, hot dogs or a piece of buchta. Sometimes they even bring their friends. Hot dogs they like, especially on Mondays when we make them. That's the best way to taste them."

8:30 a.m. The shop will be opening soon. Otto has been working on his order list for the markets. He stops at times to question his brother about the amount of meat to be ordered. Bill begins spreading sawdust behind the counter, uncovering meat in the counter, filling the egg basket, taking down the shopping bags in the front window, hanging up *prazsky* in their place.

Shortly before 9 the three other butchers arrive at the front door: Little Jerry Kostrunek, who sings to the customers in Bohemian; quiet Frankie Janouch, who prefers to work in the basement making sausage; and big Jim Tolar, who is all smiles, always. During the busy part of the week, Bob Kucera, former owner and now retired part-time butcher, will come in to give the boys a hand.

Quietly they put on their aprons and scatter quickly throughout the shop— the cooler, the back room, the freezer, the basement, the store itself. There is always work to be done. There are no chairs in butcher shops.

At 9 o'clock when Bill opens the front door, Otto is on his way to the markets. A cigar in his mouth, a long white butcher coat spread across his shoulders, he heads down Congress for Fulton street, talking of many things—the butcher shop a part of everything he knows and does.

Like skinning a calf. "Nobody skins his own calves anymore." But if you look in the cooler of the Polacek butcher shop, there in the corner hangs a black and white calf that the butchers have been cutting into all week. "It's better that way. It's fresher. We go through three calves a week."

So much of a past in a butcher shop. So much of a people with an old, old taste for the primitive, the natural, the good.

"We used to get a lot of calls for cow bags (udders), but now the government's clamped down on them. You'd cook them maybe four or five hours. Then you'd slice them and bread them. They're good.

"Suckling pig we get calls for sometime. But you can't get them real small ones anymore, 10 or 15 pounds. They're hard to get. Snout, pig tails, ears, we have plenty of. Boil them, then eat 'em with horse radish. They're good that way. Tripe we always got. Honey comb tripe and the regular kind. Offal, they call it. Very healthy stuff. Once in a while we get odd requests from kids in school. Hearts or maybe some eyes. So I'll pick some up at the market. You won't find that in the chains.

"But a lot of this stuff is hard to get. The government's always clamping down on something. A lot of these things the old-timers used to like. Most

"Say," Otto asks the poultry man, "how's the duck blood?"

"Ah, they're crazy. I hear they're still bootlegging it across the state lines, but they're crazy what they're asking for it."

"How much?"

"Eight dollars a gallon."

"Eight dollars a gallon? It's cheaper to drink wine."

In the early afternoon, Otto returns to the butcher shop. The truck is loaded down with over 1,500 pounds of meat. All the meat necessary for a busy weekend. And Otto has hand-picked it for his people.

"It's the people that keep you going. You need that contact. Everyone that comes in, you know something different about. You know maybe something personal about them. Maybe she's been married a couple of times so you kid her about that. Or maybe her mother's sick so we ask, 'How's your mother?' Then there's the young girls. We like to kid them, too. Most of the people, I think they really enjoy coming to the butcher shop." Especially on Saturdays.

Saturday morning, 8:45, a middle-aged woman stands alone outside the door of Polacek's Market. She leans against the glass window, sometimes peeks between the shopping bags that hang from the inside, trying to get a glimpse of the butchers. She can hear them in there. (What do butchers really do behind shaded doors and windows?")

Now the sun angles down the center parkway of Cermak Road. The awning of the butcher shop awaits the morning light. Now the traffic increases, and the parking places begin to fill. Saturday morning on Cermak. Sidewalks will soon be awake with men and women, little children and very old people; shopping bags—paper, leather, plastic—swinging in stride with the shopper; carts with thumping rubber wheels pulled along from store to store, bikes with baskets, and old wagons—some wooden, some red.

A few minutes before 9 o'clock, eight people (the early shoppers) stand outside the butcher shop. They watch Cermak come alive. They wait.

Bill begins removing the shopping bags from the inside window, waves to the people waiting at the door, flips up the shade, turns the lock, and opens the door to Saturday morning. And all the poetry begins:

"Good morning!"

"Good morning!"

"Nazdar!" (Hello.)

"Nazdar"

The butchers—Bill, Jim, Frankie—are lined up in white aprons behind the counter, smiling, waving, talking to the customers (beginning with weather or health), taking their numbers, listening carefully to orders—their heads cocked slightly to the side.

"Two pork shanks."

"How much is rump?"

"A dollar-twenty-five."

"Ten pork chops and two sirloins."

The noise, the sounds in a butcher shop begin almost instantly and continue 'til closing time. Jim is already at work with the hand saw. Frankie is at the meat grinder. Bill is slicing sausage with a silent hum. Jerry is speaking Czech. Otto is moving some pans around in the back.

The people keep coming. One man takes a number, checks to see how long it will be before he's waited on, then moves off to the bakery next door. He will return, perhaps in time. The late shoppers now form a second rank behind the early shoppers. And all of them, always gathering around the "V" opening where the two meat counters suddenly converge at the busiest and most visible butcher block in the shop. It is here where the meat can be closely examined, where the butcher can be seen more openly, can be whispered to, can be advised as to how big a slice to make, how much fat to trim. It is here, and only here, where the people possess the butcher, and there is no high counter to protect him. Here at the center block is your man. And he will listen.

"Jim, do you think that's enough pork for six people?" a woman asks. "My son's bringing his girl for Sunday dinner."

"Sure, this should be enough."

"Well, if not, they can fill up on dumplings."

The women, always with black leather handbags hanging from their wrists.

The meat cleaver chopping into the block with a thump! thump! thump!

Enamel trays of *jeleta* (black) and white *jaternice* in the window. An old man, eyesight fading, slowly bending his head closer and closer to read the weight of the hanging sausage. Chickens, brown and crisp from the rotisserie, piled high on the window counter. Hot *buchta*, like tiny, fat loaves of bread, are lined up in the window. Jim offers a slice to a customer.

"Good?"

"Mmm, delicious."

The radio is playing. Always there is music in this butcher shop. The old Bohemian music, when it can be found on the dial. A polka, a sad song. Otherwise, any old music will do. Jerry whistles along. Perhaps soon he will be singing.

An Italian man walks in—a Saturday morning regular. A man perhaps a bit out of place in a Bohemian butcher shop, but not really. For this is a Bohemian butcher shop of homemade Italian sausage as well. A shop that moves with the changing neighborhood, yet retains the recipes of all the people.

"Good morning," says the Italian man.

"*Come stai*," the butchers chorus He surveys the crowd, checks the numbers, takes one, waves to the butchers, "Good-by," he smiles, and walks back out with a high number. It is 9:15 and there are 12 people ahead of him.

The men usually stand around the outer fringes and quietly wait. The women crowd closer to the counters, study the meat, watch the butchers' hands, study the scale, and jockey constantly for that "V" opening.

Sounds. Butcher paper. Meat being crisply wrapped, tossed over, bound with brown tape or coarse twine. The butcher lifting, passing the thick, bulky packages to open hands on the other side of the counter. "Thank you, Bill," "Number 56?"

Sounds. Jerry, in the little brown glasses, counting *jaternice* in Czech— "*Jeden, dva, tri, ctyri, pet ...* " (one, two, three, four, five).

The Italian man walks in again, hands in pocket, hat set back smartly on his head, and continues to move among the people like an official greeter. He must still wait for his number, so again he departs for the outside, stands on the sidewalk, smiles to the people passing, and keeps a steady eye on his number through the front window.

Inside, the sound of people talking.

"If you don't have enough, and you have to leave it on the plate, it'll stay there," says Jim to a customer.

"And I want some hot dogs."

"*Tri dolary, tricet osm*," says Jerry.

"Number 59," Bill hollers. "Ah, Sylvia!"

"Lucky me," she replies.

Jerry, near the front window, commenting on an old woman moving slowly down the sidewalk. "She must be at least 80. She walks down here all the time."

"My, my."

"She goes for her *hlasatel*, and then she goes back. Every morning she goes to the 6 o'clock mass. The fellas see her sometimes and stop to give her a lift, but she says, 'No, I'd rather walk.'"

"Eighty years old?"

"Eighty."

"My, my."

And still more talk:

"Give me a small piece of tripe."

"One leg and one breast."

Bill, to a woman customer: "Your sister says hello. I just talked to her on the phone."

"No kisses this time?"

"No, darn it." Laughter, all the butchers joining in. Butchers and customers continually switching from Bohemian to English, and then back again. Bill conversing with two different customers and one other butcher at the same time. A kind of gymnastics in language and talk.

The Italian man, hands up to his forehead, peers through the window.

"Good morning, Mrs. Kriska," Bill says to a woman in a paisley babushka.

"Let's see. I got to find my list first."

"You mean you took a day off today to see the butcher?"

"Yes, I'm lonesome for those butchers ... let's see ... four pounds of round steak."

"So you took the day off?"

"Ah, they have no work."

"Now you can do your house cleaning."

"That's too hard a work."

Otto hears Mrs. Kriska's voice as he works in the back room. He jumps into the conversation for a moment: "Hello, Mrs. Kriska. Good to see you. Jerry, sing for Mrs. Kriska."

The radio is playing. It is booming, "My Wild Irish Rose." Not a Bohemian song by any means, but the melody is there, so Jerry sings along ... the saw sings, the cash register rings and keeps time, the big door to the cooler clicks open and shut in a steady rhythm.

" ... six, seven, eight, and one is 10."

The butchers, ever on the move: standing, always standing; bending down to remove meat from the counters; reaching to grab a sausage from the hook; working, working the body over the block with heavy thrusts of the arm. Dropping meat on the scale ... everything eventually hitting the scale. The head of the butcher forever craning up, studying the moving numbers—converting pounds to prices instantly. Removing pencils from behind their ears; adding it all up on the butcher paper.

"And some of your homemade liver sausage" ... the meat orders always starting with the big stuff first—the steaks, the chops, the roasts—and always ending with the small stuff, the sliced sausage, the cheese " ... and a quarter of a pound of beer sausage."

"Number 64?"

"Me, me ... here," shouts the Italian man.

"What do you know, *pisan*?" All the butchers converge upon him, for he is one of their favorites, "Same-a-thing?"

"Same-a-thing," he smiles. "Same-a-thing" is rib-eye roast, a whole one. A regular Saturday order of his.

"And five chicken legs," says the Italian's wife, who now joins him and takes on his burden of the language. The air now is electric with English, Bohemian, and Italian.

Jim holds up a steak before their eyes. It hangs like a painting. "Nice?" he asks.

"Nice," answers the Italian, who then turns to an old woman behind him. She has been waiting a long time. "Sixty-seven!" he smiles and pats her on the back, "Pretty soon, lady. Pretty soon."

Jim continues with the order, carefully selecting a dozen eggs from a wire basket, gently holding each egg. Showing it to the wife of the Italian for her approval. Heads nod. A package is finally wrapped, a bill is handed over the counter.

The Italian moves to the cashier. "Easy money," he says. "Bye! Good day!" he shouts to the butchers as he and his wife depart.

"So long, *pisan*. Same-a-thing next week?"

"Same-a-thing."

The butchers begin taking their lunch breaks at noon. One at a time they slowly drift to the back of the store, sit at the small enamel table and eat sandwiches, hot dogs, or jiffy steaks. There is always plenty to eat. A man does not go hungry in a butcher shop.

The customers will continue to come all afternoon, not as steady as morning, but picking up again in the hours near closing. Around 5:30 p.m. the butchers begin to clean up shop. Each man knowing somehow what he and everyone else must do. Jerry begins scrubbing the blocks while Frankie washes platters. There are utensils to be cleaned, machines to be washed. Bill begins sweeping the floor. Otto prepares tripe for tomorrow's soup.

A few minutes before 6, the last customer walks in. The store is empty but for this middle-aged woman. A maidenly type, on her way home from work in the Loop. A woman most likely alone in the world.

"Is it too late to grind some round steak?" she asks.

"Yes, I'm sorry," says Bill. "The grinder's all clean. How about a jiffy steak?"

"I have an ulcer. Do you think the meat would be all right for my ulcer."

"Sure. It's all good beef. There's no fat in it. No seasoning."

"Well then, I'll take one."

Bill wraps up the one steak, collects from her and goes around the counter to see her to the door. "Good night."

"Good night."

He pulls down the shade and locks the door.

Jerry, Jim, and Frankie have already left.

In a few more minutes Otto and Bill will turn off the store lights, hang up their aprons, close the back door, and head for home in the truck. They will be back at 5 a.m. on Monday to make fresh hot dogs.

But for now the butcher shop is closed. Monday it will again speak for itself. The signs advertising homemade sausage and soup and dumplings disappear in the darkness. All the real poetry is silent—including the poem that hangs above the cash register:

The talent of success
  is nothing more
Than doing what you can do
Without a thought of fame.
If it comes at all, it will come
Because it is deserved,
Not because it is sought after.

—Longfellow

Doc Cermak

Doc Cermak ... family doctor, G.P. from the old neighborhood, Bohemian. In his office in Cicero, I look at the people waiting ... the old couple holding hands, he with a cane, she wearing a pair of felt *backory* (house slippers) like my grandma always wore. They whisper to each other in Bohemian, and over and over again I hear the name "Cermak" pronounced in heavy Slavic accents.

Many times I have walked up and down Cermak Road in Cicero and Berwyn and heard the name Dr. Cermak, uttered in English and Czech by passers-by, clusters of old people on corners. I have heard his name in the strangest conversations in restaurants, bakeries and even bars.

A young couple enter the waiting room somewhat self-consiously. The husband is wearing long sideburns. She is obviously pregnant. The old couple are watching them. Everybody is watching them. She shows him a picture of a baby in *Parents* magazine and smiles and whispers. They don't understand what the hell's happening, and they're too scared to think about it. Dr. Miles Cermak will relax them, tell him a new father joke, for he has been at this business a long time, 24 years, and delivered upwards of 1,500 babies.

I remember Cermak telling my wife about the young mother who called him at 2 a.m. to tell him that her baby was crying. "Did you give her the 2 a.m. feeding?" he asked. "No," she said. "Then why don't you try feeding the kid," he advised. According to my Aunt Mil, Doc also has some good advice about naming a kid. "Call it Joe or Pete or John or Mary so the grandmas can say it. Nothing classy."

Don't call him if he's not your family doctor. "I've been discouraging new patients for at least 10 years. It sound cruel and harsh, but if you look at the appointment book, you'll see that three weeks from tonight my last appointment is 10:15 p.m. I sometimes go till midnight. That's ridiculous. I can hardly keep up with my own people."

Don't call him unless he doctored your grandmother and grandfather, your mother and father, your brothers and sisters, aunts and uncles, nieces and nephews and cousins. Your wife. Your children. For Doc Cermak is a family doctor, and they're not making his kind anymore.

He doctored and comforted my maternal grandmother from the old country, a beautiful and strong peasant-like woman who had no earthly use for doctors or help of any kind. But she trusted him because he joked with her in Bohemian.

It was my mother who first found Doc Cermak. She opened the door for my grandparents, her sisters and brothers, the children, the whole family called Papp. To this day, Doc Cermak must be visited by some member of the Papp family at least once a week. Either my mother's there to have her weight checked and con him out of some sample diet pills, or one of my aunts is waiting in the office to talk to him (about almost anything), or one of my cousins needs a checkup.

He got me through adolescence, over the hump of young manhood, signed papers for physicals, gave me shots for trips to Mexico and Europe, handled my blood tests for marriage (took on a new patient), and initiated me into the first pangs of fatherhood—an agonizing 11 hours in the father's waiting room. I recall sitting there numb when he finally sauntered in with a nurse behind him who carried a small bundle. "It's a boy," he happily announced and shook my hand. Three years later he would greet me under the same circumstances and say, "I got you a little girl this time. Now grandma will be happy. Tell her she owes me a bottle."

The small waiting room, which he shares with a foot doctor, is Physician's Office Modern. There isn't even a window to look out at the brick wall next door. Artificial light. Green walls. Two doors. Three brown Naugahyde sofas, one orange chair, a standard potted plastic plant and a table full of old magazines.

People continue to come in, quietly take a seat, and begin staring at the walls. In a few minutes, they get up, find a magazine with a particularly bright torn cover, and begin rifling through the pages, pretending to read. The endless waiting of the waiting room. An old man coughs. A woman blows her nose. A mother and daughter quietly whisper to one another. Somewhere behind the door, the faint sound of the doctor's voice.

A man hurriedly enters, raps on the tiny glass window overlooking the receptionist's desk, and exclaims, "I want to see the doctor."

"So do I," she yells back. "Sit down." And everybody in the waiting room laughs, including the man. Only Doc Cermak would find a receptionist like that. She's his kind of people.

"So what's the matter with you, today?" she asks a patient who has just walked out of the doctor's office. "Ask the doctor. He won't tell me," the patient replies. "They you'll live, you'll live," she says tartly.

The door to Cermak's office is open just a crack. The receptionist escorts the patient to one of the cubicles, then returns to her desk as the doctor can be heard escorting another patient out.

"No charge for this," I hear him say to the receptionist. I have heard him say, "No charge this time" or "This one's on me" or "I'll get you next time." What prompts him to let any office visit go by for free in an age when some doctors charge for even a phone conversation?

I begin the interview with journalistic-type questions . . . and receive all the journalistic-type answers I deserve.

When did you graduate from medical school?

"I graduated in June, 1940, and went into industrial medicine in 1941. I went into the service in March of 1943 and spent three years and a day there. I opened here in April of '46, my first and only practice. And I'm the last guy to open in this area."

Why?

"Young fellows are not going into general practice. It's either group practice for them or exotic suburbia. They set up clinics. It's a better all-around deal for them, they think. But they have trouble collecting their bills."

I would like to say: "Doc, relax. Forget this damn interview. Let's go across the street and have a drink." Instead I just let him talk.

"The neighborhood has changed," he says. "Not so many old Slavs, Bohemians, Polish. It's a second generation of foreign people. And lots of the young kids have moved out. Yet quite a few still come back to me. Well, hell, we sort of grew up together. They have trouble in these new suburbias finding doctors. They come back here complaining, 'That guy's no good,' or they're unhappy because a new doctor told them, 'Sorry, I'm all filled up.' I've had a girl come here all the way from Fox Lake to have a baby.

"The young doctors and the guys who came out 25 years ago like me, we're probably not the same type. Sure times change. The old family doctor, house calls . . . if you did three of these a day, that would be it. You can't do it today . . . I can't do it anymore. Jesus, I would just love to sit and chat with my patients, maybe just philosophizing for hours. It's not that I wouldn't like to do it. I made a two-week study 10 years ago and found out I was spending about 11 minutes per patient. Now I do 24 charts in four hours. Overall, 10 minutes per patient. About 30 patients in a five-hour session. And that's seven sessions a week."

The Doc's office, a cubicle at the far end of the hall, is extremely small. He has a desk, a couple of chairs and a table or two. Some big fish are mounted on the walls (trophies he loves to tell about). It looks like a comfortable den a man would like to be able to spend more time in.

"I don't know, the general practitioners, I guess maybe give more personal service. Maybe that's why some people still like us. To me, how long does it take to give that shot? What's a few extra seconds, a couple minutes to chat with your patient? And money isn't the ultimate. It's a by-product.

"Patients. I sort of prefer the old-timers. I've always liked them. We sort of grew old together. Of course, the young ones you don't see very much. There's not that much illness among the young ones. Same with the kids. I'll deliver them. I'll see them when they're 12 or 14, then won't see them till their marriage exam.

"I know the language well. Czech was spoken at home. When I started practicing here, it gave me a hell of a lot of satisfaction, talking with the old folks. And they have no respect for my diet, these people. Our common topic of discussion is food. A woman came in here the other day with a great big pot of *svickova* (pickled beef). But this is what you get when you're more at the personal level with people.

"I still do some house calls. A lot of people think I'm goofy. I'll take a Wednesday afternoon when it's my time off and visit a few old-timers who can't get to the office. But at least I feel I've done some good in the world and can sit down and enjoy my scotch and soda. You won't find many people who think I'm in this for the money.

"I could take my books and throw them away, and it wouldn't hurt me. These are good people. You know how grandma would always say, 'Pay the doctor.' That was always the first thing on her mind. The old-timers always pay the bill. It's the young people who have problems with charge accounts.

"Hospital costs go up more than the doctor. The doctor's bill is only a small piece of the pie. I charged $2 for an office visit when I first started."

I laughed to myself then and thought about my mother, who still tries to palm off only two bucks for an office call every week, quickly handing it to the receptionist and disappearing from the office while Cermak stands in the background mumbling about the Bohemians.

"We're the only profession in the world that's trying hard to eliminate itself. We're practicing more and more preventive medicine. The pill? Hell, any drug has certain drawbacks. I think it's unfortunate. But why take a single drug and write about the scary side reactions when you could write the same thing about penicillin? Penicillin probably has a higher death ratio than any contraceptive pill. Personally, I've been prescribing the pill now for 10 years, and I'd be hard put to name many gals who have had any serious side effects.

"As for the future, I think we'll see more and more improvements in techniques, improvements in types of drugs. Hardly any of the drugs I use today were mentioned when I was in school. Over half of today's drugs weren't even on the market 30 years ago.

"Tranquilizers? I think our whole society is living under more tension. And we've gotten sort of soft to use them. Hell, years ago we'd try to work things out with some friends over a bottle of beer. But we're more doctor-oriented now.

"There are going to be more self-care units. Everybody's going to have some kind of hospital insurance. And there will be more cures for a good number of types of cancer, saving perhaps twice of what we're saving now.

"But I'll tell you, I'm scared," he says as he points to the piles of medical magazines and journals surrounding him. "So much knowledge coming out, it just scares the hell out of me. I certainly can't begin to think that I know all of modern medicine that I'd like to know. With medicine as it is today, I can't keep up with all the latest techniques in surgery. This one stack of magazines alone represents only four days of mail. I can't begin to read this stuff.

"We talk shop at the hospital all the time: 'Say, Joe, did you try this new drug?' We just cannot find the time to keep up with it."

What about losing a patient? How does he feel about making a diagnosis of death?

"It depends on how old they are," he says. "You take a kid who suddenly develops a brain tumor ... well, it doesn't tear me apart that much. You can't practice if it does. What bothers me the most, though, is a young kid, say 8 or 10, who loses a parent. I think it's a horrible blow to kids. I hate to see a child lose a parent."

How does he handle people in the face of tragedy?

"This is where family practice comes in. You know the family, you have an understanding, a feeling for the various members, so you tailor it to the individual. If they're religious ... God wanted it. If they're not ... something scientific.

"As for telling a patient he's going to die ... I think a patient, to some extent, appreciates the truth. But I had a patient who once told me, 'Cut out the crap, Doc, and show me the charts.' And I did, and that was it. Then a few days later he said to me: 'You know, Doc, I thought I was pretty strong. I thought I could take it.'

"So I really don't believe you should say it. I think the average patient has some kind of hope. I have some kind of hope, I know that. No, you don't want to have that old death certificate hanging out of your pocket."

How long does he intend to practice?

"Forever, I guess. If, say, at 60, I feel good enough to still practice, then I'll practice for maybe the fun of practice rather than the view of making any money at it."

And that's pretty much the real story of Dr. Cermak. In our family he's kind of a folk legend. We tell Doc Cermak stories all the time. Even my father, who has been to see the Doc only once in his life to my knowledge, enjoys hearing and telling stories about Cermak and his various bouts with the Papp family.

About how Cermak likes making house call to one of my aunts because she always has the kitchen table all set for him to sit down and polish off some homemade Czech bakery goods.

About the time Cermak sent Uncle Charlie to the hospital with his bad leg, and how he entertained everybody on the floor, including Cermak. Cemak and Uncle Charlie . . . what a combination of comedians. Cermak would say, "Stay in bed," and Uncle Charlie would hop out as soon as Doc left and begin helping the nurses and running errands for the patients. He couldn't wait for visitors to come. He'd point to the patient beside him and say, "That guy in the next bed's a goner." I remember going to visit him one day, and he got out of bed, disappeared for a few seconds, and came back with a cold beer. Cermak, finally, had to let him go, bad leg or not. He was not healthy to have around the hospital.

My wife tells of the time she was in the hospital and Doc Cermak came into the maternity ward and entertained everyone, even her roommate in the next bed, who, unfortunately had one of those no-nonsense pediatricians for a doctor. The pediatrician used to come there and quietly sit down and take great pains answering the young mother's questions, recommending specific baby foods and baby books. Cermak would strut in and start off with a joke because he loved laughter. "How's your bottom today?" he might ask. Or my wife would tell him about a serious concern of hers, like my daughter's arm being blue from sleeping on it, and Cermak would come back with, "Well, if you put a rope around her neck, her eyes would pop out, too."

And there was the time my baby son was sore just after Cermak performed the ancient operation most sons receive. "You put some vaseline on it," he said, "then you wrap it in gauze. And if the gauze won't stay in place, you put a pin through it."

Sometimes I think Doc Cermak's real contribution has nothing at all to do with medicine. Sometimes I think even he doesn't put much faith in the knife, the pill, the machine. No matter what ails you, you call up Cermak and you feel better for having talked to him. And no matter how serious you may think things are, you don't get a hell of a lot of sympathy from him, only common sense and laughter.

I have a vision of calling him some day and saying: "Doc, I think this is it. I have these terrible chest pains; my breath is coming in gasps!" And Cermak will probably say, "Well, if you put a rope around your neck, your eyes will pop out, too." And I'll laugh. And it may not be a very professional diagnosis, but it's a hell of a good prescription. And Doc Cermak knows it.

Goodbye, My Ladies

They were two women he had never met, never spoken a word to.

One must have been 60 or 70 years old. She was the old woman in the corner window, and often, when he passed by, he would wave to her. She would smile sometimes, move her mouth, and lift a thin, white arm.

The other was a fat, middle-aged woman with a red umbrella, and she might suddenly appear anywhere in the neighborhood, anytime. And always with the red umbrella. She was a bundle of surprises—how she dressed, what she said, where she would turn up. But the old woman in the window was a dead certainty. She was always there waiting.

She occupied what seemed like a dayroom on the second floor of an old people's home. She wore a white hospital gown, always. Other figures in white could be seen moving around her occasionally. But she was the only one who maintained a solitary day and night watch at the window.

He would talk to her sometimes, to himself. *How are you doing, old woman? Do you get enough to eat? What kind of bird seed do they feed you in those places? Where are your friends? Does anyone ever visit you, old woman? What do you watch all day and night? What do you see? Who put you there in the first place? It's no way to live, old woman, just waiting to die. I'd open that window and jump.*

The fat woman with the red umbrella would leave her basement apartment early in the morning and wander through the neighborhood till her husband came home from work in the afternoon and brought her back. He would start searching some of the nearby streets first, and then the main street and three or four stores: a restaurant, a bakery, a dime store, a tire store. She liked the tire store best of all because in front of it was a comfortable red fireplug where she often sat, her umbrella open to whatever the weather, whatever the season.

She talked incessantly, but no one answered. Small children would be amused and then run away. Teenagers might comment on her red umbrella or her fat body, but she never listened. Most of the people her own age either avoided her or shook their heads in pity. They were sure she was out of place even though she lived in the same neighborhood for many years. They were sure it was a terrible thing that happened to her. They were sure, for the good of all, she would be better off somewhere else.

Only she seemed to like where she was, wherever the hell it was, certainly enjoyed whatever the day had to offer, and was fortunate in that she had a husband who catered to her.

Days came though when she had to be brought home in a police car because she sat down in the middle of the street, or was found holding a picnic on someone's front lawn, or decided to take a nap on someone's front steps. There was a winter day when she came into the restaurant with her open umbrella, walked behind the counter, and then waltzed over to the grill and kissed the cook.

"Well," she said, "I have a brother in Indiana, and do you know your food smells awfully good. I remember St. Joseph. My brother's going to visit with us sometime. Well, goodbye now, and say hello to Jim. I just thought I'd stop and tell you."

At night in the old people's home, someone draws a long, heavy drape that covers both windows of the dayroom. The lights go out at 9 o'clock and then the dayroom is dark. But one particular night, very late and almost a year ago, he passed by and could see two hands outstretched behind the drapes.

Good night, old woman, he said. *Get some sleep.*

The fat lady with the red umbrella sprung her final surprise many months ago. She disappeared. Everyone seems to recall her, but no one will say where she went.

The window of the dayroom has been empty now for almost a year. Occasionally an old face will look out for a minute and then move somewhere out of view.

Sometimes late at night, after too much drink, too much everything, he can be found wandering the dark alley home wishing he had a red umbrella, wondering whether a solitary nightwatch could make the whole world stand still for just a while. Sometimes he will break the silence with a loud, "Goodbye, my ladies. I miss you both. Good night."

The Slovenian Grape Festival

We are standing at the entrance to the Slovene Center, 5820 W. 35th in Cicero, a couple of unethnic, uncola looking characters, trying to find a way into the *Vinska Trgatev* (grape festival). There is a constant stream of Slovenians in regulation suits, hostess gowns and a few ethnic costumes. I can maybe pass for an Authentic Slavic Ethnic ...the darkness, the mixture of merriment and melancholia ...except for my long hair and safari coat. But my cohort, Ross, the photographer who has come along to preserve tradition on film, is already eliciting serious Slovenian stares and secret conversations in foreign tongues.

Ross, steeped in the American Indian culture, is dressed like he just came out of the Southwest (which he did), cowboy boots, Navajo turquoise and silver belt, his own handcrafted-sculpted rings, plus a *hisshi* necklace of tiny shells which, he says, is the in thing for White Man in Red Man's territory these days.

"Yeah, but this is a Slovenian rite tonight, old boy. If you find another set of *hisshi* beads at the Vinska Trgatev, I'll dance the polka on my hands," I tell him. But he just howls like a coyote and starts loading his camera while I'm figuring out how to buffalo a ticket-taker.

"I'm a guest ... so is he. I don't need a ticket. Some of my best friends are Slovenians. I'm part of the family. Hey, there goes one now ... that fat guy there in the police uniform."

"Who?" says the Slovenian guard seated at a card table by the door.

"Fat Eddie, the grouch. Tomse ... no, Thom Shea, the way you people say it."

"Oh, him? He's your friend? He ain't got no friends."

"You're telling me. I grew up with the guy on 18th and 58th. His old man, Matt Tomse, and Uncle John Zbasnik used to make wine. Eddie and I used to watch and help them drink it. I wrote a story about them once, the old Slovenian winemakers ..."

"Oh, you're the guy ..."

"Let him in, for crissake," Fat Eddie comes to my defense. "So, the freeloader finally made it. When the hell you going to work for a living like everybody else?"

"Good to see you, Eddie. Meet my friend, Ross, a Slovenian Indian. I've come to investigate a rumor that you were mellowing in your old age, Eddie."

"He's mellowing all right," says his neat wife, Marianne, the only one who can dish it back to Eddie faster than he can dish it out, and then add 10 layers of hearty laughter to really make it hurt. "All I gotta do now is wait till he's 50 years old. They say when they're 50, the Slovenians suddenly realize they're gonna die, and then they begin to live!" She pummels him with laughter.

"What's with the Keystone Kop uniform?" I ask.

"Ah, it's all part of this damn thing we do tonight. I'm supposed to arrest the grape thieves. I'll be damn if I know what a cop outfit has to do with a Slovenian wine festival, but I'm it for the night."

"Are you Slovenian?" I ask Marianne.

"I never had to be nothing till I joined this organization. That's the first thing they all want to know, 'What are you? What are you?' There are all these little groups here, you know. I'm a Slovak. What the hell's the difference?"

"Come on," says Eddie, "I'll introduce you guys to the bartenders. I'll show you around. Find Toncka," he tells Marianne. "I want him to meet Toncka. She knows all about this stuff. What are you guys drinking?"

"Anything the Slovenians are giving away tonight."

Toncka Garden (pronounced Tawnch-ka) is a beautiful, smiling lady in her 70s. I love her name immediately ... the kind of name a woman should have. (I'll take Toncka anyday to 500 sweet Debbies.)

And Toncka turns out to be one of those poetic, folk-historians who somehow continue to survive in Chicago's ethnic neighborhoods ... all the history of Slovenian customs in her head, all the songs and memories and feelings for the old country in her heart. And saving it all for occasions like this, the Vinska Trgatev, when the people, her people, the Slovenians, once again express a ritual, a rite, that now only a few oldtimers remember in the essence of its purity in Slovenian villages past ... an occasions of joy, a celebration of the good harvest.

But how does one recreate this for others? For the second, third and future generations bogged down in the plastic and concrete civilization of Chicago and suburbs?

Well, you keep all the Slovenians together in a social club, for one thing. And you meet every week. And you keep sisters and brothers and uncles and

aunts and cousins and friends as close together as possible. And you tell stories of then and now. And you dance the old dances, sing the old songs and keep the rhythm of the old music coming out of the button-box accordians, and you eat Slovenian food, washed down with homemade Slovenian wine. And you celebrate the seasonal occasions such as tonight, the Grape Festival, and you trust tradition will not die among the young.

"Slovenians are a wine-drinking people," Toncka smiles. "They are happy people."

And they continue to crowd into the Slovene Center this evening, over 200 of them before the night is over. Here and there I recognize a face from the old neighborhood ... John Kozar and his wife Rose, who still live a few doors away from my father's house ... Ann Birsa (formerly Ann Tomse, Fat Eddie's sister) and her husband, Carl ... their son, Dennis, behind the bar.

Friends, relatives, neighbors drift by, shake my hand ... we have something in common ... we're part of the Ethnic Family ... and I'm an adopted Slovenian for the night because I grew up with a Tomse and knew the Zbasniks and Kozars as well.

Time out for a drink and a brief history. Slovenia itself is one of six republics (Croatia, Serbia, Bosnia-Hercegovina, Montenegro, Macedonia) first gathered into a nation callyed Yugoslavia (Land of the South Slavs) in 1918, and fixed there somewhat firmly in place by Josip Broz Tito after World War II. It's an incredible mixture of people, customs, religious beliefs and strong individualists supposedly united under one red, white and blue flag with a big red star in the middle.

But, as a Croatian once told me, "No one will ever keep that goddam country together for long. Each group thinks it's better than the other. And, of course, the Croatians are the best."

Toncka sits serenely at the table, points to the colorful costumes some of the men and women are wearing, and tells a sweet tale of grape harvests past, the way it once was (and still is) over there in Slovenia.

"It was a natural thing, this festival. Something like Thanksgiving ... yes, like Thanksgiving here. Only nothing religious about it. It was held on the last day of the grape harvest. What you see here tonight is just a re-creation in miniature. Each village would hold their own. And oh, it was such a beautiful thing to see. You know, you could hear it from one hillside to the other ... the singing, the dancing. Now, it is more organized. Not as spontaneous as it used to be.

"After the grape festival, then the actual wine making began. But the festival itself was held around the *vinski hram* (wine cellar) which was a stone building in the middle of the vineyard. A cool place, where all the food was preserved ... sausages, ham, and, of course, last year's wine, which everyone got into.

"The new wine, you see, is not ripe till the 11th of November, St. Martin's Day. Only then can you start drinking this year's wine."

"But what about my friend, Fat Eddie, in the police uniform? And that fella in the judge's robes? Give me the whole play, the whole cast of characters," I ask.

So Toncka explains the particulars of the story, how guards were stationed during the harvest to prevent any outsiders from coming into the vineyards and stealing the grapes and the wine. Thieves who were caught were brought before the judge and fined. The fine was collected and recorded by a clerk and those who could not pay the fine were tossed in jail where they remained for so long or until someone paid the fine for them.

"Then there is the Mayor and the Mayor's Wife who are like the host and hostess for the celebration. Then all the men and women, boys and girls who represent the townspeople, the workers."

"And who are the thieves?" I ask . . . a philosophical position, a question of ethics. Toncka just smiles. I understand now . . . I'm in the midst of a Slovenian medieval morality play.

We go into the other room, the dining and dance hall where the tables and chairs are filling up rapidly, and check the vineyards which hang heavy with fruit.

To re-create the custom, they've attached an arbor to the center of the ceiling above the dancing area, with bunches of real grapes hanging ripe and ready. Apples, too, and bananas, pears, all the fruits in season. Beneath the arbor are tables ladened with food . . . sausage, bread, wine *shtruklje* (a sort of cold strudel in a bowl) for all the happy celebrators to partake of.

In one corner of the hall is a makeshift courtroom and a small room marked, Jail.

A stranger passes by and hands me a fresh beer to wash down my Scotch. The table of Zbasniks, Tomses and Birsas wave me over and tell me that their bottles of bourbon, Scotch and beer are my bottles. Drink . . . Help yourself. For a wine-loving people, there's a hell of a lot of hard whisky floating around the Vinska Trgatev tonight . . . Another American variation, I presume.

In the distance an accordian can be heard and voices begin to sing as a small procession forms near the end of the bar, the Mayor and the Mayor's Wife dressed in the national costumes of Slovenia. Her red dress, white apron and headpiece are elaborately done in beautiful handiwork. The Mayor, dressed in black velvet, displays a neat embroidered vest and a wild black hat with a decorative feather . . . a constume any Hip would gladly trade his blue denims for, I surmise, trying to put the whole scene in proper perspective.

"That feather in the Mayor's hat is from a wild rooster," Toncka explains. "It's a *krivce za klobuk* (double feather). Very rare. Very hard to find anymore. Ony the leader of the yound men is allowed to wear a feather like that. The one the Mayor's wearing, my brother-in-law sent to me in 1930."

I check Ross ... he's already got his eye on that feather.

"It's time for the Mayor to give the speech ..."

The Mayor, who is Carl Birsa, standing a little shakily from all the dancing and singing (not to mention too many visits to the *vinski hram*, manages to hush the hall as he prepares to read his speech. This Mayor, one soon perceives from his halting eloquence, has probably never given a speech before in his life, at least a speech under such conditions.

"Dear friends," he begins with a smile, a laugh, applause from the crowd. "We have come here to celebrate our annual Grape Festival. We worked hard all summer and we are happy that our vineyards are full of ripe, sweet grapes."

(He emphasizes ripe, sweet grapes, as he checks all the women in the hall with a knowing grin.) "In the orchards one can see RED, RIPE APPLES" (applause, laughs, guffaws) "SWEET PEARS and JUICY PEACHES!" (which brings down the house.) "The weather hasn't been nice all the time, but we are happy to report that the hail didn't cause any damage to our crops.

"Everybody is HAPPY NOW!" (more laughter) "OH GOD, ARE WE HAPPY!" (another off the cuff remark which cracks the Mayor up completely). "We have only one complaint. Some newcomers have settled in our village and they like to pick our grapes in the vineyards. Of course, we hired a guard, but he can't be on duty day and night So, an emergency meeting was held in our village hall. We discussed all the problems at length. We must put an end to the unauthorized picking of grapes. Our guard will get help by our townspeople lending him a hand.

"According to our by-laws, they are empowered to arrest anyone who takes fruit from our vineyards. The thief, of course, will be fined. If they don't pay the fine on the spot, they will be put in jail. To comfort you a little, because of growing inflation, fines won't be as high this year as they were last year. The smallest fine will be 25 cents. The bigger the grape, the bigger the fine. Those who steal a bunch of grapes will pay plenty.

"And now my dear friends, guard, fellows and girls ... watch carefully over our property and arrest everyone stealing and damaging our vineyards."

Applause, laughter, toasts, drinks, eats ... the music begins, the dancers dance, and everyone sings yet another song. "Toncka, what is it? What are they singing now?"

"An old Slovenian song ... 'What can they do to us if we're happy ... Nothing!"

"Oh, I like that, Toncka. I like that very much."

The whole band is on the scene now, consisting of two button-box accordians, a banjo player, a bass and a drummer. And the music they play is the old music, polkas, waltzes and occasionally something close to a jitterbug-fox trot.

As the dancers swing and circle under the arbor, here and there hands go up, somewhat secretively, and pull down an apple, a pear, a bunch of grapes. The policeman and the villagers try to keep an ever watchful eye, but it's difficult when the small, crowded world of the dance floor is packed with fruit thieves everywhere.

The Mayor himself is one of the first to be arrested and fined 50 cents ... shades of Chicago city government, "No tax," says the judge. "Scratch me off the books," says the Mayor.

And so on and on through the evening arrests are made, culprits brought before the judge found guilty, fined, recorded in the clerk's ledger and tossed into jail if the fine isn't paid. (In a few hours, the club treasury is already $50 richer.)

The object of this Slovenian game is the same as any real life game of cops and robbers: Take if you like, but don't get caught. Concealment helps. And so the dancers grab an apple and quickly try to hide it in their hand, in their pocket or, in the case of women, somewhere in the secret hideaways of their dress. To get the fruit safely back to the table is to be home free.

Fat Eddie is making a night of it, arresting fruit thieves left and right, especially women. "I knew he missed his calling in life," I tell his wife, Marianne. "Yeah," she says. "And how do you like the way he handles the merchandise."

The drinks continue to mount at a fast pace. Three fresh Scotches await me and at least two beers. I am trying my Christian best to control the tumult and the times. "Where's Ross?" I ask. "Where's the picture taker?"

"He's in jail," someone says. "He's in jail with some babe taking pictures."

I've lost Toncka, Ross, Marianne, Fat Eddie, and I'm set in the midst of these dancing, thieving Slovenians and trying to get a few more particulars down. "Who's really in charge here?" I ask aloud as Marianne comes dancing by ... "Nobody," she laughs.

"Who's the president?" I ask. "Somebody, explain this organization, please!"

"Well," ventures one Slovenian standing by, "The orignal lodge was on 27th and Lawndale. But the social club was on 23rd and Lawndale. Then the neighborhood got bad, and we got this place about three years ago."

The Mayor's brother, Johnny Birsa, comes on the scene. "Talk to John Rak," he says. "Find Gus Kramer."

"Who? Who?" I ask, in between the dancers, the judge, the fruit thieves, the free-flowing booze.

"Hi, I'm John Rak," a nice old man says, shaking my hand. "I'm the custodian."

"We're open every night but Monday," says Rak. "Tuesday night our singing group meets here. Wednesday nights the button-box accordian players come here to play and give lessons. Thursday's for card players, pinochle, poker, Friday is dinner night — chicken, fish, goulash. Saturday night, usually some kind of lodge doings or else we rent the hall out. Sunday morning we clean up. Then we have happy hour about 10 in the morning."

"Who's Gus Kramer?" I ask.

"Oh, he's like the financial secretary," says Johnny Birsa.

By all indications, it's a loose organization. Yet, if the Vinska Trgatev is any measure of its success, it sure as hell works, thanks, I'm sure, to guys like Rak and Kramer and a handful of others.

"Marianne!" I holler, but she's just been arrested. And Fat Eddie is in no hurry to bail her out. As the bass player says upon being informed of the arrest of his wife, "That's the way it goes. Let her stay there."

Only a few hours old and the Grape Festival is already bordering on chaos. How do the musicians keep going? Don't they ever take a break?

Either Johnny Birsa or Gus Kramer or Johnny Rak interrupts with another bit of folk philosophy ... "This is a dying tradition, you know. We don't like to let these things go. We try to keep all this alive for the next generation."

"How's the folks?" Johnny Kozar asks from the table.

"Fine, John, fine. How's the neighborhood these days?" I ask.

"Well, I tell you. People just don't take care of their houses the way they used to. They don't take care of their property."

I finally make it to the bar where the Colorado Kid, Dennis Birsa, slaps another Scotch in front of me. "As a card-holding character of the Now Generation," I approach him "... the counter culture, the Whole Hip Catalog, how do you dig tradition, the Vinska Trgatev?"

"Things like this, you know, I really like them. It's the same thing ... people coming together to drink, to dance, to have a good time . . . It's the same thing . . ."

And he's right, of course. It is the same thing. There's more in common between the ethnic traditions and the Hip culture than most people care to realize. How does that song go ... ? "What can they do to us if we're happy? ... Nothing." And what's that choice bit of Yugoslav philosophy as I recall? Ah, yes: Living well is the best revenge.

Back to the madness of the dance floor and the fruit thieves, where the entire Slovene Center has become courtroom and the jail will never be big enough to include all of us.

Marianne Tomse and Eddie's sister, Ann, have just been bailed out, two for a dollar. "Is that all we're worth?" pipes Ann.

Fat Eddie has just rounded up a kid, a banana stealer, and knowing how Eddie likes little kids the way W.C. Fields liked kids, I have nothing but sympathy for the young banana stealer.

"But I ate the evidence!" The wise child screams at Eddie.

"Then you better eat the goddam peels too," advises Eddie as he flings the kid in the pokey, and takes off, once again, for Hilda —the same woman he's arrested at least five times.

With his eyes focused on her, somehow he overlooks a woman right beside him who has just deposited a couple of pears in her bosom. But the Mayor doesn't miss it. He's out to lay claim to the evidence.

Somebody else tries to move in on Hilda before Fat Eddie makes the arrest. "I'll take care of this," says Eddie. "I'm having a hell of a lot of fun," he confesses as he locks himself and Hilda in jail.

"Don't believe it," Marianne cautions Hilda. "He's lost all his gusto."

"Weird dude," says Ross to me.

"Who, that guy?" pops in Johny Birsa, who is always popping in. "If you washed all your Manhattans down with a shot, you'd be weird too."

Another peak of the night's celebration is the theft of a huge wreath of fruit called the *krancel*, suspended near the edge of the arbor like a chandelier. Inflation or no inflation, the thief will pay dearly for that baby. Besides, it's almost a self-sacrifice since there's no way the thief can get away with it. He damn near needs a ladder to cut it down.

And so out of nowhere (but from behind the bar, actually), and right in front of everybody, who should steal the *krancel* but the guy who can least afford it, the guy most likely not to succeed . . . Fat Eddie's nephew, Dennis, the Colorado Kid, the hippie. Twenty-five bucks it will cost him. "Charge it," somebody says.

Dennis enters the hoosegow, with a nice chick in tow, and prepares to weather it out. "I want a lawyer," he explains to the judge and arresting officer. "I'm entitled to one phone call," he admonishes the judge. Dennis is the ony thief tonight who seems to understand the subtleties of the law.

Tasting another Scotch, I surmise that the hour of chaos is now; there is no use fighting it; my notes are written in another language entirely, and so I opt for Gestalt and the go-with-it feeling. I try humming a few bars of "How can they kill me if I'm happy? . . . No way," but I discover I can't remember the music, and I've lost the words completely.

The music . . . ah the music goes on and on and it comes out good, polkas, waltzes, and more polkas. Almost all the fruit has been stolen . . . all the officials are in jail at the moment . . . I check with the recording clerk and discover she's collected $130.80 for a grand total ("We paid about $30 for the fruit," she confides) . . . and still the music goes round and round, and the dancers keep circling, keep vocally in tune with the rhythm . . . hollering, stamping their feet, whistling . . .

"What's Ross up to these days?" I ask.

"He's dancing," I'm told.

"Dancing! He's supposed to be taking pictures, for crissake. He doesn't know a polka from a kola. He's a Corn Dancer."

Sure enough, he's doing a Western polka ... he's moving those big cowboy boots across the floor like a real Slovenian dude. "Hey, man, I love these whistlers," he yells to me in passing ... "Listen to these dudes whistling to the music, will you!"

"You have to live each day," somebody else tells me in greeting card philosophy. (Why are they laying all this heavy stuff on me? I ponder. Just when I think I'm happy?)

But oh, the fine sounds coming out of those button-box accordians. I move to a table next to the musicians, a table piled high with fruit. I taste a sweet dark grape. The music ... the soothing whines of music I must have recorded somewhere in my blood stream, going back to the ethnic celebrations of my own family, back to the music my grandparents brought from Croatia, Hungary, Yugoslavia ...

Just look at that old guy standing all alone in front of the musicians ... eyes closed ... he's somewhere else entirely ... the altered consciousness of an old man as he begins to sway in place, in time to all the old memories still so alive in his head ...

And it's still elbow to elbow on the dance floor. These people are happy!

"Hey, you see that old couple?" Marianne joins me. "They live together, but they're not married."

"I thought the Now Generation discovered that arrangement," I reflect.

"No, no, he's the one always complaining about his wife, you know. But it's not really his wife. And you know what she says, you know what she says? 'All he does is bizz and buzz and tell me how good he used to was!' "roars Marianne.

"Spoogie's gonna sing 'O ja,' " Johnny Birsa pops up to inform me.

"Who's gonna do what?"

"Spoogie ... he's gonna sing his song."

"Don't you know 'O ja'?" says Marianne. "That's like the Slovenian National Anthem. Every goddam place they go, they sing 'O ja'.

"Ya, ya, of course. How could I forget that. I used to love to hear Uncle John say, 'Ya, is gonna be nice day today, ya, ya.' "

"Well, that's what the song is about. And Spoogie's gonna sing it.'

Spoogie? I want to meet him. And the call goes out for Spoogie.

But before anyone comes up with him, there's a round of applause, laughter, groans and Slovenian cheers as a fairly young, well-dressed man approaches the table with a drink in each hand. He yells to the musicians who have just finished another polka, "I got a request! Play the theme from 'Deliverance'!"

"Now the party's a success," screams Marianne. Ronnie Zefran the undertaker is here. Every Slovenian in the joint will be buried by Zefran sooner or later."

Enter Zefran the undertaker, the only Slovenian stand-up comic to be found around the old neighborhood, St. Stephen's Church, Wolcott and 22nd Place.... Zefran's Funeral Parlor, 1941 West Cermak ... or the new neighborhood, Cicero ... wherever happy Slovenians meet.

"Yeah, watch out for me," he says. "I'm the last guy to lay you out. I got the greatest job in the world, you know."

In the midst of Zefran's routine, the word is passed around that Frankie Yankovic, the great Slovenian accordionist, is coming before the night is over.

"That's all we need," says Marianne, "Yankovic, the King of the Slovenians."

A middle-aged woman dances by and tells Zefran that she's already got her dress and a new wig put aside for him when he comes by for the final call. "Yeah, that's me," he says, "a real live undertaker. And when John over here dies," (pointing to Johnny Birsa) "its gonna take me seven days and at least four other guys to get the smile off his face, cause I know where he's gonna go . . .

And the laughter, the stories of Zefran go on and on through the early hours of morning. He's in full control, whether he stands at the table, sits or whirls around the dance floor. "Play the theme from 'Deliverance,' " he yells at the polka band once again.

Somewhere I make a mental note to myself . . . I want to attend a Ronnie Zefran funeral sometime . . .one of his close friends . . . a drinking buddy . . . shades of a Vinska Trgatev finale, I would imagine . . . a real dance of death . . .

"Hi, I'm Spoogie," someone interrupts my not so dark thoughts.

"Who?"

"Leo Kregul . . . Call me Spoogie."

"Okay, Spoogie . . . a great name. What's your song? What's your story?"

Spoogie is a bargeman. A Slovenian bargeman. I've never met anyone who works on a barge before. Sounds like a great life. But about that song, "O ja"?

"It's an oldtime song," he says. "Recently revived in Cleveland."

"Yeah," says somebody else. "Spoogie's in his glory when he can hop the barge to Cleveland just to hear all his polka bands . . . Yankovic and the rest."

"I'm gonna sing it now," he says. And Spoogie gets up to sing "O ja" much to the applause of his countrymen. It's a soft song, kind of a ballad it seems. I was expecting a wild drinking song. But no, this seems warm, bordering on the sad, though I don't understand a word of it except the constant refain, O ja, O ja . . . And almost unconsciously all the Slovenians join in, and there's finally a kind of hymn to something in the air.

Spoogie sits down to talk about the song when it's over. "It means, oh yes . . . like something really good, oh yeah," he begins.

"It means a lot of other things," says Marianne, temporarily interrupting Spoogie. "There's never been a Slovene party that hasn't sung that song. Hey, Zefran, did you measure him up yet?" she points to her husband, Fat Eddie.

"O ja," smiles Zefran.

"Oh yes," continues Spoogie, trying to unlock the lyrics of the song . . . "Oh yes, I'm always happy, happy, as long as I'm living . . . Oh yes, I'm going to always drink wine as long as I live . . . Oh yes, I'm going to always drink wine as long as I live . . . Then the woman passes by his grave and tells him to get up, get up! To drink the wine again . . . O ja . . . O ja . . ."

"O ja."

Ray Schwartzkopf: The Feather Comforter Man

Eighteenth Street, Blue Island, Pilsen, the Leader Store ... I've heard these places mentioned all my life. It was the area of the first big settlement of Czech immigrants in Chicago. Both my grandparents came from that neighborhood. Later they filtered into the 26th Street and Pulaski area (now known as the Little Village) and then into Cicero and Berwyn.

Stores sometimes reflect the unique history of a neighborhood. Stores like Ray Schwarzkopf's Leader Store at 18th and Paulina, which has been there since 1925. My grandparents shopped at the Leader Store, as did all the Bohemians in those days. They had their *periñas* (Czech feather comforters) made there. It was a store that kept them in touch with the old world and eased them into the new with modern housewares like linoleum.

Times change indeed. Neighborhoods crumble or disappear entirely. Yet some hang on. Some, like 18th Street, adapt and somehow try to keep the culture flowing.

The Bohemians pull out; the Poles follow, and so do the Yugoslavs, the Germans. Only a few of the old remain to witness the incredible transformation of their neighborhood as the Latins (Mexican and Puerto Rican) move into the old houses and take up the cheaper rents. Just a trickle at first. And then, just as it did with the Czechs and Poles, the word spreads and then the neighborhood becomes engulfed with a new wave of people and customs.

So, on a sunny Saturday morning, when almost 50 years have passed for the old Leader Store, Ray Schwarzkopf, who has spent the last 36 years there, sweeps down the sidewalk and laughs and jokes and greets the day, the people, with a touch of Spanish in his voice. A sprightly Mexican dance tune blares from the speaker above the door. "Good morning, Senor," says Ray. "Good morning, Señora."

Schwarzkopf is a bit heavy-set, gray, balding, but in tune with the times . . . maroon pants, white, wide belt, wide tie. For a man of 62, he is young. And he has that strange mixture of two cultures running through his blood — Bohemian and Jew.

And it's this urgent desire to communicate with people that contrasts so clearly with the rather taciturn Bohemian heritage. For Schwarzkopf is a merchant in love with his business, his wife Irma, his children, his employees, the 18th Street neighborhood, the whole history of his people. For Schwarzkopf realizes that to be alive, to make the personal contact, you've got to keep talking. And so he does . . . he does.

"It's like the end of an era," he say, "the Bohemian Jew. We're practically extinct. Five hundred, maybe 1,000 of us in all of Chicago.

"Bohemian Jews still have their own cemetery at Addison and Narragansett. That's about the only place you'll see them before long."

Up and down 18th Street early on a Saturday morning, the neighborhood is somewhat still. The Douglas Park "L," 18th Street stop, runs along the west side of the store; along the street you see a mingling of neighborhood life-styles: Chapala Restaurant . . . Kowalski Funeral Home . . . Super Mercado . . . Andziewicz Funeral Home . . . Casa Cardenas (furniture).

Schwarzkopf explains the stillness of Saturday morning with his own brand of neighborhood history. "The Spanish, you see, are late sleepers. They don't really get going till around noon. So it's a different shopping day entirely with them. With the Bohemians and Poles, they used to be lined up at the door early in the morning, waiting for us to open. Then they'd have the rest of the day to themselves. With the Spanish, it's the other way around. But that's all right. Good morning, Senor."

It's a three-and-a-half-story brick building which must have been quite impressive in its day. Now it shows its years, reveals its private history with an old-fashioned black fire escape and faded painted signs . . . OshKosh B'Gosh. The World's Best Work Wear . . . Leader Store Lunch Counter, Eat in Comfort . . .

The display windows are clean and sparsley decorated with a wisp of colored paper here, a sprig of plastic flowers there. But then there's the merchandise: curtains 2½-yard cottage set, $10.98; bedspreads, $8.98; women's dresses, $11.95, $7.95; and "I Can't Believe It's a Girdle" girdle, $14. There's a window of housewares, of shoes, of paintings "Made in Mexico."

And there's a window sign near the entrance to the store. Another 'sign of the times' — WANTED, SPANISH-SPEAKING SALES HELP, MEN & WOMEN.

The original Leader Store was founded by Ray's father in law, Edward Oplatka, and a partner, Emil Reinish, in 1914 on Chicago Avenue. Before that, in 1910, Oplatka got his start at another famous department store on

18th and Blue Island run by Albert Lurie.

"A lot of the Bohemian Jews came to Lurie's Department Store to work, to get their start," explains Ray. "The neighborhood was solid Bohemian and Polish. No English was spoken there at all. In 1924, the 26th Street Leader Store was opened. And in 1925 this present and last of the Leader Stores began on 18th and Paulina."

Other Leader stores were tried in various locations, including one in Berwyn on Cermak and Oak Park, which lasted for 10 years. But, Ray says, in one way or another these stores faded from the scene. Either their customers moved away, or bigger stores came in.

Schwarzkopf's entry into the Leader Store business was all very simple. "I married the boss' daughter 36 years ago," he smiles, "and I'm still working."

Schwarzkopf rolls up his sleeve and reveals a tattoo (cleaver, knife, saw, sharpening rods) on his forearm. "I started out as a butcher, just as my father did. I was instrumental in forming the butcher's union, Local 638, a Bohemian local. Solid Bohemian butchers. After my marriage to Irma, I bought out the food market and became a meat salesman. Then my father in law talked me into trying soft-goods merchandising.

"My father in law died in 1945. It's a partnership now with my brother in law, William E. Oplatka, chief of the suburban division of the State's Attorney's office. It was called the Leader Store because my father in law was a leader in bargains in the old days when they gave away soap and everything."

Ray's life is the Leader Store. He thinks the place is unique even today. Though one might consider such neighborhood department stores a thing of the past, Ray keeps the faith. "I think of it as a bit of the old days. We're the kind of store every neighborhood needs," he says.

"There's a basement we open in September for Toyland. We still make Bohemian comforters, made to order or recover, *periñas* something like the kings and queens of old Bohemia slept under. We also make drapes right in our shop before the customer's very eyes... European style. We have employees, 40, 50 years with us. And they are expert craftsmen. We also make slipcovers. We are one of the few stores left that makes such items like they did 20 or 30 years ago.

"We have our own stamp plan. Leader Store stamps ... 59 years old. You don't have to go anywhere else to redeem them. For each 10-cent purchase, we give you one stamp. When you fill the book, it's worth $2 on any merchandise in the store. No hokum. No traveling all over the city to redeem the stamps.

"We have free and immediate delivery. We cash checks free. We have budget and layaway plans. The biggest part of our business is medium-priced, nationally advertised merchandise. We are the Levi headquarters for 18th Street."

Time and again Schwarzkopf comes back to the people, the neighborhood, sounding something like a Bohemian-Jewish Carl Sandburg. "Brotherhood was practiced between us 30 years ago, before anyone knew what it was. I was more of a helper to everyone than a merchant . . . immigration problems, real estate, helping the families. And now I'm doing it all over again with the Spanish, helping them get various permits for buildings, references for people they want to bring here from Mexico, real estate problems, directing them to lawyers and proper City Hall officials, all kinds of problems.

"The neighborhood . . . let me tell you about this neighborhood. It was great, and it's still great. People ought to know about that — all those who left and are afraid to come back. Sure I had it rough when it started to change. The transitional period around nine years ago with the Czechs and the Poles on the move, the Mexicans and the Puerto Ricans coming in — it lasted almost three years. I didn't know what to do, how I was going to keep going.

"But our new customers educated us. The reason I was able to survive this terrible storm is that I'm a humble man, and so I asked our Latin customers to please advise . . . what did they want?

"You see, the Spanish are creatures of habit. They were used to shopping on Halsted, stores they knew before coming here. And I made mistakes. I bought stuff that looked typical Mexican. I tried to make cowboys out of all of them.

"And I was stuck, you see, with all this merchandise that belonged to another people . . . Bohemian comforters, the drapes and things. I had all these clothes in huge sizes . . . men's work clothes, size 50. A Latin would come in with a 29-inch waist! Christ, a Pole is *born* with a 19-inch waist!

"So I talked to the Spanish. I listened. And much to my surprise, I discovered that what the Spanish people really wanted to be was American. I'm thankful to them for telling me that. So the Poles and Czechs left, and we welcomed the Mexican and the Puerto Rican."

The only way to describe the inside of the Leader Store is to say that it is just about an exact replica of the old-fashioned neighborhood department store, pre-Zayre, pre-Korvette. The floors are wooden and worn smooth. The ceiling is ornately tin-pressed and peeling. Counters are mostly wood, completely functional, and holding all there is to display and sell. Cash registers are the old kind that whirl and ring and throw out the drawer.

The store itself is not crowded, but there is a steady and orderly turnover of shoppers. Mexican music bounces through the air.

In "women's stockings" a Latin saleswoman closes a bargain with one of the neighborhood oldtimers (either a Pole or a Bohemian). "You have here two pair stockings. You find one pair to make $3 worth," she advises the old woman, who keeps burrowing through the goods.

A young Latin salesman in "men's clothing" helps a Latin woman decide on a shirt. "You know what I can do?" he tells the woman, who is unsure of the shirt size. "I can open the shirt from the package, and you can see how big it is. And that doesn't mean you have to buy it."

The woman smiles. "Is this for your husband?" the young man asks. "No, for my son," she laughs.

"Oh, is that your son who works at the bakery?" "Si, si," she smiles. Only in a neighborhood store can relationships like this exist.

Myrtle Goode runs the first floor and much of the Leader Store, it seems; Ray has given her more and more responsibility during her 40 or so years in and out of the business.

She too remembers the years of transition, "between '61 and '65," she says. "There was a big conflict with the Poles who were left in the neighborhood. 'Why are you putting up signs in Spanish?' they would holler. 'Why don't you put up signs in Polish?' "

But she has grown with the change and has a deep admiration for the Latins. "I love working with them so much more than any other group. They have such a happy disposition. They are marvelous to work with. I have three Spanish office girls who are absolutely wonderful. I take them when they are sophomores in high school, and I train them. A couple of them are now with banks downtown. One is with Bache & Co.

"The sales people are all working straight salary and all of them above the minimum wage."

"We have never become self-service. That is important to these people. We can help them with sizes and all kinds of questions. We take a lot of layaway. They put stuff away with $2 or $3 and pay it off a little each week. Yesterday I had a woman come in who bought $90 worth of clothes to take to Mexico for her family later in the summer. She gave me $15 to hold it for her."

On the second floor are children's clothes, lingerie, fabrics, drapes, curtains, and those comforters. The man in charge of it all is a Pole, Stanley Majka, who has been with the Leader Store since 1927.

To get into the particulars of the *periňa*, the poetry of feathery sleep, one must again return to the past. There is nothing in America to equal the downy sleep under a *periňa* on a cold winter's night.

It ws one of the first Bohemian words I understood as a child ... grandma and her *periňa*. They brought these 10- and 20- pound bags of feathers with them from the old country, where heat (especially in a bedroom) was unheard of. And when they settled into the 18th Street area, the 26th Street area, even Cicero and Berwyn, their *periňas* went with them.

When their children were married, they were usually given the billowy gift of a *periňa* to last them forever after. And more likely than not, Schwarzkopf's Leader Store was involved. The feathers were divided so that new comforter's could be made or perhaps more feathers added. More likely than not, Stanley Majka handled the order ... the size, the amount of feathers and down, the color of the ticking.

Schwarzkopf laughs and testifies to the sanctity of a Bohemian's feathers.

Often the Bohemian women would come in with their treasured bundle of feathers to have a new *periňa* made or the old one recovered. Down is expensive, and they were ever suspicious lest some of theirs be lost or replaced with coarser feathers. So they would stay and watch and guard their feathers until their new *periňas* were made.

"Take my husband," Ray laughs as he imitates a Bohemian customer, "but don't take my feathers."

Stanley Majka recalls the *periňa* business of the past. "Starting in July, we used to make 1,000 a month for 6 months straight. The old-timers had 8 to 10 pounds of feathers in their old comforters, and out of that we could make 2 comforters for them. Now we average maybe 1,500 *periňas* per year. We still get orders from them from Cicero and Berwyn. The young people don't care for them, though. With central heating, they don't want them. And I haven't been able to sell them to the Spanish. The Spanish are great on Dacron.

"Thirty-five years ago we used to make *periňas* for $9.80 with your own feathers. Today, $29.80 to $34.80 with your feathers. A brand new comforter in the old days was $39 for the full size, 84x90. Today, it's $64.80. You can have it with three pounds of pure down or 50/50 — half goose feathers, half goose down."

We go into the feather-dusty room where the *periňas* are put together on a huge table about the size of three double beds, end on end. This is where Vlasta Krejci, who has been with the Leader more than 40 years and is now in her eighties, sews the cover like an envelope and stuffs the feathers in. And this is where Danny Zurawski does the superb job of intricate patterned quilting, all free-hand.

"He's an artist," says Stan. "This guy can knock out about three of these an hour. There's only two or three guys in the whole city of Chicago that can do this."

Third floor: housewares ... stoves, refrigerators, furniture, paintings of burros on velvet, pots, pans, oilcloth, dishes, luggage, and a funny Bohemian in charge named Adolph Koss, a Leader Store man since 1929.

An old Slav has come to buy a fan, and Adolph stands back and lets an attractive Mexican saleswoman handle the deal.

"Is this the regular price?" asks the old man. "Has this thing got three speeds?"

"No, two," she says. "It's $18.80 on sale."

"Is that one there a little cheaper?"

"No. This is the discount price."

"What will it be with the tax? The tax I can do without. I don't like the tax."

The saleswoman goes back to check on the tax while the old man continues mumbling to himself and plays with the switch, click ... click ...

Adolph, in the meantime, reflects on the houseware history of a neighborhood store. "We've got lots of things people don't think of anymore ... meat grinders, old pans, enamel soup kettles." One soup kettle, in fact, that holds 36 quarts. "To the Bohemians it was a stock pot. The Mexicans use them now for tamales. People still come here from Berwyn and Cicero to buy washboards, coleslaw cutters ... look, even a poppy-seed grinder ($4.98). Stovepipes. This is still a stove-heated neighborhood, do you realize that?"

The old man and the Mexican saleswoman are still at it about the fan. "It is $19.82 with the tax," she tells him. Adolph hollers back jokingly from another aisle. "You'll get the tax back in your Social Security."

The old man laughs and nods and whispers to the saleswoman.

"It's 19? Huh?" he bargains.

"You can't do that. It's already a discount price," says Adolph, smiling.

"But I want a little money left to buy couple beers," laughs the old man.

"But I want to keep you sober," laughs Adolph.

An agreement is reached, and the old man walks happily away — first to the tavern for some beer, then home to try his new fan.

Adolph continues with his enthusiasm for third floor merchandise. "Kerosene lanterns ... they still use them here. Screens ... I used to buy 86 dozen; now I buy 6 dozen. The Bohemians had screens in every window. The Spanish keep the windows wide open. The flies go in one window and out the other. Luggage! I sell more luggage today than ever. The Spanish are always going somewhere. The Bohemians and Poles stay home and paint their houses on vacation. These people go to Mexico. There's a bus just down the block that takes them."

Another Latin salesgirl calls out ... "Adolph, I put on the Polish sausages about a half hour ago. You think they're done?"

"Leave 'em on. I'll see."

There's a makeshift kitchen and table set up in the back where employees can eat and cook. "I buy the coffee," explains Adolph. "They pay pay me a dime a cup or whatever. And on Saturdays I buy the Polish sausage and some good Bohemian rye."

Latin people ... Polish sausage?

"The Spanish people love the Polish sausage ... even more than the Polish do," he laughs.

You wonder, after a while, about all these salespeople and employees who have been with Schwarzkopf for years. How does he hold on to them, especially in such an old neighborhood?

Says Adolph Koss, "I love it here. I wouldn't want to work anywhere else."

Afternoon and 18th Street. The entire neighborhood has come to life, just as Ray Schwarzkopf said it would.

"See, what did I tell you?" says Ray. "Look at all the people on the street. Hello, Andy, how are you? Hello, Señora."

If there was ever a man to measure the pulse of an old neighborhood, it's Schwarzkopf. He can lead you from place to place and recall the history of a store, a restaurant, a people, a person.

"This corner, 18th and Blue Island, this was like being in the center of Prague. Here is St. Vitus. All the Czechs went to this church. Here's St. Adalbert's, where all the Polish went. They still ring he bell in St. Adalbert's by hand. Yeah, there's this big guy who pulls it and goes up in the air. That building over there was Nemecek, the photographer. Every Bohemian, at one time or another, had his picture taken there."

You roll quietly down the streets with him in his car, and his enthusiasm seldom wanes. "Look at this street, will you? It's like a little bit of Europe. A lot of people in Chicago don't even know streets like this exist. Here's Dvorak Park, named after the famous Czech composer. Look how nicely the Spanish take care of the buildings. They are old, but they're kept up. These people are proud of them."

Here and there we pass a spattering of old Poles, their houses, their yards, immaculate. "Hey, look at there," shouts Schwarzkopf with the excitement of a man discovering some extinct species. "There's an old Bohemian. See. You can always tell them by those eight-cornered caps they wear. But for every one of him left, there's 150 Spanish now."

Yet he retains a great faith in this patch of 18th Street, something close to a personal joy. "I'm looking for that Mexican band. Yeah, every Saturday afternoon they start out down the street with this little parade. No reason. They just play, and the people give them money."

He is aware of problems, even danger lurking just outside the old neighborhood, but he refuses to give in. "Even my own kids are afraid to come here, but I tell you it's all a myth," he argues. "I'm not saying there's no crime, but it's not what you read in the newspapers and see on TV.

"Sure there's crime. Show me where there isn't any crime today. There's crime in the suburbs. But in areas like this, it's mostly myth. These are good, working people. And the area is running true to form. It always was a stepping-stone — low rentals, jobs, a place for new people to take a hold and then move on.

"It's still happening now. The Spanish are beginning to move from 18th to 26th Street, just like the Bohemians did. But how you going to tell people what's going on here? How you going to tell them not to be afraid . . . to come back and see this place? And where the hell's that Mexican band?"

The Roller Rink

He came into the neighborhood bar off Cermak Road singing, humming, reaching for the words of a half-remembered song.

It's almost midnight, she said. Where you been? I've been waiting here for three hours. How much did you have to drink? Shhh ... sit down and quit making a fool of yourself. Where you been?

You miss the point, woman. I'm merely trying to remember a song. How old am I? Who am I? Where am I going? Don't answer such questions.

You're old enough to know better, and tonight you're falling apart.

I said don't answer, woman. All you ever tell me is what I know.

So what's new?

I went roller skating.

That's a new one, all right. That's a beautiful one.

I went to Mill Bridge over in Lyons.

And I was dancing at the Melody Mill ballroom.

I was roller skating again. It must be 20 years since I was on skates.

I used to skate down the sidewalks and alleys in the neighborhood. Only my skates kept falling off, the leather straps hurt my ankles, and I could never find the key. It was always rough skating on concrete. The vibrations used to rattle the silver fillings in my teeth. Thump, thump, thump over the cracks all the time. But they still do it, don't they?

I haven't seen a kid skating down the alley in years.

That's what I'm getting at. But I mean the roller rink. "Roller rink." "Rink." Do you remember words like that? They sound so strange in my mouth.

You look like you're going to pass out. You better get another beer to hold onto.

You're right. You're beginning to get the meaning of all this. A man of my years on roller skates needs some kind of balance. Bartender, brandy.

So what happened? That's what you want me to say, isn't it? What was it like?

It was a wake. That's the only way to describe it.

Yours?

Yes, in a way. Kind of a poor man's wake, you know? Hardly anyone around to pay his respects. Maybe you recognize a face or two, but more than anything you sit alone, way in the back, and remember.

I'm almost afraid to hear what's coming.

No, no. It's still alive, is what I mean. But just barely. The roller rink. Still huddled over there on Ogden avenue in Lyons. Remember that kind of shady part of Lyons with the local night clubs where maybe Al Morgan is still singing "Jealous Heart," all those sinister looking roadside bars? And then there's Mill Bridge, right in the middle of it all. The old roller rink. Same little neon sign. Same building standing off Ogden avenue there like a huge, weathered cardboard box. I opened the front door, and it was like, like ... like nothing I could describe. I mean, the smell for one. That's the first thing. It smells exactly the way it always smelled. Not a bad smell. I don't know what it is. Just kind of a roller-skating-rink smell. Something to do with the wooden floor, I guess, and all those thousands of feet on tiny wheels going 'round and 'round and 'round forever.

So you really went back to Mill Bridge?

Woman, it was beautiful. That song ... you know, what was that song I was trying to sing?

"Far Away Places"?

Yeah, "Far Away Places." That's what I was playing when I walked up to where they were skating. I haven't heard that song in ... in ...

In 20 years.

In 20 years! All those songs! They're still alive and playing at Mill Bridge! That crazy damn organ-background sound pumping them out with that heavy rhythm: dum, da, dum, dum, da, dum! Anybody could skate to that beat! Even a drunk on wheels who's sure he's racing through hell, falling in holes ... Remember "Walking My Baby Back Home?"

Shhh ... they'll throw you out of here.

Try skating to that one sometime, baby. You can't miss. Or how about "Blues in the Night?"

It's time to go.

Stand by me in this time of crisis, woman. Things are beginning to whirl. Tonight I was roller skating.

O. K., but stop singing those songs.

I can't. What's a roller rink without music? "Blue Moon." That was another one! God, those songs just came chasing after me, all of them . . . all of those great songs I had completely forgotten. Remember "Doodle Do?"

No.

Me either. That's all I remember. But it's on the hit parade at Mill Bridge. There are people still skating to that song this very minute.

Not at 1 in the morning.

No. But tomorrow they will be.

You're really out of it, aren't you? Quiet down, you're causing a commotion.

Hey, sing us another one, old boy!

Sure, sure, be glad to. How about "Ida! Sweet as Apple Cider!"? Come on, sing! Everybody sing! See, see how they remember it? Everybody remembers it!

I'm embarrassed. I'm going.

Sit down, sit down. We're just getting started. Now — "Peg O' My Heart."

This is terrible.

"Paper Doll." "Cecilia."

This can't go on.

Where's my roller skates? Tell me, my eyes are beginning to fail me, are any of my old buddies at the bar?

Dareba's down there with his softball team. They lost again.

Dareba . . . there's a case for you. A 250-pound dumpling almost 40 years old, still parading around the bar every night in his blue and gold uniform, still trying to hit the old softball. Dareba! Get your spikes off the bar! Do you still remember Mill Bridge?

Who? Naw, I could never get her in the car.

Mill Bridge roller rink, you fathead!

O yeah, yeah. I used to get thrown out of there all the time when I was a kid. Yeah, the roller rink. Geez, that must have been . . .

Twenty years ago . . . she said.

Yeah, 20 years ago.

It's still there, Dareba. Why don't you take your old lady skating some time? It's still there. Everything . . . the music, the shoe skates, the smell. And even "Jokes." Do you remember Jokes? Joachim Fonter or something's his real name. Sounds like an alias to me.

You mean the guy who used to run the place? Always wore a white shirt and bow tie? Used to smoke with a cigarette holder, I think? He looked like he wore a toupee or something?

Yeah, yeah, yeah! That's him. Jokes! He's still there. He's the owner.

He used to tell all those corny jokes like . . . ah . . . like, "You tell 'em big wheel, you been around!"

Exactly! Exactly! And you know what, Dareba? He's still telling them! I was there tonight. And do you know what I heard him tell a kid? "You tell 'em goldfish, you've circled the globe!'"

Same old Jokes.

Honest to God, Dareba, the same old Jokes. Maybe he's a little older, but I couldn't tell. You know how dark it is in there. He still skates around like the master of ceremonies or something. He still looks like a romantic movie lead in a 1930 film. Same old Jokes.

Did he throw you out?

Come one, I'm a mild-mannered man these days. I'm no kid any more. No, but he did throw out a couple of dames who were giving him a hard time.

Same old Jokes.

Yeah. But a good guy, you know? We didn't realize it then, but he's a good man. Roller skating is his whole way of life. Just think about that for a while. He's been at it since 1939!

Some guys just never grow up.

He's still loaning money to kids for Cokes. And, you know ... I almost forgot. One of the beautiful things he did was ask a really homely dame to skate with him during one of those "Couples Only" numbers when the love-birds have the whole rink to themselves.

Yeah, listen I'll see you later. This one's on me. Gotta check with my pitcher here. He's losing his touch with the ball.

Sure, Dareba, sure. Thanks.

"Couples Only," she said. I remember that.

Remember there was that little tone signal — ding, ding, ding — and you'd look up at the board to see what the next skate was?

Yes, now I remember.

There was "Couples Only," and then there was "All Skate," the main one. Kind of a free-for-all. Everybody out there rolling at once, good and bad skaters. Guys out there for the first time, stiff-legged and falling all over the place. I saw one tonight still making the classic stop. You know, going around in circles for almost five minutes and suddenly you're dizzy and want out. You want to stop, but how do you break through that solid ring of skaters? And even if you do, how do you stop your wheels from moving you into a wall or down some disaster of steps? This kid came tearing to beat hell on the inside, made a frantic dash for the outside, sent two other kids into the wall, and then came flying in, stiff-legged, arms out straight grabbing for a post, a railing, another kid, anything to stop and keep his balance. He went right under the railing. But hung on.

I remember "All Skate." What were some of the others?

Let's see ... "Reverse All Skate." That gets kind of hairy if you can't skate. And then there were the wild ones like "Couples Tag" and "Trio."

Do the girls still wear those skating skirts?

I'm glad you asked. I want to tell you about that. About the girls, the guys, that whole sad scene.

Why sad? You sound like you had a good time.

It was sad. Like I said, I kept remembering the way it used to be. And maybe what I'm telling you now is more the way it used to be than the way it is.

Don't make me cry.

Woman, you're all heart. You know, when you get right down to it, you went roller skating at Mill Bridge on Sunday afternoon for one reason. You were in grammar school or just starting high school, and you were beginning to make it a little on your own in the world. Maybe you had a part-time job after school; maybe you even took accordion lessons like everyone else because your parents knew a musician down the block who made good money playing polkas on Saturday nights; maybe you had to stay in every night to practice and do your homework. But Sunday afternoons were yours. And one of the best scenes for a kid that age, at that time to really swing, was the roller rink. It was the safest place to hold a girl's hand.

You're going to make me cry.

No, I mean it. No one, not even your best friend, would care if you held a girl's hand during "Couples Only." And your parents would never know. They thought it was nice you were learning how to skate in between your accordion lessons and everything. They had no idea you were already so fast on wheels you could glide around the floor with your arm around some girl you were dreaming about all week.

Innocence ... please get me another drink...."

Exactly. First love, puppy love, call it what you will. But it was the roller rink that provided that first taste of freedom and love and all the excitement to go with it. Do your remember holding someone's hand for the first time? And innocent it was ... like hay rides, picnics, hide-and-seek, a walk home from school.

I'm crying.

Good. You should be. Terrible things happen to a man. Trite or popular as it sounds, the times are always changing. You will never hold hands and skate like that again. In fact, yo may not even be able to skate any more.

Stop it!

You know how many kids were skating tonight?

No.

Thirteen. That's all. Thirteen! God only knows how they found the place or why they were there. They were mostly adolescents. And mostly girls. Jokes blames it all on TV. "You have this whole generation that grew up in front of a TV set," he said. And then he laughed, "And so many young people can't stand this exotic music."

"You've got to admit "Ida! Sweet as Apple Cider!" doesn't really rock.

But it does when you're out there on skates and that damn organ is pumping out the rhythm!

How do you know?

Don't ask me. I just know. I feel it.

Did you actually skate around that rink tonight with all those kids? Over 30, fat, and as far out of shape as you are?

Never mind. I'm talking about the kids who were there. All 13 of them. Only one couple skated during "Couples Only." One! And they were hardly holding hands like they really meant it.

They'll make up for it later in the car.

Yes. That's the problem, too. Kids move from bikes to cycles to cars. There's no longer any time for skates.

Do the girls still wear skating skirts?

I forgot. That used to be one of the extra thrills for the guys, you know. Watching one of those beautiful girls who could really skate come flashing by from behind you on white skates, that short, pleated skirt just swinging away. It was enough to make any guy lose a step, fall on his face, get up, fall down again, and swear he would keep practicing with the skates till he could catch her. Maybe next time it would be just the two of them in the soft blue lights of "Couples Only," skating hand in hand to "Peg O' My Heart." He would never fall so hard again. Skating skirts? Hell, they all wear them now whether they're good skaters or not. Only they're mini-skirts. And unexciting. Maybe because the girls who were wearing them were either fat or skinny and kept falling down.

That's a shame.

You don't mean it.

I do, I do. Are you finished? Can we go now?

Where? You can't go home again.

Don't tell me. That's sad. The neighborhood and all.

I'll confess. I tried it. Bartender, one last brandy.

Tried what?

Roller skating. Tonight. At Mill Bridge.

I don't believe you.

I had to. I walked up to the window, got a pair of size 8 skates, and sneaked off to the back room, sat on a bench, and put them on. I was 12 years old again. No one was around. All 13 kids were floundering around the floor skating; only Jokes was weaving his way backward so beautifully in and out and around the 13 kids to the soft strains of "Blue Moon." I swear he was aloft. Like an angel.

Size 8 skates?

Right. They didn't fit. But I shoved them on anyway.
And then what happened?
I laced them tight around the ankle.
And?
I stood up.
Then?
I fell on my ...
No!
But I got up again. "Blue Moon" was still playing. I had to make it at least once around the rink.
But you were standing this time? All alone? On wheels?
Yes. All alone. In the back room. By the bench.
And then?
I took a step.
And?
Fell on my face. My legs folded under me like two lumps of dough.
No!
I crawled. Crawled! On my hands and knees back to the bench.
And?
Took off the skates, put on my shoes, and left. Nobody saw me. I will never go back to Mill Bridge again. Bartender, a final brandy. I'm going.
I think I'll stay a while longer.
You know ... standing here now at the bar ... after all I said ... singing, reminiscing, falling down, and all that ... you know ... as I take a step now ... it's almost as if I had wheels on my feet ... almost as if my legs were holding up and pushing me gently into the music, into a skater's glide ...
Here ... hold my hand ...

Soup

You're cold? Soup. You're tired? Soup. You're angry? Soup. You're hot? Soup. You're sick? Soup. You're loving? Soup. You're dying? Soup. You're back again? Soup. Have some soup.

Soup travels in circles, recycles beautifully, and satisfies almost every appetite.

And if hot soup in the mouth doesn't remind you of home, you don't know what soup is all about; you should remain an orphan confined to cracked bowls of thin metallic soup the rest of your life. Sooner or later it all boils down to this — Soup is people.

The Greeks have a word for soup, like everything else (Σούπα) ... only it's avgholemono (egg/lemon soup) that I'm really after.

The first time I had it was in a cafe on Omonia Square at 1 in the morning in Athens after starving for what seemed like two days and five nights in a coach of the Orient Express from Belgrade. The soup was yellow and white with little globs of rice surfacing here and there and a spoon sticking out. The first swallow damn near came up again for air. My sour taste buds were not yet ready for the Mediterranean touch of lemon. But this was the soup of the Greek people, and I did not give up.

A few years later, in a tiny Greek kitchen in Toledo, I had another round with avgholemono. This time the cook waved me into the kitchen, put his arm around my shoulder, lifted a lid on a boiling pot, smiled, and announced in his best Greek-American language, "Thiz iz the zoop!" And I've been eating avgholemono and holding it down ever since.

One day, George Mangriotis, a student in a writing class I was teaching at the College of Du Page, said he was going home to make some soup. "What kind?" I asked. "Avgholemono," he replied.

To insure George's high grade in the course, I suggested he turn over the recipe for my private file.

George Mangriotis' Avgholemono Soup

Prepare rice soup as usual.

In a small bowl, separate the white form the yolk of one egg. With an eggbeater, beat the egg white until it becomes fluffy, then add the yolk and beat some more. Squeeze the juice of a whole lemon (you may wish to use less lemon) in the bowl with the egg and mix well.

The secret of this recipe is to mix the egg and lemon with the hot soup slowly so as not to cook the egg. Start adding soup from the pot into the bowl with a ladle while stirring the egg and the lemon. When the bowl is almost full, pour it into the pot slowly while mixing the soup. The avgholemono soup is now ready to eat.

"Thank you, George. I tried it, and it didn't work. It was the first direction of yours that threw me ... " I used a can of beef bouillon for the base with the rice. I think I should have used chicken. And I know the real secret is lamb, but I just didn't happen to have a hunk handy.

But let's hear it for Navy Bean! For me, bean soup means Thursday, because that's when they used to serve it at the Knotty Pine, 24 W. Burlington Avenue, La Grange, one of my old hamburger hangouts. You'll see that little red sign on the wall, Bean Soup. You'll find Bob behind the grill, Kirk holding court at the counter, and Homer washing dishes and giving his opinion on just about everything from God to the police. (They're about equal in Homer's eyes.)

For 30 cents the waitress brings some crackers and a hot bowl of beige-looking navy bean soup, to which I add a little pepper, some salt, and more pepper. I scoop up a spoonful and marvel again at the simplicity, the satisfaction of just plain beans falling apart softly in my mouth.

There are more elaborate recipes, I am sure, but navy bean soup, according to Bob, remains:

"A 1-pound bag of beans ... but this varies. If it's cold, I double it. I let the beans soak overnight on Wednesday. Salt, pepper, a whole onion peeled. Let it boil. Simmer 2, 3, 4 hours. Remove the onion, if you care, and it's ready to serve."

As a fellow Knotty Piner used to say to me at the counter, "This soup clears up more than just the sinuses."

A few cold, wintry days later, I'm back in the high rent district, honk-tonkying it along Wells, and turn in at 1246, Bowl & Roll, to answer yet another call for soup.

This is one of Chef Louie Szathmary's restaurants (he is famed for The Bakery), and it is run by his brother in law, Marsh Kobata. There are three soups on the menu, chicken, bean with sausage or ham hock, and beef. And though I'm no great lover of chicken, I decide to opt for it just to see what a continental chef can do.

Well, half a bird is better than none, and that's how much you find slightly submerged in your big bowl of chicken soup going for $1.50. As the matchbook states, "Soups You Couldn't Finish Without a Fork and Knife." There are plenty of beautiful noodles (shaped by Kluski's) chunks of carrots, celery, hunks of turnip, and the whole show garnished with a sprinkle of parsley and bright green peas.

This chicken soup's got everything going for it, everything in it including the bottom end of the bird I'm not particularly fond of. Nevertheless, it stares me in the face and begs for some kind of acknowledgement.

The kind Kobata takes a seat to tell me everything about his soup except the specifics of how ... the internal soft machinery of soup.

He furnishes me with some soup statistics, like it's a quart-size bowl of soup he serves, that beef (at $1.75) outsells chicken, that (checking his soup diary) last year on this date he sold 53 bowls of chicken soup, and that on February 27, 1971, he ladled out 394 bowls of soup, 210 beef, 92 chicken, and the rest, bean.

"It's all made at The Bakery," is his final revelation. And The Bakery is a secret stronghold of Hungarian heritage that I'm not about to attempt for the moment since I'm full, up to the delicious depths, of chicken soup, Near North Style. And so I set a sudden course for the old neighborhood.

Tripe soup is incomparable. So, it's back to Bohemia and the small Czech restaurants and butcher shops strung out along Cermak Road in Cicero and Berwyn. The Pelikan restaurant, 5639 W. Cermak Road, on Saturday night is my usual stop. Here big Frank Desensky, owner, host, cook, keeps his firm hand in the soup pot.

Frank, from East Bohemia, opened his first restaurant on Cermak Road in 1952. He learned to cook in Rome.

"I had good government job in Old Country," says Frank. "Before I come to America I told I should learn something else, so I learn cooking with Bohemian chef in Rome. Is why I know to cook Italian too."

"But tripe, Frank? What's the tale of tripe?"

"Is good Old Country soup. Italians make, too, but not same. In Old Country people who no live in city come to town maybe Saturday and take vith them tripe soup. Some people no can take it meal, so that it tripe soup. Is popular soup, yes.

"I make it five gallons for Saturday. At old restaurant, you remember, by savings and loan? I make it 15 gallon and all gone one day. Lots of tripe there ... but different business. So for five gallon tripe soup I cook 12 pounds tripe. On Saturday I here at 4 in morning. I make tripe soup about 6. Before tripe, I roast some duck, some pork."

"What's the tip on tripe, Frank?"

"Twelve pounds tripe I cook. Maybe three big onions ... fry in lard first. Six, what you say ... spoons ... big spoons of paprika. Beef soup as stock. I cook some meat, some bones, you know ... this is base."

"Put it all together, Frank, which comes first?"

"Well, there is beef base, then there is tripe cooking, and then I fry onions with paprika together and put it in some flour ... how much? You know, hand like this. Everything I have just in my head. Three or four garlic, two big spoons marjoram, one teaspoon white peppercorn, one teaspoon ground caraway seed."

"And that's it?"

"Usually I cook tripe two hours. I cut it up like noodle slices and when soup is ready, I drop it in tripe and cook some more and some salt. Is hard explain. Is just tripe soup, you know?"

Yes, is just tripe soup, but with a rich, golden brown substance to it that immediately attacks the eyes, then the nose, and finally the taste buds. Tripe itself is, of course, a cow's stomach lining — rather slippery stuff that lurks somewhere in the bottom of the bowl. It has to be coaxed to the surface and will just as easily slip off the spoon. And once it's under the bite of the back molars, there's no way to describe the sensation of tripe ... something like hot, well-seasoned innertubes, I should guess. At times, under dental pressure, tripe may even turn on you and sound a kind of squeak.

"Some people don't eat with mouth," philosophizes Frank. "Some eat only with eyes ... every plate they want it perfect picture."

Farther west along Cermak Road, at 7018½, I return to the Plaza Dining Room, one of the smallest, least expensive, best Bohemian restaurants anywhere. Ann Nachtigall, proprietress, makes a liver dumpling soup that's worth slurping about. Though she can speak only two, maybe three words of English, she communicates through her cooking. You eat and you understand Ann and everything else.

I work through her head waitress (and interpreter), Ann Mudra, in an attempt to get to the bottom of a bowl of liver dumpling soup, but again I'm met with a razzle-dazzle recipe that seems to have no limits. Who cares? Eat. Just eat your soup.

The sign on the door says CLOSED at 10 in the morning, as shoppers, the mailman, other people dribble in for a cup of coffee, homemade bakery, dumplings and eggs, and even soup for breakfast. I try to get down some kind of recipe from Ann Mudra. I ask her in English how much liver, for example, and she calls out the question in Bohemian to Ann Nachtigall, in the kitchen, who is busily preparing a meat loaf and roasting a second set of a dozen ducks. Hands are tossed in the air.

Finally, I'm pressed into the kitchen, ladled out a bowl of liver dumpling soup, and afforded a view of the stove and environs.

There is a six gallon caldron of beef stock boiling (I understand this is at the bottom of liver dumpling soup). Ann, the owner, stirs and then brings up for inspection a hunk of beef that must weigh 5 or 10 pounds. There's more beef ... and at least two other caldrons going as well.

There are finely ground onions in that stock (as I try to decipher Bohemian kitchen talk) and celery and carrots. And now the cook is showing me a huge pan loaded with fresh liver. This, too, must be ground fine, and to it is added onions (fine) and pepper and salt and bread crumbs. Then the liver dumplings are hand rolled and dumped into the soup. And somehow it all cooks, all comes together. (Twenty cents small, one dumpling; 25 cents large, two dumplings; 50 cents for a container to go; and people coming in all the time with their own pots to be filled.)

So liver dumpling soup, Monday, Thursday, and Saturday at the Plaza Dining Room, is the best recipe I can get for the neighborhood soup lovers.

For the last few years, home for me has also been Door County. And home, when you face right up to it, is anywhere you sit down at a kitchen table with family and friends and soup.

At 20 below zero on a white, wintry morning in Door, I get a call from my lonely 88-year-old neighbor, Charley Root, who lives with his dog, Happy, about a mile away on the back forty along the eastern edge of my woods.

He calls almost every morning, and usually I'm staring at the typewriter or the birch and chickadees outside my window. Usually I'm hungry and always ripe for conversation.

"Herb?" his voice comes crackling and thinly strung out through the wires. (He has always called me Herb and I've never bothered to correct him.)

"HELLO, CHARLEY. HOW YOU FEELING?" I holler, since he doesn't wear his hearing aid and claims he can hear better without it.

"Oh, not so good. Feeling kinda tough today. Jeez, I got up this morning and had such a pain in my head, I pred'near fell I was so dizzy."

"MAYBE YOU BETTER GO SEE DOC FARMER AGAIN FOR A SHOT. YOU WANT ME TO DRIVE YOU?"

"No. Maybe I better get a new head instead," he laughs.

"PRETTY COLD IN THE HOUSE?"

"Jeez, I should say so. Kitchen pipes all frozen up. But the bathroom's okay. I went and stuck a electric heater under the pipes."

"A GOOD DAY FOR SOUP."

"Gosh, yes. I was just makin' a pot of potato soup for lunch."

"KEEP THE STOVE HOT, CHARLEY, I'LL BE RIGHT OVER."

After hiking through the snow for about five minutes, my mustache frozen and white like a wire brush, I sit in Charley's dark, somewhat depressing kitchen, thawing my tight face and catching the drops from my mustache, and watch the old man move around with Happy at his feet.

There are mousetraps set on the counter, a half bottle of Mogen David I gave him a few months ago, and a bag of his great popcorn which he popped especially for my wife and kids.

"HOW MANY POTATOES IN THERE, CHARLEY?"

"As many as I can get a hold of," he laughs.

"WHAT ELSE?"

"Oh, a couple a cups of milk. Then I put some flour in it to make it nice and thick. You gotta mash them potatoes with this," he says, rummaging through a drawer of tools to find whatever it is. "Now what did I do with that damn thing?"

"HOW'S THE MICE?"

"Oh, they're still around. Come winter, they come inside. They'll always be around ... longer'n I will, I guess."

"WHAT YOU NEED AROUND THIS KITCHEN IS A WILD WOMAN, CHARLEY. I'M GONNA BRING YOU ONE FROM CHICAGO SOMETIME."

"Yeah, I should say. Only don't bring one too wild," he grins.

"WHAT ELSE YOU GOT IN THAT SOUP?"

"Some salt and some onions. Here, try some," and he hands me a spoon, and we both attack the bubbling pot. Two friends, a cold day, and a pot of hot potato soup. What more can a man ask?

"A LITTLE MORE SALT, CHARLEY."

He adds the salt, stirs, takes the pot off the flame, and fills a few bowls — Happy's dish as well.

"She sure likes my potato soup," he smiles.

"I LIKE YOUR STYLE, CHARLEY. WHAT ABOUT THE MICE?"

"The hell with them. Let them scratch for their own."

Back in my own kitchen, it's one of those days when the kids are happy, the dog is asleep on the sofa, and the wife is saintly and stoical. At the same time it is another day with no check in sight . . . which means another supper of Kraft Dinner or maybe tuna fish casserole.

And just when things seem a little too grim, I descend from my attic retreat, put on my Panama hat and announce: "Surprise! It's Mexican Magic Soup time!" The kitchen clears miraculously as I search for the soup pot.

I rummage through the cabinet for every bean in sight, pinto, kidney, whatever looks like good bean material. Soak 'em. Get them nice and fat. And then cook them.

Next the refrigerator . . . what's left? . . . Some parsley, onion, about three or four tomatoes that look like they need more sun . . . some bell peppers, a little Parmesan cheese, and a slightly sick Zucchini. Everything's possible for my Mexican Magic Soup.

Back to the cabinet for spice and such. The dog is up and barking, the children are fighting, the wife is screaming, the sun has just taken cover under one lone cloud.

Garlic! One, two, three, four, five, six cloves . . . everything into the boiling bean pot. A shot of olive oil, some chili powder. Taste time . . . mmmm . . . more chili powder. Salt, pepper, pepper, salt . . . mmm . . . pepper. Oregano? Why not? Paprika? Of course, it's in the blood.

There's a little homemade wine left from fisherman and friend Chet Elquist, so I throw in a snort of that for old time's sake. And a shot of tabasco for Constable Johnny Gonzales, just in case he comes around.

For two or three hours it boils, and the kitchen is steeped in a heavy aroma that brings back memories of a soupy summer of Mexico sun, and finally we sup on soup. Magic.

Still not out of the woods; still not out of the kitchen. Visitors have arrived! My Aunt Lorry, a fantastic cook with the great Slavic cache of Grandma's Old World recipes in her head, and Uncle Arnie, a true soup man and lover of home cooking.

In the house hardly 10 minutes, the car barely unpacked, Aunt Lorry takes her commanding position in the kitchen, flings on an apron, fills a cup of coffee, lights a cigaret, and the whole house surrenders.

For openers she whips together an Italian dish of palenta. And follows that with a new dish each day ... often twice a day: standing rib roast and mushroom gravy, Bohemian chop suey, reuben sandwiches, crepes stuffed with cottage cheese and baked in strawberries, roast leg of lamb, all kinds of bakery, all kinds of soup. I concentrate on a week of heartburn, laughter, cursing, family gossip, and the sensation of soup.

By the third day, Aunt Lorry (a psychic, a Capricorn, a true believer in astrology, tarot, tea leaves, the transmigration of the soul) picks up my vibrations. She senses I am dying for a pot of her homemade potato mushroom soup. Grandma used to make it, and Aunt Lorry has somehow gleaned the unwritten recipe from a past that includes kitchens near Cermak Road in Cicero, 30th Street and Pulaski Road in Chicago, Three Oaks, Michigan, 18th and Lomis Streets, and even beyond that to kitchens as far away as Yugoslavia, Hungary, and Bohemia.

"I know what you want. Get me some goddam mushrooms," says Aunt Lorry (she has a touch of the old and the touch of the Now about her). "Bramborova polivka (potato soup)," she announces, and heads for the bag of potatoes on the porch.

"I came prepared," she says and pulls two chive plants from out of nowhere. "I got 'em at Dominick's in Chicago. Grandma always grew her own chives on the farm, remember? Then in winter she'd have them growing in the house so she'd have chives all year long."

She is chopping the chives, she is telling my wife to put the shorn plants on the windowsill and keep them growing, she is moving now into a bag of onions.

And all the while she is discussing astrology, sex, her two daughters, her sisters, her brothers, her neighbors, and her favorite nephew (me) and what my future holds: a few more years of Kraft dinner and, after that, the world!

Uncle Arnie has suggested she write down the soup recipe so he can have it Xeroxed at work. And she has told Uncle Arnie to go to hell. "You think I want everybody at your place to see my recipe? Only No. 1 nephew, that's all."

She is into dicing the potatoes now, chopping celery, washing, soaking, draining the dry mushrooms, putting together a batter of eggs and flour for the famous dumpling drop.

Meanwhile, she moves the conversation from a quick review of "Black Elk Speaks," to the herbs Grandma used to use before there were health stores, to the sexual properties of vitamin E. "Hell yes, it must do something for you."

Pots are boiling, lids are dropping, she hands my son a carton of potato peels. "Here, for your mommy's compost pile" ... and the soup is recycled.

Around the old oak table we talk about the way things are and used to be, and all of this, our words, our laughter, our fears, joy, and love, go into the soup and give us nourishment.

Amidst all the talk, I sneak the written recipe she has jotted down for my wife and rush upstairs to make a quick copy:

Aunt Lorry's Potato Mushroom Soup

1/4 cup butter or margarine

1/2 cup chopped onion

3 medium stalks of celery chopped.

1 1/2 cups or a nice big handful of dried mushrooms that have been washed and drained. I always boil mine about 30 to 40 minutes depending on how tough they are. Cook till tender and drain.

1 tablespoon caraway seed

1/4 cup of flour

3 cups of water — Here's how I do mine: 1 1/2 cup of water, 1 1/2 cup of milk, 3 cups cubed raw potatoes ... more or less depending on what No. 1 nephew likes

Salt and pepper to taste

1 cup of milk ... or I use half & half

Chopped chives or, if you don't have, chop off the tops of some green onions

Optional: egg droppings.

In large sauce pan, saute onion and celery, caraway seed, and mushrooms in butter, covered till tender. Gradually add water to flour, stirring until smooth. Add flour mixture, potatoes, salt, and pepper to sauted vegetables and chives. Cover. Bring to a boil and simmer for about 20 minutes, until potatoes are tender. Stir in half & half. Heat thoroughly. Most of the time I make the egg droppings. I think you'll find you could serve this soup for a king ... King Nephew No. 1, of course!

                                                                                    A.L.

Darkness, dinner time, a two-gallon white enamel pot of Aunt Lorry's potato mushroom soup on the round table ... and a kind of silence now, a certain sanctity for soup. Some rye bread from the old neighborhood, a tub of whipped butter. Aunt Lorry stirs the pot and fills all the bowls once, twice.

The potatoes are soft, the mushrooms are plentiful (she's doubled the recipe) and black and marvelous to taste, all of it just like Grandma used to make ... as far back as family taste buds can remember.

"I talked to Chef Louie of The Bakery a while ago in Chicago," I tell Aunt Lorry. "A great Hungarian, something like Grandpa. You must meet him sometime. He has the dark eyes, you know, like us, like all the Papps. He speaks in a beautiful, broken English with big pauses in between for poetry. You have to keep filling in those spaces for yourself. 'When you look in the caves of Southern France,' he said, 'Africa ... a tremendous amount of bowls ... a tribal thing ... a pot to stir. When you think of the methods of cooking ... when the tribe cooks, that's a barbecue ... when the individual cooks, that's something on the spit over the fire ... when the family cooks, that's soup.' Maybe it doesn't make much sense. But maybe it does."

Aunt Lorry bores in with her black eyes and smiles her secret smile. She knows what Chef Louie's all about without ever having met him. She knows what the cave paintings are about without ever having seen them. Her spirit has been around a long, long time.

She stirs the pot with all her soul and silently settles for the transmigration of soup.

Discovering Father

He was a white collar worker. That was always very important to him, to me in my growing years. My father worked in a bank — the Continental Bank of Chicago. He wore a clean white shirt with a starched collar and cuffs to work each day, and always some shade of gray suit and conservative tie. Nothing very loud.

He was not a man who wished to attract attention. Color, stripes, checks were always "racetrack clothes" to him.

"There is nothing neater than a clean white shirt," my father believes.

He left the house for work quite early each morning, walking to the Douglas Park El. The same elevated ride each morning, each afternoon, stop after stop, year after year after year: Laramie, Cicero, Pulaski, California, Western, Ashland, the Loop and back again.

In my boyhood, I often met him in the afternoon coming home from work, walking down the street with his hat brim always turned up and a newspaper under his arm. His shirt still looked fresh and his tie was perfectly in place. "Christ, I could wear the same white shirt for a week straight, and it would still be spotless," he would admonish me for the way I treated a white shirt in just a matter of hours.

He had but one luxury, my father. A Chinaman on Lombard and Cermak who laundered and starched five of my father's shirts each week. And there was a Saturday morning ritual of going to the Chinaman with the shirts.

We never looked like father and son. And as the years increased, the differences grew even greater. We didn't act alike, talk alike think alike, dress alike. Even today, a father myself, my own father still tells me to put on a clean white shirt, polish my shoes and get a haircut.

I hate white shirts, polished shoes and haircuts. I have never been particularly convinced that any of that mattered. Somewhere around my young manhood years, it became a stand-off between us. My father knew he couldn't tell me anything, and I knew that a long time before. Somewhere at this point, with luck, you begin to try to understand and love the old man for what he isn't. Today, in silence, we seem to be forever looking at each other from a distance, wondering just how we got to be who we are.

We never did a great deal together. It was that kind of post-depression, pre-suburbia relationship. He went to work at the bank, and I went to school. Weekend and holidays, he worked around the house while I found my own friends to play with. He was never a domineering father or the least bit violent. Just quiet, and sometimes curt. I was expected to look neat, keep my hair combed, my shoes polished, go to church and school . . . and keep my dirty hands off the clean walls. "Christ, can't you stand up? What do you have to hold onto the walls for?"

My father never said to me, "Son, let's play some baseball!" . . . or "Would you like to go to the show?" . . . or "How about the zoo on Sunday and the circus when it comes to town?" My father had no concept of fun. Uncles played ball with you. Grandmas and grandpas took you to zoos and parades.

And I don't hold this against him, then or now. But as I continue to discover myself in a father role of my own, I suddenly realize how little of my childhood was touched by a father who was mostly a white collar worker all his life, and a man who never learned how to play.

Once, as a very small child, I remember him demonstrating an old fashioned toy, part top, part yo-yo as I recall, that he set in a seesaw motion on a piece of string with stick handles and then shot it up in the air, only to catch it again, spinning, on the piece of string. I was 3 or 4, and I can see him doing that outside our old apartment in Chicago at 31st and Hamlin.

A few times he let me sit in his lap and "drive" his old '32 Ford.

Occasionally, on a summer picnic, he would resurrect an old softball that he had carefully preserved in the trunk of his car, and he and I would play catch, along with my Uncle Bill, who was a real pro and knew all the fancy stuff. My Uncle Bill, now, was a man who knew how to play. And it must have hurt my father immensely, because I favored my uncle so.

That, however, was the extent of father and son at play. There was a pair of old black iceskates in the attic, racers that he claimed were his. But I never saw him ice skate. And there was some brand-new fishing tackle put away in a shoebox. But he never took me fishing.

Yet just a year ago, one Sunday afternoon, I saw him take the comic section of the newspaper, and with a few deft strokes, make a nifty kite for my son. What's more, they went out to the backyard then, and the damn thing flew! I was stunned and overjoyed in the spontaneous mystery of his performance.

My father's whole life was the bank. He started at the Continental Bank of

Chicago in 1925. He was 16 years old. It was the only job he ever had. Neither my mother nor I were ever sure just where the bank was, what he did there, or why he seemed to love his work so. To this day, I feel the faith in his work, the faith in that bank, was greater than the faith he so diligently professed in church.

My mother never did visit him at the bank, and I must have been 19 or 20 before I finally ventured into that hallowed building, uninvited, and asked the information desk to ring George Blei, and tell him that his son was here.

He came down on the elevator, as I recall, with a rather surprised look on his face ... which I read at the time as "Now what the hell am I going to do with him here?" But what he did do was give me a quick tour of the various departments (I remember the "hardware" department best of all, where all the coins rolled in ... and I can't forget the stacks and stacks of fresh, green currency), introducing me, somewhat embarrassingly, to bank officers, tellers, and people in his own department.

"I'd like you to meet my son," he said. And the words, the revelation, came as somewhat of a shock to all of us.

He went from bank messenger to supervisor of the payroll division in all the time he spent there. I never knew just what the hell a bank "officer" was, but it seemed to be a particular position of power and prestige that my father revered, and I was certain that some day my father would be one. There would be no stopping him, a man so dedicated to his work.

Only later, when I began to go to college, when college graduates began to infiltrate the bank in great numbers, did I begin to realize some of the silence of my father when it came to moving ahead in the banking business.

Officers came out of wealthy families; officers were frequently educated in good eastern universities and moved up in banking through management programs; officers were a class apart from us. You could change into a clean white shirt every hour, and still not make the grade. "If you brought in a million-dollar account, I suppose they'd make you an officer right away," he once said to me. I always hoped to run into a friend with a million dollars to set my old man up. But my father never became an officer.

My mother would characterize all the George Bleis in the world as "Just goddam workhorses," because she understood the real working world from the vantage point of an assembly line. Workhorse or not, my father still had style.

He didn't like the young punks coming out of college, demanding all kinds of fringe benefits. He could never understand why so many high school graduates failed to stay with the bank and make it a career. The last 10 or 15 years, especially, he could not comprehend why there was such a tremendous turnover at the bank. "Now what more could they want? Paid vacation, hospitalization, pension, profit sharing, plus all the paid holidays. People are just never satisfied."

The whole work ethic was changing, but my father still hung on to the way it was with him. I know he saw men younger, unexperienced, moving faster and further than he. George Blei rose as far as he would go in the early '50s, and from that point on the bank would keep him in a hold position, interest accruing of course.

Styles changed, gray flannel suits, ivy league suits, wild sport coats, pink shirts, striped shirts, wide collar, tab collar, cuff links; wing tip shoes, cordovans, suede boots, platforms; wide ties, bowties, skinny ties, knit ties, and back to wide ties and bow ties. "I've still got boxes of old wide ties up in the attic, and now they're back in style again," he said. George Blei just stood still, shook his head, and continued doing his job. He didn't understand the full-circle philosophy, but he lived it.

"The clothes these people are wearing in the bank these days, Christ, they ought to be sent home." The short skirts in his own office bothered him to no end. But I think he loved them.

I know he cringed when the computers came marching in. He was never a believer in machinery being better than any man. To this day he would rather work figures out in his head than resort to an adding machine, or even worse, a pocket calculator. "The stuff is always breaking down," he would say about the computers.

His last years at the bank must have been filled with ominous threats to a way of work that was fast disappearing.

Mandatory retirement came for my father a few months ago at age 65. My father who had worked 48 years, 7 months and 30 days at the same bank. My father who has never known any other job. My father who is 65 years old, looks 50, and can do as much physical work as a man 30. My father who has no other interests, no hobbies, nothing save work. My father suddenly comes home one afternoon, drops the newspaper on the dining room table, hangs up his suit, and takes off his white shirt for good.

"I don't want a retirement party," said my father. "The bank doesn't owe me a thing. They gave me a job. That's all I wanted." My father, a company man to the end.

But they did give him a retirement party. And he did attend. Along with more banking friends and co-workers than I ever knew he had. There were testimonials of all sorts. And they all added up to: George Blei who did his job and did it well. "150 percent co-operation," claimed one banker. Still, "It is time to say so long to George Blei ..." And the Continental Bank will never hire another man like him.

On his first application he had to answer questions like: Have you ever been financially embarrassed? Has he good associates? Is he obedient?

My father's references included a steamfitter, a molder, an organ tuner, a housewife and a tinsmith. He was making $1,350 a year at the time of his

marriage, seven years later. (A bank official explained the fiscal responsibilities of a married man to him at that same time.)

I learned more about my father on the night of his retirement party than I
ever knew before.

He was a prolific writer of suggestions, one of the speakers said. From May,
1940, to January, 1941, he turned in about a dozen suggestions for which he
was awarded the sum of $30.

"The suggestions covered a wide range of subjects, from adding a number 6
to the checks issued to pensioners so that they could be sorted more easily in
the Proof Division, to installing an extra towel rack in one of the men's wash-
rooms." He also suggested that when an employee had to work late, his toll
call home should be paid for by the bank. (Ah, the Bohemian in my father.)

George Blei also accumulated close to 600 days sick leave in his 48 years
with the bank. He used up about 110 of these days, and more than half of
those in just the last two years when he was hospitalized twice, and probably
stretched it a bit because he knew the time of his working days was running
out. And this was his only sin against the bank.

His virtue goes unrecorded. Entitled to four, five, six weeks of paid vacation a year, he seldom took the time. Two weeks was enough for him. He had
to get back to the bank. There was just too much work sitting there.

"One of my last impressions of George," continued the speaker, "is that
nothing was impossible to be done. However, when you came to him with a
project, he had a standard reaction: 'We can't do it. It will take two weeks. We
don't have the information.' But by the time you had called the individual who
had requested the information to say it couldn't be done, the fellow would say,
'George just delivered it to me.'"

There was much good natured laughter over these revelations at my father's
retirement dinner. He and I both laughed, though we both knew how serious
the nature of work and responsibility was to him.

"One thing that did not appear on his application," concluded the speaker,
for the last laugh on George Blei and the bank, "was the fact that he suffered
from insomnia, because I do not know how to explain the fact that he was
always in to work at 7 a.m."

True and false. He never suffered from insomnia. But banker's hours were a
myth my father never perpetuated. He was at the breakfast table every
morning by 5:15. At a quarter to 6, you could hear the front door click shut as
he stepped out and down the dark sidewalk toward the L which would get him
to the bank at least two hours before the doors opened.

As his retirement drew closer, he grew even worse. "I don't know what I'm
going to do with him," confessed my mother to me one afternoon. "He's getting up at 4 in the morning now, and leaving for work at 5! He must think the
bank can't go on without him. Well, he'll soon see."

They gave my father an old adding machine at his retirement dinner. They gave him the name-plate from his desk. The big gift was, of course, a gold watch. My father probably has 20 watches. But what else can you give a man who has no other desires but work and has never been known to be late for anything?

He thanked everyone. He made a little speech . . . something else I had never known he could do. He told them he was surprised he had so many friends, that he would miss them, and that he loved them. I was not prepared for any of these feelings. He concluded, matter-of-factly, with a statement that I'm sure meant more than a final laugh to him: "I'll probably wake up Friday morning and come down to work."

In my young manhood, I, too, once considered the security and sanity of my father's calling and tried following his footsteps in banking. Getting up at 6, riding the L downtown, starting out as a messenger, taking courses in banking, hoping for the future. I lasted less than 6 months. The work was so incredibly boring, the daily trek downtown so maddening, that I was willing to accept eternal poverty to save me from such a future as my father's.

I was part of the generation that placed no value in the relationship between dedicated employee and protective employer, who would never receive a pension from anyone because it was not worth sacrificing my life to the Company, and a future which grows less and less certain.

My father slowly became aware of this and even today cannot accept the insecurity of my life as compared to his. (Though I would like to think at times he envies me.)

He spends his retirement "working around the house," which is his usual reply whenever you ask what he is doing. He spends his retirement the same way he spent his vacations — painting windows, painting every room and closet in the house, washing everything within reach, "so it's nice and clean," making and finding work almost too deliberately. "You got to keep busy," he told me the other day, as he began painting the stairway to the attic.

I bought him a book of essays on walking during his last stay in the hospital because he likes to walk a lot. I wanted to capitalize on that. Start somewhere.

I've tried to interest him in birds during the last few years. He was always a compulsive bird feeder, tossing loaves of stale bread and bakery to them in the backyard each morning before going to work. I've bought him bird books, showed him feeders to make, suggested different kinds of seed. This too is perhaps a beginning.

More than anything, though, I would wish him adventure of all sorts. I would like him to live some of the life his son has been able to live. But he seems to harbor some deep fear of change and the unknown. Forty-eight years on a job may have taken more of a toll than he cares to consider or even imagine. I'm afraid he may never learn how to play.

Lately I've noticed in the afternoons how he puts on a white shirt and tie before taking a walk for his newspaper and returning home for dinner. "I always like to be neat," he tells me.

Driving down Cermak Road, I've spotted him off in the distance any number of times, walking for his paper in his white shirt and tie, looking for all the world like an honest working man, refusing to admit he has no place to go, nothing to do, and nowhere to be, now, ahead of time.

The Croatian Picnic

You call this a picnic, my son? Just the four of us sitting here on a bench at a wayside counting trucks, drinking Kool-Aid from a Tupperware container and beer from flip-top cans, eating cold baloney sandwiches of foam rubber bread, listening to the Raiders sing "Indian Reservation?" on a one-station Japanese radio? This is a *picnic?*

Only the old-timers knew how to throw a picnic. A real picnic has its own style, like folk theater.

You take the Slavs, the Germans, the Greeks, the French, the Italians ... they know what the hell a picnic is. The Indians understood why *life* was a picnic. They consorted with all the elements ... nature, man, animal, music, joy.

Pass me another can of noisy beer ... pssssssst! I remember when you could *see* beer, quiet beer sold in buckets, with foam that looked like whipped cream.

I remember Pilsen Park, a picnic grove on 26th Street where my grandparents went to sing and dance and drink and eat and play cards and talk the old language and escape to the Old-World villages from where they came.

My family always referred to each other as "the tribe." "Let's throw a picnic," someone would say, "and invite the whole tribe."

Today, Pilsen Park is a shopping center. Polonia Grove on 46th and Archer is used mostly for concerts. Worse yet, old-timers tend to keep their picnics to themselves.

Take the Croatian picnic I went to in Chicago the other day. I sent vibrations out via Slavic and Serbo-Croats of my own tribe scattered through city and suburbs and let it be known that I had a terrible hunger for roast lamb on the spit. Was anybody picknicking like that any more? Or had all the world succumbed to charcoal-burnt hamburgers and Styrofoam ice chests?

The Croatians came through. I made contact with the family, Kalmeta. The wife, Mary, told me about a picnic grove, Jugoslav Hall, at 5540 S. Narragansett, where Croatian clubs picnic on Sundays throughout the summer. Her father in law, Božo Kalmeta, was caretaker; her husband, Tony, was president of Lodge No. 53, Hrvat Primorac, and a picnic was coming up.

Will you be roasting lambs?

"Oh yes. And maybe a pig. But this will be just a small picnic."

Will there be music and drinking and dancing and homemade bakery and old men sitting in the shade of trees?

"Oh yes. They start roasting the lambs about 5 or 5:30 in the morning. My father in law or Tony will be there to let you in. Most of the people begin coming around 12. It's open to the public."

It feels a little strange to be driving down Cermak Road toward Harlem before a sunrise so silent you can hear the stoplights click. Even at this hour, there are men on wooden benches, waiting for buses they will never board, enjoying a quiet early morning picnic in themselves.

There's a Dunkin Donut crowd of three. a man walking and talking to his dog, and a couple of cops in White Castle, eating a breakfast of burgers.

Sunrise on Harlem Avenue, turning onto Archer, heading for Narragansett, trying to remember the taste of roast lamb.

Božo Kalmeta has not yet arrived, so I take in the neighborhood on foot, once, twice around the block. Two robins confer in the middle of the street, a rabbit stares at me from a backyard garden feast, a cat slinks home down a gangway.

The benches inside the fenced grove take on an eerie glow of silver from the mercury streetlamps bordering the grounds. It is day but the trees still hold fast to the night. All the firemen are asleep across the street in Engine Co. No. 32. The grove is only about a quarter of a block in size. There are about 46 trees. A small picnic, indeed.

As for history, this grove was here almost 50 years ago, when the neighborhood wasn't, when this was called countryside. Even my Hungarian grandfather ate, drank, danced, and picnicked in these woods.

Tony Kalmeta meets me outside the gate. Božo Kalmeta, the father, is already inside the hall, turing on lights, complaining about the mess the last group left.

So first there is Božo and then Tony; and later Tony's wife, Mary, and the younger children; and later their oldest daughter, her husband and their child; and later Mary's sister and her husband, Mark, and later Božo's wife, Della.

And that is how ethnic picnics are peopled — with blood ties, if you're lucky: grandfathers, grandmothers, mothers, fathers, sisters, brothers, uncles, aunts, cousins, children, grandchildren, great-grandchildren. And that is one way old picnics are preserved.

But a picnic is all kinds of people. The relationships are varied but firm and all tied to a common background, a common tongue.

And father and son are already deep into those sounds as they discuss the number of lambs to be roasted and who will be around to help. You hear names such as Nick, Darvin, Billie . . . .

They will roast only 10 lambs today and no pig. Lodge No. 53 is small, only 80 members, most of them old-timers. The younger ones number around 20 and include Tony and the two other men who will help roast the lambs.

"Last year we roasted 12 lambs and a pig, and we got stuck," says Tony. "Today, with good weather, maybe we'll sell out."

Darvin Churlin and his twin brother, Carl, enter the grove about 6 a.m. They do no look alike. Darvin seems to tower over Carl, looks darker, tougher, talks louder, and nourishes a kind of sweet contempt for everything.

Carl, short with a slight mustache, has the touch of the old-time, low-keyed, comic about him. They are 36 years old. Darvin drives a truck in Chicago for Nighthawk Freight ("a friendly old Croatian firm," he says) while Carl works as a telegraph operator at Chicago's Union Station.

They were reared at the Croatian Fraternal Union Orphanage in Des Plaines, where they learned to roast lambs at picnics under the strict tutelage of an old man named Mirko — a great name for an old man. It sounds like miracle.

Darvin, who seems to relish the old way of life, buries his arm elbow deep in the lamb. (Carl takes it all in silently, smiles, and may suddenly make a joke, even raise his fist and yell, "Croatian power!") Darvin stands tall at a table inside the shack (the pit area where the lambs are to be roasted and later chopped and served), puts on a white apron, and begins emptying a blue plastic shopping bag of the tools of his art — an ax, a pick, two long, sharp knives, a meat cleaver, something called a "spaga," which serves as a needle. Also, a ball of heavy twine and a 5-pound package of salt.

He hefts a 40-pound bag of charcoal, drops it under the first spit, slices it open with a knife, pours a can of fluid, and tosses a match. A picnic without fire is no picnic.

"Who the hell's gonna handle the fire today? I gotta do everything?" he asks.

"Billie," says Božo. "Billie will come."

"He better."

Just outside the pit Tony and his father are cleaning off a long table for the lambs. Carl carries the first one from the ice cooler and drops it on the table.

"How many?" asks Darvin.

"Ten," says Tony.

"You sure?" asks Božo. "No look like no 10 to me. Look like eight."

"Well, there better be 10," says Tony.

"Ten's enough," says Darvin.

"What the hell's the difference," says Carl.

Nick Vukelic, another old-timer and past president of the lodge, comes on the scene, and there is some kidding in Croatian, some laughter, some cursing, and Nick says in broken English, "I come to tie lambs."

Immediately an argument starts between him and Darvin about how the lambs are to be tied to the spit. In English, in Croatian, in fierce gestures, the fight explodes across the Croatian generation gap.

"All right, let him tie, let him tie," says Darvin.

"And you can bet that the lamb breaks, and then I have to go over that goddam fire and tie it right."

"No, no, no," says Nick.

"Yeah, yeah, yeah," says Darvin. "Last year you tied 'em and five fell in the fire!"

"Nick," says Carl, as diplomatically as possible, but joking with him all the while, acting out the part, "you're the past president of the lodge. You're supposed to walk around the grove like this with a straw hat and your hands behind your back and a big cigar in your mouth."

Nick brushes him off in Croatian. Darvin returns the gesture and shouts in English: "MY JOB IS TO TIE THE BASTARDS AND CHOP THEM! THAT'S WHAT I'M HERE FOR!"

They both tie, Darvin watching the old man closely out of the corner of his eye.

The tie-down begins with a wooden shaft about 5 feet long which is jammed through the tail end of the lamb, passed through the open rib cage, and out beneath the neck. The lamb is punctured with the spaga-needle in at least two places on both sides of the backbone, before the twine is inserted and the actual tying takes place. The twine goes around the shaft, around the backbone, and is pulled to the breaking point before knotting on the inside.

Darvin has tied the neck and is already moving to the back legs of his lamb while Nick is still wrestling with the shaft and backbone of his.

Another argument develops about how much fat to take out of the inside. Nick feels a little should be left in; Božo says, "Take it all out"; Darvin yells: "There are too goddam many people telling me what to do! I'm not gettin' paid for this, you know. I'm doin' this for the lodge. Nick, just tie those lambs and be quiet. I'll take out what I want to take out." He pulls out a handful of guts.

"This stuff is good," says Darvin. "Later we fry this up for breakfast."

"*Zigerica*, that's called," says Tony, "lungs, heart, liver, spleen. You chop it up in a pan of olive oil, add some parsley, some wine ... stir it up, fry it. It's good."

"*Zigerica*, that's called," says Tony, "lungs, heart, liver, spleen. You chop it up in a pan of olive oil, add some parsley, some wine ... stir it up, fry it. It's good."

"*Zigerica*!" yells Carl, just for the hell of it, because it's one of those strong sounding Slavic words that hits the air like a spark.

"You gotta leave a little fat in," explains Darvin. "But this stuff" (a handful of lardy looking stuff near the back end) "I always tear out. Leaves a bad taste to the lamb."

The preparation of the lambs continues. And no matter how many old-timers lend their wisdom or how many early-morning stragglers mill around the table, it's Darvin in charge all the way.

He keeps a constant pace, a supercharged chatter of English, Croatian, and pure Chicago cussedness that sometimes begins in simple instruction and often borders on folk philosophy.

"Now you wash 'em and salt 'em. Nick, give a hand. Carl, go get a rag and some water. Where's the salt? Tony, get the salt. Nick, if those goddam lambs you tied break, I'm gonna throw you on the fire to pick up the pieces.

"How do you like that hat on Božo, huh? He thinks he's in the movies. All the old-timers do. Pa had a hat like that, huh, Carl. Didn't the old man used to dress sharp? We used to laugh at Pa and his Edwardian suits, his spats, his big ties. These guys today with their way-out clothes ... hell, the old man dressed like that 20 years ago! Right, Carl? Throw a handful of salt like this, you see. Then wash it in, wash it down, rub it in ...."

The back legs are slipped into each other between the bone and the tendon, then tied to the spit. The front legs are tied directly to the spit after the forelegs have been broken off. More salt. Then the belly of the lamb is closed with the broken forelegs. Two neat slices are made on both sides of the chest and the bones slipped through to close the gap tight.

Darvin cuts slits into the front and rear shanks and stuffs them full of salt with his finger. Nick is about to tell him something about salting when Darvin hits him with a couple of untranslatable Croatian curses.

"You can't change people," continues Darvin. "Especially the Yugoslavs, the Croatians, the Serbs, the whole bunch. I was over there. You'll never unite that goddam country ... all kinds of rivalries between. Just like here. Same old thing ... north and south, black and white. They'll never be united ... can't change people.

"I like the old-timers, don't get me wrong about Nick. It's nice of him to come down here and give me a hand. You don't see any of the younger guys here, do you? It's these guys who've been doin' this all their lives. I like to do these picnics for the club. Anybody else I'd charge at least 20 bucks. All this Old-World crap ... it's in my blood.

"Put a lotta water on it," he tells Carl and Tony. "Rub that salt in good or else it'll all fall off in the fire. And if the skin ain't good, the lamb ain't good. What time is it? We're doing all right. Put the lambs on around 6, they should be done by 12."

They carry the first lamb to the fire, one man on each end of the shaft, holding the lamb like some ancient sacrifice, fixing it into its proper place on the lower rack, the fire glowing a steady red just to the side of the spit, never right underneath it; then turning on the motor (once this was done by hand at half hour intervals), watching the lamb make its first slow, somewhat jerky revolution ... the fire reflecting a deep pink off the raw meat.

There are two fires going, another about to be started. It is still early with a cool wind blowing through the pit area but you can begin to feel the fire, smell the lamb burning (at least 5 pounds of it to dissipate in juice and atmosphere) and imagine the heat later in the day with 10 lambs and five fires going.

The men carry more fresh lambs from the cooler and repeat again and again the process of breaking the forelegs, bending/tying the lamb to the spit, cleaning out the fat and guts, washing, salting, and closing up the cavity with bones.

And the conversation never falters. Such work, such celebration does not require silence. There is a Croatian harmony and good feeling in the air, a kind of do-you-remember camaraderie.

"Hey, remember Matievic?" says Darvin. Heads nod, language shifts again to Croatian and Nick laughs and shakes his head. Matievic, so the story unfolds, was an artist at tying down lambs. "Matievic can tie lamb in three minutes!" says Božo. "He ought to, for crissake," says Darvin, "he was a butcher, wasn't he?" "Yeah," says Carl, "and when he got mad he'd throw a goddam hatchet at you."

"What about Mirko, huh, Carl?" says Darvin. He's the one who taught me all this stuff. Remember for the big picnic, getting up at midnight and watching Mirko start roasting the lambs?"

"He'd throw a goddam crowbar at you, anything," says Carl. "He'd work the hell out of you."

"Yeah, but he really liked us," says Darvin. "He was kind of a father to us. He could really roast lamb."

"But, Darv, you're the best of the younger guys," says Tony. "There's nobody else doin' it."

Darvin pretends he doesn't hear the compliment. He says: "It'd be nice if Mirko showed up today. I'd like to see the old bastard again."

But Darvin has learned a lot about the Old-World art of cooking. He keeps in practice.

"I do this sometimes on weekends. For two lambs, I get 20 bucks. I got two lambs and two pigs to roast at Fox Lake next week. I bring all my own gear. With pigs you gotta be careful. I got a friend who roasted a pig by hand for 18 hours and the damn thing was still raw. A pig's gotta age. You gotta leave it hang for two weeks at 39 degrees. With a pig you gotta break down the molecules, let 'em hang.

"I get all my lambs from Nea-Agora on Taylor Street. They're good lambs. 'Don't do me any goddam favors,' I tell him. I bought over 300 lambs from him this year already. He wanted to give me a leg of lamb on him. 'Just send me good lambs, 35 to 40 pounds,' I tell him. 'Don't bring me no babies or no goddam goats. I don't want any favors ... just good lambs or you'll get the goddam things back, roasted.' "

Darvin has ideas on seasoning as well: "I'm not puttin' any garlic in these 'cause there's too many old-timers in the club that can't take it anymore. It's good with garlic, though. You just stick the pieces in all around the lamb. The Italians baste it with Worcestershire Sauce, oregano, a mixture of all kinds of stuff. I saw the Czechs once take lamb fat, mix it with chicken fat, then mix it with Open Pit Sauce. It was good."

Nick suddenly butts in with a little early-morning picnic philosophy: "I do everything that is good for the people. Money is money but people is people."

Suddenly Darvin jumps in with, "We're in good shape ... 7:30, five lambs on ... take a break."

Carl goes through a broken English DP routine: "Ya, meat cutters union! Break time! Ve break now!"

But Božo is not about to let the men give up. "Bring 'nother lamb here! Don't leave fire burn for nawthing!"

At 7:45 Nick says: "I go home now and make breakfast. Be back later."

"Yeah," says Darvin. "You better be back to catch those goddam lambs you tied."

While the men are soaking up the peace and quiet in even so small a sanctuary of nature, an old man in a straw hat approaches. He moves slowly, stops, straightens his glasses, and pushes forward with a cane.

"Hey!" shouts Carl. "Will you look at this! Mirko, the old master lamb roaster!"

Darvin yells at him in Croatian.

Mirko Kolak, 73, stops at the table, looks Carl straight in the eye and says, "You fulla crap."

Mirko, the taskmaster of picnics past, pokes Darvin in the ribs with his cane and says: "You goddam lazy sonofabitch. I do this all by myself. No help."

"I can do it all by myself, too," says Darvin.

"You can't even sign your name by yourself, you bastard," says Mirko.

"How do you spell Matievic's name?' Tony asks him.

"How I should know to spell Matievic? I got trouble spelling my own," says Mirko.

Darvin, one can sense, revels in getting Mirko riled up, even if he must suffer the old man's curses.

"We're the only young guys who follow our nationality," he tells Mirko.

Mirko ignores the remark. "Why don't you do the job right?" he shouts at Darvin. "Use wire, not string!"

"I know. I wanted to use wire like the old days, but they can't afford it."

"You was a no good kid sonofabitch at the orphanage, and you gonna die no good," he tells Darvin.

"And they're gonna bury me right next to you," laughs Darvin.

"You not going into any cemetery I go," says Mirko. "They gonna throw you in the ditch!"

Mirko moves around the table as the master he was, and even Darvin steps aside. "Make room, make room," he tells Darvin. "Put more salt in there! And if you gonna use string, goddam it, use the next size! How many lambs you got?"

"Ten," says Darvin.

"Ten?" says Mirko. "I put 90 on! Ninety!"

"I've had 25 on," says Darvin.

"I put 90 on from 12 midnight to 5 in the morning. You remember that? At the orphanage, you remember? Ninety? You through now, all through? Then clean the table," and he hits him again with the cane.

"I still got your meat cleaver," Darvin tells Mirko. "I keep it nice and sharp. Only use if for special picnics."

"Ya, I gave it to you."

"You never gave me anything. I bought it," says Darvin, and they both break up in laughter.

By 8:45, all 10 lambs are on the fire.

Mirko, no longer supervising, comes over to me, rubs his forehead, and confesses just how much the two brothers mean to him: "That big one, he used to beat the hell out of the small one at the orphanage. But the big one, he was always there to help me roast the lambs for the picnic. Twelve o'clock he get out of bed and say, 'Mirko, I help you' Ninety I roast once. Eighty-six lambs and four pigs. Hot like hell. Sweat. Everything smell, lamb, lamb. So bad, I couldn't eat! When I finish, I go out and eat hamburger instead. Ya, 90 at one time. But let me tell you, nothing is forever." And Mirko moves off to a bench in the shade of a catalpa tree.

Billie, the fireman and an old Bohemian at heart, is now inside the pit feeding the fire, spreading out the coals between the turning lambs. The heat has risen considerably. Darvin, Billie, and Carl are wrinkling their faces in sweat.

"See that lamb that Nick tied?" points Darvin. "The sonofabitch is falling. He tied the leg wrong, see? Now the goddam thing's coming down, and Nick is nowhere around."

"We stop. I get," says Billie.

"No, gimmie the string," says Darvin. "I'll go around the back there and try to tie it."

While the lambs are roasting, two of the women are inside the kitchen of the hall getting the bakery ready. Antoinette Cuculich and Betty are putting apple and cheese strudel into the oven.

Some nationalities, some women, make strudel with a crust that hits the table like 10 pounds of stale bread. But the art of the strudel is a delicate balance — the weight of the filling, either apple or cheese, balanced by the airiness, almost the transparency, of the layers of flaky, crispy crust.

Show me a wet, soggy crust, and I'll show you a lump of a strudel.

Show me a crust that floats into your mouth yet holds the heavy, sweat cinnamony taste of apple, the chewy cheesiness of cheese, and I'll show you a strudel you can stomach, mouthful after mouthful, like cotton candy.

Antoinette makes that kind of strudel. She has 10 of them going for the picnic. She slips me a warm slice of cheese strudel, and I am tempted to forgo the roast lamb.

What's the secret of strudel, Antoinette?

She smiles. Ethnic people classify their recipes with a tougher code than the Pentagon's. But there is always a way to weaken an ethnic woman ... look hungry, be grateful for whatever she gives you, tell her you wish your mother could bake like that. Then ask, in all sincerity, "Is it very hard to make?"

More than likely she'll try to recall the recipe: "Three cups of flour, ¼ cup of oil, 2 tablespoons of sugar, ½ teaspoon of salt, 2 cups of lukewarm water. Knead together for 15 minutes. Let it rest for an hour and a half at room temperature. then stretch it out on a table. As for filling (apple), 3 pounds of apples, a teaspoon of cinnamon, 1 cup of sugar, about a ½ pound of butter for the whole works. As for cheese, 2 pounds of it, ½ pint of sour cream, ½ cup of sugar, 3 eggs, mix the sugar in the cheese, with a pinch of salt. This should make about 5½ pounds of apple strudel, about 35 pieces."

But the final secret rests with the soft touch of the strudelmaker. Even she doesn't know that secret.

At 10:30 the grove takes on more sun. The cool breeze brushes the leaves, scatters light between the trees. More old-timers arrive, gesturing — for such is the visual nature of their language — talking the old talk, the words and syllables that jump and sizzle and ignite the very air above them.

At 11:15 Billie is adding more coal, the temperature is now 110, 120 in the pit area. Darvin is preparing *zigerica*, barbecuing it instead of frying . . . it's time for the cooks to eat.

Carl is holding a sirloin over the hot coals between the lambs. "Won't be long for this." And Darvin is pouring olive oil into a pot and filling it with swiss chard from his own garden.

The smell of lamb slowly turning on the fire, the sound of skin sizzling, the

juicy crispiness of it all, and the smoke, the terrible heat, recalls what Darvin said some hours ago.

"Getting drunk on the heat," he called it. "The smell of lamb, the fire, you go crazy after a while. Especially when you're chopping and people are out there yelling their orders. You go a little nuts in the heat. You don't care what you tell 'em."

At 11:30, Darvin sets the scale into which he will drop the pieces of hot lamb. "I want it right *on* there, not an ounce over! I don't want nobody tellin' me I'm cheatin' him."

There is a price list scratched on cardboard near the cashier's window: 1 (lb.)—$2.25; 1½—$3.40; 2—$4.50; 2½—$5.65; 5—$11.25....

Billie the fireman places a bottle of cold beer near the coals. "You can't drink it cold like that. It'll kill a man."

People are beginning to congregate inside and around the pit area. Darvin is roasting; he is getting hotter by the second as people begin pressing him, getting in his way, asking for special cuts. Darvin will have no part of that. "When I'm doin' the roasting, no one gets no special favors! No one!"

"When be ready the lamb?" asks a woman, again.

Darvin ignores the remark as an insult to his artistry. But then, over his shoulder, the heat rising, he gives her the back of his lip: "I told you 12 o'clock! TWELVE O'CLOCK, GODDAM IT!"

The scent of the dripping roast lamb ... no wonder the Croatians are restless outside the pit, the smoke wafting over the grove. They press their noses to the screen like children and are rewarded with the sight of shoulder bones beginning to crack, through skin burnt to a mouth dazzling succulence. It's enough to make the savage in any man tear off a hunk right from the spit, burnt hands and all, and gorge himself while the juice drips down his chin.

My God! How can a man picnic on baloney sandwiches! Such an obscenity of the primitive pleasure that is *Picnic*!

Now it is 11:55, and Darvin has locked himself in the pit to keep out the people asking for special favors.

Meanwhile, in the grove, the aura of Picnic begins to stir the air. One woman finds a place in the shade while her husband waits in line for the lamb. Another begins wiping down a bench, setting a tablecloth, placing a big blue roaster for the lamb in the center of the table. Even the firemen look hungry across the street and pick up a kind of quiet alarm as they stare into the grove from the station house.

At one minute before noon, Carl and Darvin are sitting in the alley behind the pit area eating *zigerica* and swiss cheese, topping it off with sirloin.

At 10 minutes after, the two brothers enter the firepit and the action begins. You can sense the delight in Darvin as he lingers over the lamb Carl and Billie have carried from the spit and dropped on the butcher block. Now for the cleaver, the knife, and the ax. WAAAAAAUMMPHF!

The people call out their orders, and Darvin listens, argues, sweats, swears, and all the while hacking, piling the hot, juicy lamb on paper plates, dumping it onto the scale, wiping his hands on his apron, telling the cashier, "Okay, 5 pounds, $11.25!"

With the lamb is served a handful of raw, green onions and another handful of bread, white or rye. You buy cold beer to wash it down, then carry the hot lamb to your table and begin eating with your bare hands. No utensils furnished. Anyway, meat like this is best savored this way.

The lamb goes fast. Especially the legs.

"No more leg?" someone asks.

"If you want leg, you wait," says Darvin. "I ain't cuttin' another one up yet. All I got is ribs left. Who want ribs? ANYBODY, RIBS?"

He makes a quick deal with a woman. "Tell you what, I'll give you 2 pounds of ribs now and 4 pounds of leg later." She takes it. "That's some nice meat I gave you, lady. You can't complain."

They're all yelling in Croatian now, Billie, Carl, Darvin, the people in line, the heat beginning to affect all of them ... a roast lamb mania taking hold. And Darvin not only roasting, chopping, weighing but also fiercely bargaining with everyone, something like a Turkish rug man in the market streets of Istanbul.

"But it's a beautiful piece of lamb, beautiful." Heads of prospective buyers are sticking in the window, two at a time, examining the butcher's bargain. Darvin's hands, dripping with lamb, turns the choice cut first this way, then that, smacking his lips. "I'll take it," somebody says.

"I got ribs now only," he yells again. "Ribs, ribs."

"Put up another one," somebody tells him.

"I'm not choppin' another one, goddamn it, till I get rid of these ribs!"

"I'll take them," says a woman in the middle of the line with an empty pot.

Carl, standing in the background, counterpointing the haggling with occasional shouts in Croatian, seems completely caught up in the madness.

"No checks, please!" he yells and laughs. "And no dinars! Only cold American cash!"

Darvin, scraping the butcher block clean of meaty scraps, tasting them: "Lotta good meat here. Who wants some scraps? SCRAPS? I'LL GIVE YOU A POUND OF SCRAPS FOR THE PRICE OF HALF A POUND!"

"I'll take it."

"You gotta good deal. BRING UP ANOTHER LAMB!" Slap, chop, crunch, goes the bone. "Who wants legs? I got legs.... How many pounds? Two pounds a leg. Wait your turn, lady, wait your turn .... You got a little better than 4½ pounds, okay?"

"Oh, that's too much," says the man.

"That's too bad. What the hell you want me to do? You want it or not? Look, it's beautiful lamb...."

Silence ... the smell overpowering. "Give it to me."

In 20 minutes, two lambs have been chopped and sold. And there is already a complaint. An old man hollers at Darvin: "All bones, for crissake. You gave me 2 pounds of bones!"

"You wanted ribs, you got ribs," Darvin tell him.

"Yeah, but for crissake, no meat! No meat!"

"Somebody's got to eat the bone," says Darvin.

"HOT LAMB, HOT LAMB," hawks Carl. "NO DINARS, PLEASE!"

Food is the pinnacle of Picnic, whether it be hot dogs over the fire, roast lamb, or cold baloney sandwiches. The major problem is always, "What should we eat?" But once that has been settled, once the lamb, seasoned with raw onions, buried in bread, has been ingested, topped with beer, laid gently to rest with strudel and hot coffee ... once the body has picnicked, it's time for the spirit to stretch the afternoon away under the sun and shade. Although one may occasionally add beer to keep body and spirit in proper picnic perspective.

And so the Croatians at the Jugoslav Hall Picnic Grove settle down to the tranquil phase of their Sunday afternoon picnic. Children play hard, to be sure. Young and middle-aged marrieds swap stories and dreams of their homes, their families, their future. Old-timers soak it all in, recall picnics past, take note of who is still around and who isn't, and dream, too, of when they will make another trip to the old country.

"I'll go next year, maybe to Zagreb, and see my nephew."

A quiet card game slowly unfolds at one of the picnic benches. NO GAMBLING PLEASE POLICE ORDER states a sign posted high on a tree, almost out of sight.

"What's the matter, Charley," chides the dealer, a wizened old man in a funny fedora, always laughing, moving the cards expertly, even though his right hand has only the little finger.

"Charley lose three in a row," he grins, and there is the sound of loose change exchanged in closed fists and buried in pockets.

One man reads the Sunday paper, a man and a wife play cards, a mother hollers at a child to get down off the table before he breaks his neck, a father plays catch with his son, a man sits alone in the corner of the grove, takes off his shoes and socks, stretches, and begins reading a book.

Nick returns (Darvin giving him hell for the lambs he tied) and walks around the grove, small-talking it in Croatian with the people, nodding, shaking hands, acting the way Carl told him past presidents of Lodge No. 53 were supposed to act.

Mirko removes his hat, rests his cane on the picnic bench, and sits folded over in conversation with one of his cronies. The hands all the time moving.

By 2:30 Darvin is down to three lambs. How do you tell when they're done, I ask him. How do you know when to take them off the spit?

"When the juice has run all out of them, see? How dry .... Then you take the front legs and push them in like this and listen if they crack."

There are 150 people in the small grove and more still coming. The whole family of Kalmeta is there, plus who knows how many other families.

Across the street, in a world far away, the firemen take out their trucks for a Sunday airing, then put them back in again.

Music. Around 3 o'clock, Louie Vucinic's Balkan Tamburitza Orchestra assembles almost magically at the northwest corner of the grove. There are five pieces: concertina, bass, and three guitar-like stringed instruments of different shapes and sizes, the prima, the tamburitza, and a cello-sounding guitar. The music they make is impossible to describe.

If you like the music from "Zorba," it is something like that. If you like the music from "Dr. Zhivago," it is something like that. It is old music, quick, plunky, high-tight-stringy music ... earthy, bouncy Balkan ... fields, flowers, mountains, village, laughter, love, the full circle of human expression.

And with the music, with the drinking, with the eating, with the whole purity of Old-World picnicking, comes the singing ... *"Vrati Mi Srce"* *(Return to me my love ...)*. The musicians singing, the men with too many beers joining in, clustering around the band; old Nick in front of them all, rocking in place, remembering.

I listen carefully to Tony's brother in law, Mark Skeva, who has played the Balkan music, feels it intensely, knows exactly what sound each instrument can make, and understands how music, especially the music that nourished you from a child on, is a kind of soul music, too.

"It means a lot to me, the old music," he says. "I go to different places all over the city to still hear it. I hate to see it die out. In fact, about the only thing I'll miss on leaving life is this ... I'll miss the music."

By 4 o'clock in the afternoon all the lamb is gone. "Fifteen," says Darvin as he begins to clean up. "I could have chopped 15 today."

And the dancing. Only one couple at first. An old man in a brown suit and a hefty woman in a bright, flowered dress. They step slowly in time to the music ... to the sunlight ... to the picnic.

Another hot card game develops at the south end of the grove. Some of the picnic regulars, says Tony. "I think that's all the hell they ever do is go to picnics every Sunday just to play cards."

There are more dancers, most of them old-timers. Occasionally a young couple, though picnics like this, it seems, no longer serve as celebration for the young.

Yet celebrations of earth and life remain the same. Symbols do not change.

The men, at the moment, are singing a "round" song ... a melody that never seems to end ....

And next the women dance the *Kolo*, an old, old circle dance, feet hopping, stepping, gliding around and around and around; and there is one girl in the group wearing a T-shirt with a peace symbol.

And you have Darvin, a young brave, cleaning the knives, and ready to roast two lambs and two pigs come next Sunday . . . .

And you have Mirko, an old chieftain, surveying the whole ritual from a picnic bench under a late sun, knowing damn well that though "nothing is forever," there are some things men do in peace and joy that do not die.

Epilogue: Where the Old Still Dance

I am sitting at the bar of Old Prague in Cicero on a late autumn night, a stranger in my own neighborhood. Years have passed since I lived within the stories of this book. My visits home are not as frequent as they used to be.

I rarely return to write stories of the neighborhood for newspapers and magazines anymore. For various reasons, my life as a freelance writer in search of the ethnic heart of his old neighborhood has ended. There is little chance that time will ever come again. I am reminded of the words of Mirko, the old master lambroaster of Croatian picnics past: "Nothing is forever."

Old Prague was one of my mother's favorite restaurants on Cermak Road, though she knew and enjoyed most of them. She went to Old Prague for lunch, for banquets, parties, get-togethers with her sisters, Millie and Lorry. On Saturday evenings, after church, she often had dinner there with my father and friends. I would join them if I was in the neighborhood. She knew the owner, the waitresses, the cooks, the bartenders, Frankie the accordian player, cops, local politicians, cab drivers, you name them, and spoke their languages — English, Czech, or the language of the streets. She was that kind of person.

She worked at Western Electric, in the factory, for 25 years. And when she retired (never fond of sitting home) she found another job almost immediately as the front desk receptionist of Western National Bank, a few blocks from home, where (she convinced the bank) she could greet customers in five languages. It was a perfect job for a woman whose whole life was people — and the bakeries, butcher shops, clothing stores, all the life along Cermak Road.

Through the years, the family attended many celebrations at Old Prague. My parents held their 50th wedding anniversary there in June of 1982. Brothers, sisters, uncles, aunts, cousins, grandchildren, friends, neighbors, nuns, parish priests, doctors, were in attendance. Frankie played the accordian and the family danced, just like old times. Then on January 15, 1983, seven months later to the day, many of the same people gathered in the same back room of Old Prague for a more solemn dinner in memory of my mother, Emily Blei. who was buried at Mt. Auburn, south of the neighborhood in Stickney, that same day.

With her passing, came a significant loss of the neighborhood way of life for me. She was my source; stories, recipes, restaurants, gossip, jokes, language, customs, food, family history, friends, church functions, politics, neighbors, stories, tips on horses, contacts of all kinds I needed to pursue many of the stories I wished to tell. "My son the writer," she would introduce me to one Cermak Road denizen after another. She was my voice with the old-timers, the Czech langauge crackling from her mouth. The mother tongue. Much of the neighborhood was reborn for me through her eyes. Much of her spirit resides in this book.

The neighborhood continues to slip away from me. I picture the two-flats, houses, bungalows on my street where my friends once lived and realize that all of them have moved to distant suburbs, distant states. A handful of neighbors remain: Tamse, Zbasnik, Kozar, Kachlic.

I see some of these people occasionally on my visits, wave to them on the street, perhaps while walking with my father on a late Friday afternoon in spring, stopping by to pick up his friend, John Cilik, on the next block. Then the three of us are off to one of the many Bohemian restaurants on Cermak Road for a senior citizen discount dinner, before 5 o'clock.

The neighborhood seems very much the same to me at those times. The houses are well-maintained, the lawns trimmed, the gardens beautiful, the people friendly. Occasionally, if I listen carefully, I can still hear the sound of Czech on the street. I could come back to all this, I tell myself. I could still live here, I daydream.

I overlook, no doubt, the occasional derelict house, an apartment building boarded up, broken sidewalks, abandoned stores along Cermak, some back yards and alleys filled with junk, side streets clogged with parked cars; some of the new neighborhood immigrants content to have a roof over their heads and the hell with painting the garage, repairing windows and doors, planting flowers, cutting lawns. Then there's the outbreak of vandalism, garage break-ins, drugs, gangs, corruption, the past and the present as the neighborhood of Cicero struggles to survive, to live up and down its name.

The old hometown is in the national news again. The shadow of Al Capone and the mob remains, prompting even President Reagan to cancel a visit for fear of his image. The image of Cicero (anti-law, anti-black) will not go away, though a settlement of sorts was reached in March of 1986 between the Town of Cicero and the federal government regarding jobs and open housing for minorities. It remains to be seen, of course, just when and how that will be implemented. Change, though inevitable, will no doubt be a wearing-down process (economically, socially, politically) rather than an overnight reality. As what was once Cicero fades, disappears, dies off, what Cicero could become hangs in the balance.

Still a 'border town' of dancing girls and all-night bars, hookers and horse players — as evidenced along the still seamy side of Cicero Avenue and 12th Street? Still a burg where crime does pay with a mafia influence? Drugs, prostitution, gambling, graft? (The more things change, the more they remain the same? True and false.) The dark side of the heart of the neighborhood is the dark side in the heart of us all. Who knows when the light will come?

Change? Perhaps in the social fabric as the Last of the Mohicans, the last of the old Bohemians, Poles, Slovenians, Croatians, Germans, Italians die off, sell out, move with their children to distant suburbs, go into nursing and retirement homes, buy condos in Florida and Arizona, abandon a way of life they knew intimately and perpetuated for a generation or two.

Realtors in the neighborhood today will tell you that 50% of the housing sales are to Hispanic families, another large portion to Orientals. Most of the sales are to families in the medium-to-low income bracket. In this way, perhaps, does an old neighborhood begin to make adjustments.

At times I entertain the notion that in years to come Cicero might become a kind of Old Town. Young professionals working in Chicago will discover the potential of this neighborhood as an "in" place to live — less than ten miles from downtown on the Eisenhower Expressway; minutes from the Loop on the Douglas Park El; minutes away too via the Burlington; excellent shopping, restaurants, services; an Old World atmosphere; brick bungalows, many of which remain architectural wonders of stained glass and beautiful interior details of oak woodwork; an authentic ethnic culture which might be preserved and encouraged for its full European flavor, for truly there is no place, so self-contained, quite like it in all of Chicago. These new "professional neighborhood folk" then will begin to buy into the area, re-hab the buildings that need it, preserve the past, and see to it that local government begins to function along more democratic lines. And that there will be room for all.

I share my concerns with a neighborhood friend, Madeline Rowe, living now in Naperville. She too has a single parent still living in Cicero. "Norb," she writes, "I think any dreams we have of saving the ethnic neighborhood will vanish shortly — when this last stand of seniors are gone."

Dining on a late Friday afternoon with my father, in his mid-70's, and his friend, John Cilik, in his 80's, delighting in the way the three of us still savor traditional Bohemian delicasies like liver dumpling soup, roast duck, roast pork, dumplings and sauerkraut, washed down by cold pilsner, topped off with hot coffee and homemade kolacky sprinkled with powdered sugar, I glance around the room and discover how many tables-for-one there are, a widow or widower eating alone. Of all the diners present, I am the youngest, though my hair too is turning grey. The restaurant is half full. What's to become of all this?

In my darkest dreams I envision a time when my father is gone, the remaining relatives have moved, and I am an old man, alone, afraid, sequestered behind triple-locked doors in my father's house of hardwork and fond memories, continually attacked by roving gangs because the house, newly painted and well-maintained, is the last bastion of peace, pride, and order in a neighborhood gone lawless, gone derelict, gone ghetto. All the irrational, inbred fears of my father, of the old neighbors, have been realized. Small fires burn throughout the day and night. The smell of smoke is everywhere. In the darkness of the kitchen or the basement I await the shattering of a window, the battering of a door in a final confrontation of a new order of change, of chaos, that will leave me dead, the rooms ransacked, and the house on fire.

But alone at the bar in Old Prague this October night, all these thoughts (enhanced by drink) serve notice that the hour is late, my time is up. I should call it a night, walk back to the house, try not to wake my father, catch a few hours' sleep on the sofa, a hit the road again tomorrow — stopping first at Fingerhut's for a loaf of Babi's rye, then Vesecky's for houska and coffeecakes before I leave the neighborhood.

But a man at the bar I had not noticed strikes up a conversation. We engage in the usual talk: weather, sports, and you-from-around-here? He is; I used to be. And I leave it at that, appreciating the silence again, hoping to finish my drink and depart with a nod; hoping to avoid the dreaded question of What's your name? or What do you do? for no other reason than I like privacy, anonymity, which the neighborhood always afforded me. The writer's life and work is so strange, I find it difficult to explain.

But before I've emptied my glass, he's bought me a drink, and I acknowledge my approval with a raised glass, all the while wondering whether to talk or not to talk because he seems like a good guy who loves and needs a neighborhood bar at this hour as much as I do.

I used to write about this place, I finally respond.

You mean Old Prague?

Well, everything. Cermak Road. The neighborhood.

Are you the guy who did that thing on the bakery?

I nod yes, and for the next hour we are old neighborhood cronies, swapping names and streets, schools and baseball teams, restaurants, friends we may or may not have in comon — Don Malicki, remember him? He's with the "force" —living in the way things were, and to some degree still are. Nothing can orient a stranger as much as a mention of the old neighborhood. Everyone finds his way back there.

At one point in the conversation he begins telling me about a place he's heard of in the neighborhood, somewhere on the southside, maybe 25th? He's not sure. He hasn't been there himself. Maybe just off Cermak, down Lombard. Anyway, a tavern with a small hall in the back where on Saturday nights the old people come to dance.

You ought to write about that, he says.

I smile and nod yes, and finally bid my farewell, hoping to meet him again someday, under the same circumstances. Only next time we won't be strangers.

But the deed is done, the seed planted, and the image remains: a place where the old still dance.

I leave Old Prague, but instead of heading east and walking home a few blocks, I turn down Cermak in the opposite direction. A few lights burn in the store windows. Again I am playing games up and down the street, trying to remember where certain places once were — the bookie parlor just east of Old Prague, Kral's Music Store, United Auto and the two brothers lost amongst all the parts — and stores I may or may not be passing up ahead. Is the Troy store still there? No, that's now McDonald's. What about Ondrus? Where was the Balkan Music store? That's still there, down in Berwyn.

Cermak Road itself is brightly lit, with only an occasional car going by. The street is so deserted I can stand in the middle where the streetcars used to run and looking west toward Harlem, watch the stoplights change in sequence . . . red to green.

I have not walked Cermak this distance in many years. Though it is very late, with a sharpness of fall in the air, it is not cold, and I am invigorated by the walk, feeling good to be on the street again. I pass many stores that became stories for me. Some blocks ahead. I know a darkened Vesecky's Bakery awaits me through the front window, while in a brightly lit room in back, bakers covered with flour coax the oven-warm aromas of fresh bakery to greet the neighborhood morning.

Perhaps it's the drink in me, but I am even tempting the night to some degree. (Read it all in the next Cicero Life. Visiting Writer Mugged — or worse — in His Old Neighborhood). I am sauntering. I am a bit of the young neighborhood tough from years ago. I am remembering lines from Sandburg's "Chicago" . . . "They tell me you are wicked . . . they tell me you are brutal . . . Fierce as a dog with tongue lapping for action, cunning as a savage, pitted against the wilderness. . . . " And I am daring my old *neighborhood now, in this hour, to come and get me, show me what it's got. If it's as tough as many of the neighbors say, locked and double-locked in their houses, afraid to walk the streets after dark, show me. Come out of the darkened doorway, alleyway, gangway. Stalk my steps. I've got maybe $20 to my name, just your average working-stiff trying to make ends meet. A blue-collar man who works seven days a week on a typing machine. Come and get me.*

The bogeyman fails to appear, and I walk all the way, untouched, to the one restaurant I know is still open at this hour, my late night neighborhood haunt during my years of expatriation: the Seneca, on the corner of Cermak and Oak Park Avenue, where the food is always good, the people real, the talk (of horses) cheap, the newspaper stand always open, and where an empty booth can always be found at this hour next to the always clean large windows, where I can enjoy a steaming cup of coffee and my favorite special sandwich, "Steve's," named after the owner himself, and all the while look out on the neon neighborhood streets in the quietest hours before dawn. It's my "Clean, Well-Lighted Place," my "Nighthawks," and it has nourished my late night spirit well, holding me close to the neighborhood in those early morning hours when I feel that gnawing need to belong here again.

The old people keep dancing in my head. What a story it would make! For awhile I'm a freelancer in touch with my old neighborhood again, my own territory of reality and folklore I had to abandon some years ago. Stories come at me from everywhere. I feel the need to get them down on paper, shape them, find the heartbeat, pick up the result at this very newstand on Saturday night, come into a window booth of the Seneca, open the paper to the story over a cup of coffee, and find satisfaction in the words and illustrations: the magic of publication. To be alive, a writer in place, in that way again!

I consider walking back to the house to get the car and check out the possibilities of a story on the old dancers. Already I see them, know exactly how they're dressed, and hear the music. I am certain I would find the place. I would sit in the car out front and make notes: immediate impressions, the specific address, whatever I was already feeling even before making the initial contact with the people and the very scene where some Saturday night soon I would return to watch oldtimers dance, to talk with them, to put their words and my words in a small black notebook, to maybe even dance the last dance myself, then go home and early the next morning, tell just what it was I saw and felt, and what meaning it might have for us all.

But as I stare out the large glass window of the Seneca at this hour, the neighborhood vision fades into darkness before my eyes, leaving me inside the brightly lit restaurant with only a reflection of myself in the glass: no longer the neighborhood kid or the young man. Only a grey mustachioed writer who doesn't live here anymore and will never write about this place in such a way again. I am faced, too, with the realization that there is really nowhere to go these days with a story concerning the last of the neighborhood oldtimers dancing their final hours away.

The newspapers and magazines, as I knew them, have changed or disappeared. Almost all my editors (Herman Kogan, John Fink, Dick Takeuchi) with hearts big enough to encourage the young writer to stake out his own territory and pursue, always, the human element of the story, have left the scene. I mourn the loss of all of this. Especially the golden years of the Chicago Tribune's *Sunday Magazine under the editorship of John Fink.*

But the true faith of a writer is his own imagination. It is his beginning and ending and beginning again. His godhead. In this way, each day, does he transform the world and himself. And one way or another he lives to tell it. Somewhere Camus once said, "A writer's work is nothing but a long journey to recover through the detours of art the two or three simple and great images which first gained access to his heart."

So somewhere in the neighborhood I see a story unfolding: a dozen more men and women, widows and widowers in their late 60's, 70's and 80's, the last of the oldtimers, ethnics everyone of them, still speaking their native tongue. I see them gather in a small hall behind a corner tavern. They drink, they eat, they smoke, they play cards, they laugh, they reminisce. They feel their age. The men are dressed in baggy suits, white shirts and ties, polished shoes. The women wear ill-fitting wigs or show off newly permed and tinted hair. Their nails are polished red or pink, their wrists and fingers filled with costume jewelery. They are heavily made-up (or just a pat or two of powder on the cheeks) and heavily perfumed. They are dressed in billowy blue or beige or flowery chiffon dresses.

An old man, slightly inebriated, sits in a far corner of the room with a mother-of-pearl concertina in his lap, pushing and pulling red bellows of the button box, his eyes closed, his foot marking time, singing softly to himself, his shoulders swaying with the rhythm of the song. People smile at him from a

distance. He is the magic of the ceremony, part jester, part spirit, part poet.

The music he makes is the old music, the music of Bohemia, the music of Frankie Yankovic, of Lawrence Welk. Old waltzes, mazurkas, polkas. Nobody ever told these people that sentiment is a false virtue. It has held families, customs, entire neighborhoods together. It has kept individuals from falling apart. And the music releases this emotion like a blessing to the old.

Nobody in the neighborhood remembers these songs anymore but the old ones. The man sitting alone, both hands on the cane between his knees, thumping to the tune of the concertina. The two widows dancing together (they outnumber the men two to one), each lost in her own world, their eyes welling up, feeling both sadness and joy but making no sense of it.

Some of them, standing or sitting, sing along in Czech and English, while others move toward the floor as the concertina man begins a slow introduction to a song dispelling more good memories. There is a small chorus of "ahs" a gentle hand-clapping as the concertina man himself appears to drift aloft like a village musician in a Chagall painting, filling the sky with "The Blue Skirt Waltz":

> *I dream of that night with you,*
> *lady when first we met,*
> *we danced in a world of blue,*
> *how can my heart forget?*

And the whole room swirls slowly with the concertina man, the music, the dancers, swirls with old memories, old loves, old desires.

The men see themselves as young and virile, dancing in Pilsen Park or the old country, holding beautiful, young, dark-eyed Czechoslovak maidens costumed in lace blouses, embroidered skirts and aprons, black vests laced with red silk ribbons.

The women are smiling and whispering to their men, "My name is Vlasta Novotny, my family comes from Bohemia," or Moravia, or Slovakia.

> *Blue were the skies and*
> *blue were your eyes,*
> *just like the blue skirt you wore.*

> *Come back, blue lady*
> *come back,*
> *don't be blue anymore.*

In this way only does a writer hope to keep a neighborhood from changing. Living, remembering, telling stories.

Imagining a past that was and is.

Keeping it forever in words.

ACKNOWLEDGEMENTS

Some of these pieces appeared in slightly different form, and/or under different titles, in the following publications: "Bohemia on Cermak Road" and "Carnival Time" in *The Chicago Daily News*; "The Bakery," "Shorty the Locksmith," "Softball," "Tony the Shoemaker," "In Praise of Sausage," "The Houby Hunt," "The Polka King," "Requiem for the Neighborhood Winemaker," "The Butcher Shop," "Doc Cermak," "The Feather Comforter Man," "The Roller Rink," "Soup," and "The Croatian Picnic" in *The Chicago Tribune Sunday Magazine*; "Neighborhood Games," "Cicero," "Cereal," "Soda Pop," "The Garlic Eaters," "Playing the Horses," "Joey the Peddler," "Thanksgiving," "The Ice Cream Man," "The Latin Mass," "Tennis," "The Slovenian Grape Festival," and "Discovering Father" in *The Chicago Sun-Times Midwest Magazine*; "Man on the Moon," "The Local Show," "The Neighborhood Pub" and "Goodbye My Ladies" in *Chicagoland Magazine*; and "The Savings and Loan" and "Sokol: The Flying Czech" in *Chicago* magazine. The author is grateful to these periodicals for permission to reprint these pieces here.